THE TERRITORIAL DIMENSION IN UNITED KINGDOM POLITICS

The contributors

JIM BULPITT, University of Warwick
BRIAN W. HOGWOOD, University of Strathclyde
J. BARRY JONES, University of Wales Institute of Science and Technology
MICHAEL J. KEATING, University of Strathclyde
JAMES G. KELLAS, University of Glasgow
IAN MCALLISTER, Australian National University (formerly University of Strathclyde)
PETER MADGWICK, Oxford Polytechnic (formerly University College of Wales, Aberystwyth)
WILLIAM L. MILLER, University of Strathclyde
PHILLIP RAWKINS, Ryerson Polytechnical Institute, Toronto
RICHARD ROSE, University of Strathclyde

A publication of the Political Studies Association Work Group on United Kingdom Politics

THE TERRITORIAL DIMENSION IN UNITED KINGDOM POLITICS

Edited by

Peter Madgwick

Oxford Polytechnic

and

Richard Rose

University of Strathclyde

First published 1982 by
THE MACMILLAN PRESS LTD
London and Basingstoke
Companies and representatives
throughout the world

ISBN 0 333 29403 3

Printed by Woolnough Bookbinding,
Wellingborough, Northants

Contents

Acknowledgements

Like the United Kingdom, this book is the product of an amalgam of peoples. The ten authors have diverse origins, being from England, Scotland, Wales, Northern Ireland and even from the other side of the thirteen American colonies. A wide-ranging group of authors is necessary to embrace a wide-ranging subject. Whilst politics in England may be studied in a single London postal district, SW1, the politics of the United Kingdom covers a far greater expanse of territory. To examine the subject properly, authors must be at home in Cardiff, Edinburgh and Belfast as well as Westminster.

Like its subject, this book is the product of a lengthy gestation process. It reflects five years of continuing discussion among members of the Work Group on United Kingdom Politics. The Work Group was founded under the auspices of the Political Studies Association as a forum for the serious and rigorous examination of the variety of ways in which the United Kingdom is governed. We have not isolated Scottish politics, Welsh politics, Ulster politics, or English politics; scholars interested in each of these subjects have been brought together to examine collectively the network of institutions that constitutes the United Kingdom.

The editors have had the pleasure of acting as co-convenors of Work Group discussions of up to two dozen papers at annual conferences at the Universities of Strathclyde, Warwick, the University College of Wales, Aberystwyth, and the University of Wales Institute of Science and Technology, Cardiff. Two major publications have already been issued on behalf of the Work Group by the Centre for the Study of Public Policy at the University of Strathclyde: *A Research Register of Territorial Politics in the United Kingdom* by J. Barry Jones, and *A Bibliography of United Kingdom Politics* by Laurence Pollock and Ian McAllister. These publications reflect the widespread interest in the subject outside as well as within the United Kingdom.

This book is the culmination of a dialogue about the diversity of the United Kingdom and what holds it together. The Social Science Research Council provided funds for our first two annual meetings. The Nuffield Foundation deserves special thanks for a grant to support continuing activities of the

Work Group, trusting that if we kept talking to each other long enough and exchanging papers into the bargain, a book would result. Here it is.

PETER MADGWICK   RICHARD ROSE

Introduction

PETER MADGWICK and RICHARD ROSE

Territory is an essential dimension of government. A modern state can no more exist without territorial limits and divisions than a society could exist without division into social classes. Territory is important politically. The land contributes to national identity and images and symbols of community. Politicians demand equitable treatment of all regions of a country, and institutions of governance must be able to deliver the benefits of public policy to all of its parts. In the competition for electoral advantage, political parties articulate demands for particular areas as well as for the country as a whole. Pressure groups voice what their members want – and where these demands should be met.

To understand the United Kingdom in its entirety we must therefore understand its parts – England, Scotland, Wales and Northern Ireland. We must also understand the institutions that unite one and one-fifth islands into a single state. Understanding England is insufficient for an understanding of the United Kingdom. England is, as it were, the sleeping partner in the politics of the United Kingdom. There is no need for an English office in the gallery of Whitehall ministries, for English voices and values are not absent in the making of government policies. Scotland, Wales and Northern Ireland, because they are smaller, take a disproportionate interest in the territorial dimension of events at Westminster. There are Secretaries of State for Scotland, Wales and Northern Ireland to speak for each nation at Westminster, and to speak for Westminster in each nation.

Historically, the United Kingdom is a composite of nations, that is, communities of people with a distinctive social identity, and distinctive political institutions too. To describe the United Kingdom as a multi-national state is to call attention to those things that differentiate its parts. Wales lost its status as a separate principality in 1536, but did not thereby lose its Welsh identity. A greater or lesser portion of Ireland has been more or less under the Crown for 800 years, yet still remains politically distinctive. Scotland and England co-existed as two separate Kingdoms with

1

one monarch for a century before the Union of 1707 abolished the Scots Parliament, but not the communal base of Scottish identity. Whereas most subjects of the Crown in the non-English parts of the United Kingdom live easily with both a national identity and a British identity, in England there is confusion: the terms English and British tend to be used without recognition that England by itself is different from the United Kingdom.

Nations like classes must be understood in terms of the political relationships between them, whether characterised by mutual benefit or by conflict, or by both. National differences do not necessarily lead to conflicts between nations. The persistence of the United Kingdom for centuries is proof of that. The secession of the territory now forming the 26 counties of the Republic of Ireland strengthened the unity of the remaining parts. Politically, the crucial point to understand about the United Kingdom is its continuing capacity to act as a unitary state, notwithstanding its multi-national composition.

When Westminster was an Imperial Parliament, managing territories scattered across the globe was a major concern. Secretaries of State for India, the Colonies, the Dominions and the Commonwealth preceded the entry of a Secretary of State for Wales into the Cabinet. The end of the empire has made Westminster less conscious of its responsibilities as the central authority for diverse nations and peoples. Membership of the European Community has yet to awaken a new consciousness of territo-rial politics. Community politics is not perceived at Westminster in terri-torial terms, but as a controversy about money and material benefits. The Community is a bargaining arena, not a state like the United King-dom.

The primary political concerns at Westminster today are not territorial but functional: the management of the economy and the distribution of material benefits. Functional disagreements about health, education, pensions, unemployment and industrial policies are endemic in modern government. Political controversy would remain even if the whole of the United Kingdom were reduced in territorial extent to the boundaries of the Greater London Council. Yet there is a territorial dimension in every functional policy. Political grievances can be articulated in territorial terms, such as complaints about Welsh unemployment or Scottish housing. The substantive problem remains housing or unemployment, but the demand for action is limited territorially. The question thus arises: how are the benefits of public policy to be distributed throughout the United Kingdom, given differences in needs and resources between more and less prosperous parts? Ironically, economic differences between parts of the United Kingdom can lead to demands for greater centralisation, for only the United Kingdom Treasury has the authority and the money to redistribute resources from better off to less well off areas.

The institutions of United Kingdom government also reflect recognition of territorial divisions. Every Member of Parliament represents a territorial constituency. Collectively, party discipline gives an individual MP less scope for acting as a representative than a United States Congressman, but MPs sometimes do express territorial grievances of their constituents. The multitudinous institutional instruments of the Crown-in-Parliament involve varying degrees of 'distancing' or decentralisation from Whitehall. Local government, not Whitehall, is chiefly and immediately responsible for delivery of such major services as education, social work, fire and police. The National Health Service is separate from Whitehall and significant national and territorial dimensions are built into its management structure. Nationalised industries too reflect territorial biases; this is especially evident in coal and in steel, where a concentration of investment and employment makes the future of particular steel mills important for local economies. The Cabinet itself shows a territorial consciousness. Notwithstanding the unitary authority of the Crown-in-Parliament, there are three territorially denomi-nated ministers in Cabinet, representing Scotland, Wales and Northern Ireland. Their presence in the British Cabinet is a recognition of the territorial dimension in government and a commitment by these ministers to maintain the authority of Westminster.

In a sense, the United Kingdom is a fifth 'nation' in Westminster. Most studies of 'British' politics concentrate upon the politics of the largest single nation, England. Studies of Scotland, Wales and Northern Ireland often view government from the perspective of one national component of the United Kingdom or, even more narrowly, from the view of a nationalist (that is, secessionist) minority within that nation. The relationships between Westminster and its constituent national parts are usually neglected, even though they are very different from relationships between local government and central government departments and essential for the exercise of powers of the United Kingdom government.

The attempts of Westminster to reform the government of the United Kingdom emphasise the need to understand (or to avoid misunderstanding) how the United Kingdom works. Knowledge is a precondition of successful reform. The failure of Westminster has been spectacular in Northern Ireland, where ignorance has been greatest. Since the eruption of the troubles there in 1968, Westminster has vacillated between two alternatives: conciliation and coercion. Each has failed. In Great Britain, single by-election victories by Nationalists in Wales and Scotland in 1966 and 1967, respectively, led the Labour government of the day to appoint a Royal Commission on the

Constitution to examine what need there was to reform the government of the United Kingdom. The Commission sat on the question for more than four years before producing a Report that split five ways in its principal recommendations; the Report was ignored.

The enactment of Devolution measures for Scotland and Wales in 1978 was evidence of reform without commitment to fundamental change. The Devolution Acts gave Scottish and Welsh assemblies secondary powers that Westminster was happy to shed, but no power over matters of substance to central government. Moreover, another devolution bill had been filibustered to death a year previously, when 43 backbench Labour MPs revolted against the weak lead given by the Labour government. Opposition was based on conservative and traditional preferences for 'the Union as it is' and an anxiety about the political consequences of taking a step along a path that could turn into a slippery slope culminating in a transformation of Westminster or the territorial boundaries of the United Kingdom. There were also criticisms of how (or whether) devolution might work, and some dislike, especially among MPs from the North of England, of the seeming advantage that Scottish and Welsh assertiveness claimed. Only a political imperative of the highest order – the need to maintain Liberal and Nationalist support to prevent the fall of a minority Labour government – secured passage in 1978 of the second of the two devolution proposals put to Parliament.

Ironically, Westminster's efforts to produce concessions to nationalist protests against its authority have emphasised the strength of Unionist sentiment, outside England as much or more than within it. In Wales, Plaid Cymru, the Welsh Nationalist Party, consistently wins only one-tenth of the popular vote. In the 1 March 1979 Devolution Referendum, 80 per cent of the Welsh voting opposed the limited amount of devolution on offer. In Scotland, the electoral support of the Scottish National Party was slight until 1970. Notwithstanding the rise of the party since then, the unionist parties of Scotland have consistently won the great bulk of the vote, and the great bulk of the seats. In 1979, these parties won 69 of 71 seats, and 82 per cent of the popular vote. In the Devolution Referendum, the Scottish electorate divided into three almost equal parts. The largest single group of those eligible to vote, 36.4 per cent, did not cast a ballot. Of those voting, 32.9 per cent voted yes (that is, 51.6 per cent of votes cast) and 30.8 per cent of the eligible electorate voted against devolution (that is, 48.4 per cent of votes cast). In Northern Ireland, the 1973 Referendum on the border showed that 98.9 per cent of the votes (and 57.5 per cent of all names on the electoral register) wished Northern Ireland to remain part of the United Kingdom; 1.1 per cent (or 0.6 per cent of the electorate) voted for union with the Republic of

Ireland. Every subsequent election in Northern Ireland has shown a majority of votes supporting candidates pledged to maintain the United Kingdom and opposing strenuously Westminster's proposals for 'power-sharing' and 'an Irish dimension', which they deem a derogation from Northern Ireland's status as an integral part of the United Kingdom.

In the 1980s the union of nations that constitutes the United Kingdom remains – but the union does not still stand as it did. The Devolution Acts have shown that Westminster will, if pushed, accept change in the institutions of governance of Great Britain. In Northern Ireland, Westminster has voided the Stormont Parliament that provided a buffer between it and the problems of the Province for half a century, and has yet to find a way to remove the problems or put another buffer in Stormont's place. Parliament is still in possession of all its authority, and Unionists in Scotland, Wales and Northern Ireland have demonstrated their ability to resist proposals perceived as threatening the United Kingdom. But the events of the 1970s have offered encouragement to those favouring fundamental changes in the United Kingdom.

The object of this book is to examine carefully the ways in which politics differs among the four nations of the United Kingdom, and how the distinctive parts fit together to form a United Kingdom. The first half of the book concentrates upon government and the policy process. A study of the Welsh and Scottish Offices by James Kellas and Peter Madgwick emphasises the flexibility of Westminster. It has distinctive territorial departments to oversee policies divided among half a dozen or more departments for England. Notwithstanding very different institutional histories, both the Welsh and Scottish Offices have adopted similar means of integration into British government. Three case studies show how government differs according to the policy at hand. Industrial policy is about the economy and the boundaries of an economy are not limited by administrative maps; Brian Hogwood examines how Westminster has tried to develop policies that recognise the territorial dimension in many industrial problems (such as decaying and growth regions) yet also support central economic goals. Language is a distinctive problem in Wales, for it is the only bilingual nation in the United Kingdom. While Welsh is a minority language, one-fifth of the population speaks it, and language can be used as a badge of identity. The chapter on the politics of language by Peter Madgwick and Phillip Rawkins emphasises just how different is this issue from what Westminster sees as its primary concerns. For generations, Northern Ireland too was delegated *de facto* responsibility for a *sine qua non* of government, maintaining internal security. Since direct rule of Northern Ireland in 1972, Westminster has itself been responsible for defending Northern Ireland.

Richard Rose's chapter raises basic questions about whether the state that Westminster is committed to defend is the United Kingdom, or simply the part that constitutes Great Britain.

Because government rests upon the consent of the governed, political parties have a unique role to play in mobilising support for – or against – the United Kingdom. Whereas the competition for votes in England does not threaten the constitution of the United Kingdom, in Scotland and Wales party competition is two-dimensional. Conservative, Labour and Liberal parties compete for votes by advocating alternative economic policies. Nationalist parties emphasise a different dimension, advocating national independence, and have forced British parties to fight on this dimension too. In Northern Ireland, dispute about the Constitution is the first and only dimension differentiating parties, as the recurring failure to develop a Labour Party there demonstrates. Successive chapters by Jim Bulpitt and by Barry Jones and Michael Keating deal with the Conservatives and Labour as parties seeking support throughout Great Britain. The comparative study of Nationalist parties by Ian McAllister tests to what extent nationalists only have in common a desire to become independent of Westminster. William L. Miller examines the extent to which differences in party competition and social structure in each of the four nations of the United Kingdom lead to substantial variations in electoral choice.

Throughout this book, attention is concentrated upon relationships between parts of the United Kingdom and Westminster. For example, the Northern Ireland problem is here considered as part of a United Kingdom problem: what does a government do when a subordinate part of its territory is insubordinate? Whilst recognising the importance of events within Scotland, Wales or Northern Ireland, it none the less remains true that the political significance of such events is greater, in so far as they are not only 'local' or 'national' concerns, but affect as well the government of the United Kingdom at Westminster.

Part I
The Policy Process

1 Territorial Ministries: the Scottish and Welsh Offices

JAMES G. KELLAS and PETER MADGWICK

I THE NATURE AND COMPARABILITY OF THE OFFICES

To compare the Scottish and Welsh is to imply that they are similar in important respects. Nevertheless, it is difficult to give them a descriptive label which does not beg significant questions or over-simplify reality. 'Country', 'national' and 'intermediary' are all misleading or inadequate. 'Scenes from provincial life' are here presented, but 'provincial' is an English term, approximate and pejorative. Photographs of the two Offices would no doubt give substance to a title-page, but the two Offices are housed in at least four major buildings, only one of which is architecturally distinguished.

The Scottish Office, headed by a Secretary for Scotland, was established in 1885. Today it has grown to a staff of about 10,000. The Scottish Office administers a nation of five million people with its own systems of law, local government, education and religion. It has executive responsibility for major services, including housing, roads, education, health, law and order, agriculture and fisheries; for discretionary aid to industry and the Scottish Development Agency. The United Kingdom government retains powers over the economy, including oil, taxation and legislation. There are 71 Members of Parliament (14 more than strict proportion to population would allow). Scottish Bills are considered at second reading by the Scottish Grand Committee (all Scottish MPs) and there are two Scottish legislative Standing Committees and a Select Committee on Scottish Affairs. The Scottish Ministers answer Parliamentary Questions on a regular if infrequent basis.

The Welsh Office is newer, smaller, and concerned with a nation more integrated with England than is Scotland, and with less than three million people. The Welsh Office is roughly a quarter of the size of the Scottish Office in numbers of staff. It has almost the same executive responsibilities as the Scottish Office, except for law and order. The Welsh Office was established in 1964. There are 36 Welsh Members of Parliament (five more than its proportionate due). They rarely have Welsh Bills to consider but there are general debates in a Welsh Grand Committee, an annual debate on the floor of the House, an occasional Welsh Question Time and, since 1979, the Select Committee on Welsh Affairs.

The two Offices differ in significant ways, arising mostly from differences in the nation which each serves. Scotland, with over 5 million people, has nearly twice the population of Wales; it shares with Wales an uneven distribution, and sharp contrasts between industrial and urban areas and a great half-deserted countryside. The reorganisation of local government in Wales has moderated the old preponderance of Glamorgan (almost one-third the population of Wales), while Scotland has by a similar process acquired a new, huge region, Strathclyde, containing almost half the population of Scotland. Both countries suffer from the decline of major industries, but Scotland has seen new economic and, less surely, political, opportunities in North Sea oil. For both countries, London is now close in travelling time, but historically Scotland is by far the more remote, cut off by a significant historic border, and demographically and socially little integrated with England. Scotland, with its own forms of religious life and systems of law and education, is an historic nation with features of statehood still remaining, and well-defined boundaries. Wales is also an historic nation, but centuries of integration have made it, in many respects, part of an integrated polity called England-and-Wales. At the same time, the existence of the Welsh language (spoken by about a fifth of Welsh people) is a uniquely powerful differentiating and centrifugal force.

The Scottish and Welsh Offices reflect the most significant of these differences. The Scottish Office is fully formed by comparison with the Welsh Office, and altogether more 'beefy', as a Welsh Office official has remarked. It owes its superior size partly to the relative size of Scotland's population and territory, and partly to the possession of functions beyond those of the Welsh Office, notably in the Home Office fields of law and order, including prisons and the police. Whether the fact of size makes a significant operational difference is speculative. It is arguable that the size of the Scottish Office and its organisation into five large administrative departments make it rather less 'corporate' than the Welsh Office. But 'corporateness' is an elusive and unmeasurable quality, and the difference might not in practice matter much. In any case, the territorial offices are of their nature more corporate in organisation and style than the giant functional departments based in London. Similarly, the political relationships of the two Offices are probably affected by their size and the proximity of the people they govern, so that the relations of officials with ministers, and of both ministers and officials with local government, are marked by informality, friendliness, even intimacy, in the two territorial Offices, compared with Whitehall departments.

The functions of the Welsh Office expanded rapidly from its foundation in 1964 to the late 1970s. By then, the two Offices differed little in their executive responsibilities, but the Scottish Office is indubitably the senior department. It has more senior ministers and civil servants, and it serves a political constituency twice the size of Wales, and one that has recently proved more Nationalist. Such considerations have tended to give the Scottish Office more weight than the Welsh Office in British government.

The Scottish and Welsh Offices are territorial ministries in a system of government which is now mainly related to function. They fit an historical tradition in which some nations of the United Kingdom have had distinctive administrative and governmental institutions. The Offices are asymmetrical parts of a system of government which itself lacks symmetry; consider the various forms of local authority, the government of Northern Ireland, the malapportionment of Parliamentary seats, and so on. They might be (and sometimes are) regarded as anomalous to the extent that the functional departments for England, which has no English Office, are regarded as standard. The two Offices thus fit awkwardly into the government of the United Kingdom.

Both Offices were based on pre-existing administrative structures, for example, the Scottish Education Department, and the Welsh Office of the Ministry of Housing and Local Government. The time-lag between the foundation of the two Offices, in 1885 and 1964, reflects the earlier development of Scottish institutions, the closer administrative integration of Wales with England, and the reluctance of Westminster to initiate devolution.

The characteristic functions of Scottish and Welsh Offices can be discerned in the circumstances of their establishment. First, they recognised the distinctiveness of their territories for the purpose of government (more simply, the Offices are there because Scotland and Wales are there, as constituent nations of the United Kingdom). Second, they entered the processes of government, as special territorial interests. Third, they were interposed between Whitehall and Scottish and Welsh local government, or, to be precise, they were 'out-posed', as central government intendants in the territory of local government.

The primary function of the Offices (the first historically) is the national or 'country' function: the Office relates to a territory recognised for this purpose as distinct. In the context of the United Kingdom, this is a recognition of national differences within the Union. The original model was the Scottish Secretaryship at the end of the nineteenth century, usually a Scottish notable carrying out his duties mainly in London, paid significantly less than most of his Cabinet colleagues, obliged 'to think of Upper Silesia as well as . . . Auchtermuchty' (according to a Scottish Secretary quoted in Hanham, 1969, p. 53) and expected to cruise the isles in the summer. In practice, Hanham comments, Scottish Secretaries dealt at first with petty complaints, made themselves visible by land as well as by sea, and sponsored minor administrative reforms. Visibility raised expectations. The Secretary of State ran the front office, waved the flag, became (often in a prosaic way) a minor national figure, at least a territorial notable. Outside the particular scope of his statutory duties there is a much more dubious area, wrote a Scottish Permanent Under-Secretary of the 1950s, 'a sort of no-man's land into which the Secretary of State may have to venture because . . . he is properly regarded as Scotland's Minister' (Milne, 1957, p. 7). Historically, this may have looked like colonial governorship. However, Scotland and Wales are not colonies but integral parts of a modern, complex and interventionist government. The two Secretaries have therefore significant functions as executives, based in the Cabinet, but concerned with territories distant from Westminster.

II THE OFFICES AND THE SECRETARIES

The Scottish and Welsh Offices follow the British Civil Service tradition. Their officials belong to the Home Civil Service, are recruited by the Civil Service Commission, and are promoted in the senior ranks by central Whitehall committees. They accept the conventions of bureaucratic language, and inter-departmental negotiation and in-fighting; the extreme interpretation of the 'impartiality attainable by officials' (Johnson, 1977, p. 100), and its only qualification, the propriety of strong departmental loyalties.

Both Offices also show signs of an indigenous bureaucratic culture. Except for a few officials posted to the London offices, they work a long way from Whitehall, and often have personal and family reasons for treating their bureaucratic exile as a home posting. If the pipes are heard in the Scottish Office, the harp is not unheard in the corridors of the Welsh Office.

Questions of tradition and culture are difficult to establish, but there is evidence, as well as historical sense, to support their significance. The Offices derived some character from the circumstances of their foundation and development. Only two Scottish Secretaries have not been Scots (Sir

George Trevelyan and Ernest Brown), and the Civil Service is very largely Scottish and Scottish-educated (see Kellas, 1975, p. 39). Hanham (1969, p. 68) refers to a 'slightly old-fashioned bureaucratic flavour about the Scottish Office'. Historically, it developed as a centre of administration. The bureaucratic structure had to be built. Certainly, the evidence to the Crowther Commission of the two Permanent Secretaries might suggest a difference in outlook between the two Offices. The Scottish Permanent Under-Secretary sharply attacked the ability of an Assembly to assess priorities in resource allocation. 'Would not the advocates of every particular branch of expenditure not ask for more, and without ever suggesting where it might come from?' (Commission on the Constitution, 1970, Scotland, p. 21). By contrast, the Welsh Permanent Secretary showed an optimistic faith in democracy in expounding the classic case for the accountability of public servants: 'a public servant . . . ought always to have at the back of his mind the thought that he may be called to account for his actions to a body which consists of freely elected representatives of the people he is serving' (ibid., Wales, p. 10). By comparison with the sceptical realism of the Scottish Office, the Welsh Office appears to have 'a slightly old-fashioned democratic flavour' about it.

The Scottish Office is an old-established institution, set in a historic capital city and drawing on a distinctive governing class. The Welsh Office is different in all respects. It was established as the recent tide of nationalism began to flow, and its formative early years were coloured by the heady aspirations of nationalists, devolutionists and regional planners. This was no time to settle for the role of a Treasury or DOE outpost. The Office took a Welsh character from its staff. The senior posts were mostly (but not exclusively) held by persons of Welsh birth or connections, and at the very top bi-lingualism was a decided advantage. Moreover, the Welsh Office reflected for ten of its early years the dominance of the Labour party in Wales, and the high standing of some Welsh politicians in the British Labour Party. In the Callaghan government, both Prime Minister and Deputy Leader sat for Welsh constituencies; so too did the Speaker, a former Secretary of State for Wales. Yet, if the Welsh Office had political drive and cultural pride behind it, it still lacked the substantial institutional base of the Scottish Office.

In both Offices, the Secretary enjoys the constitutional responsibility of a Cabinet Minister in Britain, with all its implications of power, and a special territorial visibility as well. Given the nature of the media in Britain, focussed on London and the 'great game' of Westminster politics, the Scottish and Welsh Secretaries are almost invisible at Westminster, and unknown to the mass public. But to the smaller publics of their nations, especially the political elites, they are significant figures. The media, substantial in Scotland and not negligible in Wales, exploit the Secretaries' constant readiness to be filmed and interviewed, and create pro-consuls out of sometimes unlikely material. Even so, the Secretaries of State are less widely known among their own people than are the major Westminster figures.

The Secretaries spend most of their working time (four days in the week) in London, the arena where they count least. This division in the working life of the Secretaries is significant in administration and politics. Administratively, the Secretary is removed both from his territory and from what is now the major part of his department. Modern communications have not totally bridged the gap. This is not surprising since informal communication, talking in an undirected way around a subject, 'rubbing shoulders', and so on, is a necessary part of government. Politically, the Secretary lives amidst the battles of the Cabinet and its committees. There are two views on this part of a Secretary's work. In one he is a relatively junior minister whose place in the Cabinet is a gesture not to be taken too seriously (see, for example, the slightly disparaging references in Crossman's Diary, 1976, p. 779). One test of his standing would be the blackmailing efficacy of a threat of resignation, a threat which a Prime Minister might bear with equanimity.

The other view is that there is no substitute in the British system for a place in the Cabinet, and even a minister lacking seniority may, with skill, exploit the advantages of superior information and 'knowing the ropes', at ease in the highest circles of government. This latter view exaggerates the importance of the Cabinet itself, except at moments of crisis, compared with the Cabinet committees and less formal groups. In these, the two Secretaries are at some disadvantage since they do not sit on the Economic Strategy (or Policy) Committee (the Cabinet's 'first team'), but on the junior committee concerned with tactics of industrial implementation (Bruce Page, in the *New Statesman*, 21 July 1978). This may in fact suit their prime concerns, which are more to do with implementation than high strategy. For any greater leverage, the Secretaries must rely not on the status of their offices, but on their standing in the party and among senior politicians, especially the Prime Minister.

The Scottish and Welsh Secretaries' success depends on their political position and personal resources. Here there are some differences between the parties. Labour Secretaries in both Offices have drawn strength from the dominant position of their parties in Scotland and Wales. They have had more Members of Parliament to support them, and have triumphed over keener competition for their jobs. In Scotland, Conservative Secretaries have enjoyed fair support, though only once, in 1955–9, with a majority over Labour. Conservative Secretaries have sometimes seemed uneasy, certainly in Wales, as in 1970–4, when the Secretary of State did not sit for a Welsh constituency. But the Conservatives enjoyed a substantial growth of electoral support in Wales in 1979, and looked altogether more confident claimants to the Welsh Office. In Scotland Conservative Secretaries have often been Anglicised Scots, educated in England, and 'untypical of the mass of Conservatives in Scotland' (Kellas, 1975, p. 42). Nevertheless, they have shown 'a surprising pride in many things Scottish. Most of the increase in powers of the Scottish Office has come under Conservative governments' (ibid., pp. 43–4). Perversely, Labour Secretaries in Scotland, and perhaps in Wales too, have sometimes, in their territorial enthusiasms, misrepresented the ambivalent attitude of the Labour Party in the two countries towards nationalism.

Some consequences flow from the partisan nature of the system in which the Offices work. Governments look to Scotland and Wales as one kind of constituency for whose support they must work – either in the specific 'pork-barrel' sense of rendering services for votes, or more generally in the proper British mode of care and concern for the country in response to support. This perception from London of party strategy is more significant than any special relationship with territorial groups of Members of Parliament. These exist, but the procedures and traditions of Parliament and the Parliamentary parties do not encourage MPs to act with any force or consistency in such groups. A Member serves his country by serving his party and his constituency, and his country is normally the United Kingdom.

Personal qualities are more difficult to evaluate. Labour Secretaries of State have been professional politicians of some seniority – notably, but uniquely so, the so-called Charter Secretary of State for Wales, James Griffiths. In Scotland, according to Pottinger, Hector McNeil was the first professional politician to be Scottish Secretary, and the one most likely to have gone on to higher office. Some Secretaries have chosen to be positive promoters of the interests of their territories, risking the weariness and irritation of their colleagues. Others have taken a more modest and diplomatic approach, concerned not to overplay their hand, perhaps mindful too of the common good. Tom Johnston boasted that the Treasury 'ran to take the cat's milk away when they heard us coming', and is credited with having (in war-time of course) secured more for his country than any recent holder of the office. Those were great days for the Scottish Office, compared with the early 1960s, under Michael Noble, when the Scottish Office 'found itself in the unusual role of spectator as independent cohorts [including even the Scottish Council] took their way South to lay their representations before Great Britain Departments. The myth of a benevolent, semi-omniscient

Scotland's Minister was impaired, and it is doubtful whether the mythology . . . has been – or can be – completely restored' (Pottinger, 1979, p. 156).

In Wales, Labour Secretaries at least have not followed this modest approach. But the history of the Offices may not be a reliable guide to their future. In the 1960s and 1970s, the two Offices have developed into established, that is, settled and accepted, legitimate, parts of British government. They are still obviously quite low in the Whitehall pecking order, but they are known, tolerated, at least no longer disdained. While relationships with Whitehall are still necessarily uneasy, especially after the devolution arguments, the two Offices are better fitted into the system and no longer simply territorial pressure groups hoping to frighten the Treasury cat. This is a matter of political and economic necessity. As in the nineteenth century, the Secretaries must think of, if not speak for, Upper Silesia as well as Auchtermuchty. But, in altered circumstances, Upper Silesia means now St Helens and Merseyside and their numerous equivalents. Politicians who seek influence outside the territories need to rise above the restrictions on political thought and enterprise imposed by a territorial department.

III THE COMPETITION FOR ECONOMIC ADVANTAGE

Being Scotland's or Wales' Minister has come to have a hard economic meaning. Symbolic politics, never potent in the major British parties, gave way to the politics of economic advantage. This has been the second function of the Scottish and Welsh Offices. Secretaries of State, and their Offices, were expected to win goods for their country – industrial development, roads and railways, housing, jobs, hospitals, schools. The justification, in terms of rational policy-making, was not to seek undue advantage, but to remedy geographical and historical disadvantages in the name of a 'regional economic policy' intended to secure 'territorial justice', that is, a distribution of resources deemed equitable for residents of the United Kingdom in its less advantaged Scottish and Welsh parts.

During the hearings in Scotland of the Commission on the Constitution, the Chairman (Lord Crowther) asked of the then Permanent Under-Secretary at the Scottish Office: 'Is it your impression that in this process of negotiation which goes on – or bitter in-fighting, as I have heard it described – Scotland gains by having the Scottish Office specifically to represent it?' Sir Douglas Haddow replied: 'I think undoubtedly yes' (Commission on the Constitution, 1970, p. 24). In fact, the Scottish Office was sometimes rather coy about this side of its work. The Office's written evidence had referred to

Scottish Office support for projects in Scotland coming within the sphere of other central departments: '. . . it is not unusual for the Scottish Office to support the Great Britain Department concerned, at official or ministerial level, in seeking the necessary authority'. One of the Commissioners, Mrs Trenaman, expressed her admiration for the drafting of this passage with its careful playing down of the process of lobbying. Sir Douglas, after drawing back for a moment ('Frankly, I am not sure how proper it is for me . . .'), gave as an example the Dounreay prototype fast reactor; and then, with uncharacteristic candour, asserted, 'The Scottish Office finger would usually be in the pie' (ibid., p. 10).

With few exceptions, Scottish Secretaries of State have always fought for economic benefits for Scotland. For example, Hector McNeil intervened personally and vigorously to bring an IBM factory to Greenock, when the Board of Trade favoured St Helens in Lancashire (Pottinger, 1979, p. 127). As a consequence, Scottish Office morale rose (no inquiries were called for about morale in St Helens in the absence of a Secretary of State for North-west England). In any case, the Welsh were already on their way to this battleground, seeking a share of the spoils. In the House of Commons in June 1964, James Callaghan paid tribute to the economic achievements of the Scottish Office, but hinted at competition to come.

> . . . I know that as initially planned by the Ministry of Transport, the Severn Bridge was to precede the Forth Bridge. This was the original intention. But because, in my view, of the presence of the Secretary of State for Scotland in the Cabinet, Scotland got the Forth Bridge ahead of the Severn Bridge.
>
> I am not arguing whether that was right or wrong. What I am saying is that the argument was never properly put and that there was no Welsh voice at the time carrying weight in the Government in respect of the timing of these projects. I believe that a Secretary of State for Wales would carry a substantial voice in the Cabinet, as he should . . .
>
> (Hansard, vol. 697, col. 748, 25 June 1964)

By the end of that year, the Labour government had established the new Welsh Office. Its civil servants adopted loyalties similar to those of their Scottish Office colleagues, and slid easily into the battle vocabulary associated with this role. More important, Welsh interests were well represented in the Cabinet, and the first Secretary of State, James Griffith, was a senior and much-respected politician. Pottinger comments rue-fully, ' . . . the Welsh influence in Wilson's Cabinet was strong'. This Welsh influence secured some notable gains for Wales in the mid-1960s. Crossman records the allocation of the new Mint to Llantrisant in South Wales and the disappointment of the Scottish Secretary:

Tuesday, April 18th, 1967
Cabinet was due to continue the discussion of the Common Market. In fact we spent most of our time discussing the future of the Royal Mint. It has been decided to move it and its 1,400 skilled workers out of London and the choice has narrowed to Llantrisant at the end of the Rhondda Valley, Washington New Town in the North-East, and Cumbernauld near Glasgow. Not unnaturally the Cabinet Committee was completely split. The Chancellor and the Treasury officials said there was no doubt the people in the Mint themselves would prefer South Wales if they had to move at all. But the Chancellor's credibility was somewhat undermined by the fact that he represents a Cardiff constituency. Michael Stewart for the D.E.A. said that on the whole in terms of dispersal policy the strongest case for was the North-East, and Willie Ross, as Secretary of State for Scotland, insisted on Cumbernauld.   (Crossman, 1976, pp. 317–18)

However, English colleagues, both political and official, were not entirely unaware of, or indifferent to, these Scottish and Welsh pressures. Wilson's government brought England into the share-out. For example, three aluminium smelters were given, one each to the three nations. The Severn Bridge, opened in 1966, was to be matched, following a promise made by a Labour Minister just before the Hull by-election in 1966, by a Humber bridge, the world's longest suspension bridge, albeit with Britain's highest toll charges.

Crossman saw the pressures of territorial interests leading to a British form of pork-barrel politics. His diary entries at this period are illuminating. The Prime Minister, he recorded, wanted Merseyside to remain a Development Area,' . . . this was a highly political subject, elections were coming up and we must look at this with open political eyes' (Crossman, 1977, p. 444). Crossman spoke of marginal seats and unemployment elsewhere (in his own constituency in Coventry, for example!). It was best, with a dwindling budget, to change nothing, but 'so many promises have been made in Blackburn or Humberside, in Yorkshire, in Derbyshire . . .'. There is little doubt that something like the American 'pork-barrel' had developed in Britain since the 1960s. It arose from the distribution of economic goods under regional economic planning, and involved a mild politicisation of that process. But this politicised distribution of economic opportunities was still only a modest variation to the working of the whole economy, a marginal adjustment to the pronounced leaning of the economy towards the South-east of England.

There was indeed some exaggeration of the extent of redistribution to Scotland and Wales. Before their home audiences, Scottish and Welsh Secretaries liked to claim credit for the good they had done – like American Congressmen for whom 'credit-claiming is highly important . . . much of congressional life is a relentless search for opportunities to engage in it' (Mayhew, 1974, pp. 52– 3). But Wales was not a desert before the Secretary of State came on the scene; thus, the great extension of the steel industry in South Wales was carried out under private enterprise in the 1950s with some subsidies from the Conservative government offered eventually to Scotland as well. If governments have looked kindly on Scotland and Wales, their concern for England has been not ungenerous. For example, government aid to British Leyland in the English Midlands far outweighed its assistance to Chrysler in Scotland and Ford in Wales. In the steel industry, Redcar not Hunterston was chosen for expansion. Nationalist advance and agitation over devolution intensified the pressures for redistribution, but exposed it to critical appraisal, especially by the less prosperous English regions. Altogether, the pork-barrel began to shrink almost as soon as it was perceived.

In any case, the British pork-barrel differs from the American original. In American politics, the pork-barrel has a precise function. Government funds and projects are distributed in exchange for political support. This is a person-to-person contract between President and Senator or Congressman. There are thus good reasons why so many members of the US armed forces find themselves stationed in places such as Georgia and Texas where Congressmen have long taken a prudent interest in military affairs. There is a hard political logic in this system, and more powerful criteria than rationality and equity apply.

In Britain, by contrast, no very precise political bargain is implicit in the distribution of pork. The parties to the bargain are indistinct – on one side the government, the Secretaries of State, the Offices or the Party; on the other, Scotland or Wales, a particular constituency, the Party. The currency is not a parliamentary vote but diffuse support or gratitude. The British pork-barrel was used in the strict and proper American sense only when the minority Labour government was looking desperately to build a majority in the House of Commons in its last months, November 1978 – March 1979. Moreover, in Britain the procedures of distribution are complex and largely bureaucratic (see Chapter 2), and criteria of equity, territorial justice and economic sense, together with general confusion, exclude simple political bargains. The development of regional economic planning allows 'pork-barrel' politics to be translated into terms which command wider support in the Cabinet.

Good politics is not necessarily just or equitable government, and a civil servant may prefer a different administrative style. Pottinger, for one, wished that the Scottish Secretary should not be seen by colleagues, or the public, solely as a pork-factor. The original functions of the Scottish Office (agriculture, health, etc.) were well administered, but there was little credit or public recognition of this.

> The Scottish health and legal aid services, to take two instances at random, are more efficient in terms of cost benefit than in England. It is when public opinion forces Scottish Ministers to appear to do what they have no power to accomplish (e.g. in promoting economic growth) that they adopt postures that arouse dissent.   (Pottinger, 1979, p. 195)

> [For the last fifty years] those who have been Secretary of State have relentlessly tried to exercise their geographical function to secure advantageous treatment for Scotland. They have been skilful . . . in bartering their support for Cabinet colleagues' proposals in exchange for reciprocity on Scottish measures. It is regrettable that the public judge them by the number of visible projects, the stripmill or the smelter, that they have brought to Scotland . . . the Scottish Office record is not a discreditable one, but it does not help when other Departments become weary of the sound of the piper.   (ibid., pp. 196–7).

The politics of pork is indeed dangerous for political reputations, since consistent success in the competition is unlikely; and the competition itself is unsettling to the policy process. Even the immediate political advantages are uncertain, since those who lose are resentful, and those who gain may be ungrateful. The reactors, smelters, engine plants, vehicle licensing centres, motorways and the like stand as monuments to the politics of pork. Most are good in themselves; a few might have been better elsewhere. Evident success on the part of Scotland or Wales leads to countervailing pressure from England, and a restriction of competitive opportunities.

Indeed, the 'pork-barrel' was an episode in British territorial politics, exaggerated by territorial ministers and cynical observers. The reality was that the English and the Treasury would not tolerate the pork-barrel in the long run, the English because it was not to their advantage, the Treasury because it was not good government as they saw it. In any case, by far the most costly of the major goods being distributed were not glamorous 'one-off' capital projects, but the continuing flow of current expenditure on the welfare services. For these massive expenditures, the Treasury devised a formula (the 'Barnett formula' – see Section IV) which promised to combine territorial equity with Treasury control. This was not exactly the revenge of the English, nor even the closing of the pork-barrel. Rather it was the protection of major recurrent expenditures from the threat of formal irregularity implied by the pork-barrel. The latter did not vanish, it was fenced off. The financial procedures for the major continuous spending programmes are related to population and to needs.

IV THE RELATIONSHIP WITH WHITEHALL: FINANCE

The Scottish and Welsh Offices work within a highly centralised constitutional and political framework. The power of government is concentrated in the Cabinet, supported by the House of Commons. The convention of ministerial responsibility draws power to the Minister on the ground (now to some extent a fiction) that he is answerable to Parliament. Ministerial power is, for the most part, exercised by the Civil Service, secure in its monopoly, anonymity and corporate spirit. The convention of collective responsibility binds the Minister to the Cabinet. Constitutional arrangements are reinforced by the collectivist, equalising drives of the modern state, and underpinned by a centralised structure of political parties. This extreme concentration of power – an institution, a tradition and a style – is the first condition of the politics of the United Kingdom. Yet it is not inconsistent with asymmetrical territorial administrations and some devolution of power to local authorities. But this is not always explicit and fully acknowledged, and is indeed subject to the overriding authority of the sovereign Crown-in-Parliament.

At the core of the relationship is the government's provision of finance for the public services in Scotland and Wales. The central processes are the determination of overall spending patterns in the major public expenditure committee of the Cabinet, and subsequently the Cabinet; the allocation of a 'block' for most Scottish and Welsh expenditures, and the specific allocation to local authorities in the Rate Support Grant (RSG). This may seem another form of the pork-barrel, but the procedures are administratively sophisticated, complex and secretive, the goods are widely distributed and not so easily identifiable. The process is a long way from the sudden and much publicised allocation by Ministerial intervention of a new industrial plant or an administrative unit. The pork-barrel is about giving benefits to particular territories, but the style is to do with favours, the soliciting of support, bribes even. The procedures for deciding public expenditure have little of that character, but they are political in the sense that they are concerned with the territorial allocation of benefits, and they have some of the character of negotiation rather than simply consultation. Competitive bids are made and fought for. In the end, the Cabinet has the final word on the global totals, and the method by which territorial allocations will be made.

The Offices enter the negotiations determined to do their best for their country within what is formally a settlement for all of Great Britain. In the recent past, Scotland and, in some respects, Wales have certainly done better than England (see Table 1.1). But the English regions may well suspect that

TABLE 1.1   Comparison of public expenditure in the four nations of the United Kingdom, in six main programmes

	England	Scotland	Wales	Northern Ireland
A. Per capita public expenditure	100	122	106	135
B. Relative needs	100	116	109	131
Relation of expenditure to needs		+6	−3	+4

A. Per capita public expenditure, 1976–7, at 1978 survey prices, expressed as a percentage of expenditure in England.
B. Relative needs, as indicated by 'measurable objective factors' (the Needs Assessment Formula).
Source: H. M. Treasury (1979) pp. 6, 45.

unfair advantages are being won. Hence 'the dark secret' of Scottish and Welsh government. The phrase was John Mackintosh's, and referred to the budget procedures being examined by the Select Committee on Scottish Affairs in 1969. Specifically, he referred both to the total of the Scottish budget, and to the possibilities of flexibility within it. Sir Douglas Haddow was asked if Scotland did better by what was, at that time, the method of building a budget function by function, rather than by negotiating a (more visible) total budget. He replied: 'I should hate an affirmative answer to come to the notice of the English colleagues of members of this committee' (quoted in Keating, 1976, p. 138, who gives further illustrations of this point).

The 'dark secret' did not, in fact, survive the 1970s unnoticed and intact. The development of a 'block' for much of Scottish and Welsh expenditure, with a formula for increases and decreases (described below), arose in the context of devolution; but it marked an attempt to 'normalise', that is, to provide a more or less predictable and equitable framework for, these negotiations. Thus, some part of the secret is out. These changes are described in the Minutes of Evidence to the Select Committee on Scottish Affairs, 7 July 1980 (referred to as SCSA).

Until 1978, public expenditure under the control of the Secretaries of State for Scotland and for Wales (amounting to over 60 per cent of all identifiable public expenditure in these countries) was allocated on the basis of 'needs', as determined by the British Government collectively. A Treasury Study carried out 1977–9 (*Needs Assessment Study – Report*, H. M. Treasury, 1979) found that under this system Scotland was receiving in the 1970s something over 20 per cent more public expenditure per head in six main programmes* than was England, with Wales much nearer the English average. When an assessment of needs was taken into the reckoning, Scotland was still receiving (in 1976–7) 6 per cent more per head than England, while Wales was 3 per cent under (see Table 1.1). Of course, the assessment of needs is controversial and 'does not provide a method of determining allocations, but is a display of relevant data intended to help towards better-informed judgments' (ibid., p. 30).

In the meantime, however, a change had taken place in the determination of a portion of the expenditure for the Scottish and Welsh Offices. In 1978, a formula was introduced which linked Scottish and Welsh expenditures in the 'needs-assessed' services to those of England. Once identified as comparable, these expenditures are subject to a 'block arrangement', whereby a fixed proportion of the changes in English or English/Welsh expenditures go to Scotland and Wales. Although built up on individual service allocations, this block of money is not tied to the same services in Scotland and Wales as in England, and can be moved between services should the Secretaries of State for Scotland or Wales wish.

This is something like the old 'Goschen formula', whereby 11/80ths of education expenditures in England and Wales automatically came to Scotland, although that was tied for use in education there. The new formula is 10/85ths of the increases or decreases only in services which are comparable with those in England, and 10/90ths where the comparison is with England and Wales. Put another way, the ratios between England, Scotland and Wales are 85 : 10 : 5 (Northern Ireland is outside the system). This ratio is obviously based on population, which in 1978 was England, 46.3 million (85.4 per cent of Great Britain); Scotland, 5.2 million (9.6 per cent); Wales 2.7 million (5.0 per cent). The formula-based method was

---

* Health and Personal Social Services; Education (excluding Universities); Housing; Other Environmental Services; Roads and Transport (excluding railways); Law, Order and Protective Services. Thus industry, agriculture, fisheries and social security (for example) were not included.

brought in to facilitate negotiations for the block funds under devolution, but it has stayed to serve the present system of British government.

The new arrangement has been named the 'Barnett formula' (Heald, 1980) after the Chief Secretary under whom it was developed. The earlier, more covert and unpredictable system (the 'dark secret'), could be labelled the 'Haddow negotiation'. The 'Barnett formula' in effect is used to adjust patterns of expenditure built up under 'Haddow' by a combination of pressure for advantage and an assessment of need.

The new arrangement reveals something about the powers of the Scottish and Welsh Offices and more broadly about the nature of the United Kingdom. The occasional triumphs of pork-barrel politics are put in perspective; and plainly, by this test, Wales has not done as well as Scotland or Northern Ireland. Furthermore, some Welsh services are compared separately with those in England, while others are taken together with those of England, in a comparison with Scotland. This reduces the freedom of the Welsh Office, as there are fewer purely Welsh Office expenditures than Scottish Office expenditures, and thus less for the Welsh Secretary to control and reallocate, should he so wish.

The 'comparable programmes' cover about 95 per cent of the Secretary of State for Scotland's expenditures, and a somewhat lower proportion of those of the Secretary of State for Wales. Outside these there is no formula allocation, and the case is argued, as before, on the basis of needs. But this amounts to only 5 per cent of the total expenditure, although including some of the most sensitive subjects (e.g. aid to industry, fishing). While these may be considered to be largely determined by United Kingdom and EEC policies, and therefore not to be changed at the discretion of the Scottish or Welsh Secretaries in the manner of the block services, paradoxically it is also argued by the Government that these programmes are not comparable with those in England (SCSA, p. 41, para. 3). Thus a peculiarly Scottish or Welsh dimension in policy is determined by United Kingdom or EEC consider-ations, or by "Haddow negotiations' as of old.

The broader significance of the change to a 'formula' and block approach in the allocation of public expenditure to the Scottish and Welsh Offices is illustrated by the answers given by the Rt Hon. George Younger, the Secretary of State for Scotland, to the Select Committee on Scottish Affairs on 7 July 1980. Thus, he spoke about the old system, which was built up on the basis of Treasury consent to individual programmes, with limited ability to change expenditures between programmes.

Mr Hughes: Is it not the case that previous Secretaries of State have banged the table in Cabinet for Scotland and therefore

	built up this higher per capita expenditure and at the same time maintained the capacity to switch programmes?
Mr Younger:	That is not so. As I understand it, in 1978 there was a change. Certainly I remember on the previous occasion I was in the Scottish Office [as Parliamentary Under-Secretary of State, 1970–4] switching programmes within the Scottish Office's responsibility required Treasury permission. This was not by any means easy to obtain, and a great deal of trouble took place in trying to get it. We have now the ability to do this without permission. (SCSA, p. 62, para. 46).

Part of the reason for the change seems to have been that the days of 'banging the table' were ceasing to have their effect (p. 63, para. 50), but undoubtedly it was the preparation for devolution which inspired the present block arrangement. For it was within the philosophy of devolution to allocate funds to Scotland and Wales in a block fund with reference to comparable expenditures in England, and then to allow the devolved bodies to spend the money the way they wished.

There seems to be a stark choice in the mind of the Scottish Secretary between the old and the new methods.

Mr Hughes:	Is the Secretary of State not a little worried that the application of this rigid formula might make it more difficult for him to get additional money for special programmes?
Mr Younger:	I am not so worried, because if I were to give up such a facility I would have to give up the ability to switch between my individual programmes; and that I do not wish to do, because Scottish needs are often very different; Scottish priorities are often very different. I would not wish to have my priorities dictated to me by my Whitehall colleagues. I now have complete control over those priorities myself. (ibid., p. 63, para. 47)

It is not clear where the balance of advantage lies between the two methods. Under the old, Scotland built up a per capita (but needs-related) advantage over England of about 20 per cent. This base is maintained, for the formula applies only to changes in expenditure, and is not applied to the total amount. In a period of rising public expenditure, Scotland would move nearer the

10 : 85 ratio with England, which is in line with population, thus reducing the present ratio of expenditures. In a period of cuts, the reverse would happen, and Scotland, while suffering in absolute terms, would gain relative to England. However, even on the 'convergence' path, an official of the Scottish Office (J. E. Fraser) predicted that in ten years there would still be only a movement of half a per cent or one per cent towards a population ratio (p. 62, para. 43). The Secretary of State for Scotland added:

> *Mr Younger*: As long as the whole of the Scottish programme remains as it is, above the level of other programmes in other parts of the UK, it must be to my advantage to have that larger overall programme and be able to switch money inside it, than to have a steadily lessening programme but to have to argue each thing individually. That would be a bad bargain for us. (ibid., p. 63, para. 49)

The whole arrangement is a curious mixture of Treasury control and decentralisation. There is no clear resolution of the problem of Scottish or Welsh as opposed to English priorities, and indeed it is largely English priorities which determine changes in the amount of money going to Scotland and Wales under the blocks. So a new and distinctive Scottish or Welsh need must be financed out of the existing block at the expense of another service, or await a new English need, with its accompanying increase in the block under the formula. There seems to be no way now to get additional money for Scotland and Wales if new, special needs arise, which fall within the block allocation.

> *Mr Younger*: If I wanted to spend a lot more money on, say, nursery education or roads, it would not be open to me to ask for a special slice of money for roads without sacrificing the general power I have over my block as a whole; one cannot have it both ways. (ibid., p. 60, para. 36)

Of course, the Scottish Secretary in his own words is 'involved' in the deliberations on the 'British functional programmes', but it may be questioned how much weight the new system gives him, especially as 'special Scottish needs' in areas of spending within comparable expenditures can no longer be used to boost existing block allocations. At a time of rising public expenditure in England, both Scotland and Wales 'ride free' with every English increase, irrespective of corresponding needs in these countries. Equally, when expenditure declines, Scotland and Wales must suffer British cuts.

V THE CENTRAL–LOCAL GOVERNMENT RELATIONSHIP

The Offices work within a central–local government relationship which is heavily weighted towards the centre. The relationship is based on the legislative and financial supremacy of the centre, modified by negotiating procedures and continuing consultation. The Layfield Report on Local Government Finance and the Central Policy Review Staff Report on Central–Local Relations testify in different ways to the power of the centre. At the same time, there is a strong tradition favouring some independence for local government. Partly, this is a rhetorical accompaniment to ministerial and mayoral speeches, splendid for prize-giving and similar occasions. It is touchingly and now quaintly memorialised in the naming of innumerable schools after forgotten aldermen – schools built by tax-payers' money with the permission of, and to standards set by, the central government. But it is partly, too, a collection of procedures, which are intended to establish strict central control of total expenditure, but within that to allow a measure of local choice. Thus, the good intentions of centralisers are modified, or at least confused, by the equally well-meaning decentralisers. Sometimes they are the same people. (Within every centraliser . . . .) The system ends as centralisation with an erratically bad conscience.

There is, in consequence, a certain political ambivalence about the two Offices. They are part of central government. This is evident in their constitution as Cabinet ministries, and in the status of their officials. They share in central power. But they are geographically apart from the centre, administering a distinct and distant territory. Their functions – overseeing, advisory, defensive and paternal – impel the Offices toward local government. This tendency for the local–central boundary to soften or shift seems more apparent in these Offices than in English regional offices, and distinguishes one from the other.

The relationship of the Scottish and Welsh Offices with local government ranges through a variety of communications and consultations, from suggestions on how to cut down trees to the vetoing of costly woodwork in council housing; the planning of major roads and the choice by the Office of which plans may be implemented. If the Offices act as Paymasters to the local authorities, the Offices must themselves look to the Treasury as their own Paymaster. The Offices are necessarily locked into the central financial procedures for the determination of the distribution of public expenditure.

But these centralised processes for the allocation of resources mainly expended by local government are softened, and the degree of influence of the Offices is enhanced, by the conscious and energetic engagement of the Offices in a network of communication and consultation with local government.

This network is intended to secure government through discussion and consent, which for local government may amount to reluctant acquiescence in central direction or comparatively free choice accompanied by generous measures of advice and guidance. The objective for central government is control, but the ambiguities of the system give scope for manoeuvre to all the participants. The ambiguities include some vagueness about the crucial 'oversight' relationship, and about the actual content and detail of decisions. However, this comparatively bland consultative relationship has hardened and sharpened since 1979, under a Conservative government. Central government has been transformed from a plurality of spending departments seeking control with consent to the Treasury seeking strict control of expenditure.

Most of the time policy itself is not at issue. The Offices are concerned with implementation, with commanding local authorities to spend less or encouraging them to spend more; with the practical details of programmes; more rarely with the allocation of resources, and the questions of rationality and equity involved. A Scottish Office programme manager is quoted as saying: 'Policy is a matter for them [the local authorities]. My concern is with the maximum uptake of resources in my particular area. They know what local needs are, and I can't judge them' (quoted in A. Midwinter, 1979, p. 27). 'Policy' here clearly refers to local, tactical choice, not central, grand strategy. Within an imposed strategy, there is still a good deal of tactical talk. Professor J. D. Stewart (1977) has drawn attention to: ' . . . the strange imbalance of a system which provided a channel of communication about details of architectural design for a particular school, but not for the discussion of the overall allocation of resources between programmes'. Consultation on the technical details of implementation outweighs consultation on resource allocation. Here the Offices are following not only the limitations of their position in the structure, but also the professional self-denial of the British civil servant.

VI AN ASSESSMENT

A simple judgement of the effectiveness of the two departments is not possible, but some general points are relevant to an assessment.

(i) The intermediary has the potential of any middle tier for the improvement of articulation, communication, responsiveness, as well as delay, confusion of responsibility and obfuscation of communication. In practice, the system of consultation in which the Offices are so heavily engaged is slow, cumbersome and a drain on manpower. At the same time, it assists a sensitive adjustment to needs and grievances both in the nations and in the localities, and is a major ingredient of a consensual style of government. It moderates the full thrust of central control in some areas of policy at some times.

(ii) The role of the Secretary of State is crucial to the integration of the Offices in the British system of government; but this process goes on mainly in Cabinet and inter-departmental committees, as part of the 'secret centre' of British government. At the central–local level, sporadic ministerial intervention is sometimes apparent in matters such as the allocation of schools, the siting of roads and the like. This concern with small decisions has been explained as a reaction to the sheer difficulty of affecting or even taking the larger decisions. However, the tightening of central controls on local government expenditure has multiplied such 'small decisions', and made them politically sensitive.

(iii) The struggle for territorial advantages in economic policy, described here as the politics of the pork-barrel, suffers the disadvantages implied by that analogy. Scotland and Wales now compete with each other, as well as with Northern Ireland and the English regions. Hence the advantages of a system of redistribution of resources are accompanied by a growing politicisation of the competition for resources.

In all these judgements, it is easy to look for and overemphasise the dramatic, to find either a sharp and substantial role, or a passive, insignificant role. But power is, most of the time, diffuse and insubstantial. The Welsh and Scottish Offices are small and peripheral parts of a large and complex system. There is very little drama. For most of the time, the two Offices are engaged in the humdrum business of implementing policies decided elsewhere and introducing modest variations where they can to suit the conditions, needs and idiosyncrasies of the two countries. The Scottish and Welsh Offices do not have to be judged by the standards of high politics.

Accountability is more easily judged than effectiveness. The Offices are accountable in the classic constitutional sense, through the responsibility of the Ministers collectively to the Cabinet and individually to Parliament. The Offices are also accountable in the classic British bureaucratic sense to the Treasury. This is a powerful form of accountability, in fact, an aspect of central control. It has grown much tighter through the system of cash limits, though modified by the increased freedom to allocate (less) cash among the services. The relationship with the Treasury has little to do with accountability in a democratic sense, except in so far as the Treasury itself is 'responsible' to Parliament. The fight for increased power for the Offices is a fight against the Treasury, an inter-bureaucratic battle, rather than a struggle for democratic responsibility.

The Offices are further accountable, in the sense of political responsiveness, to local governments. There are a few reinforcements of such responsiveness. The Offices have to 'live with' officials and councillors, and proceed with formal consultations with the local· authority associations. 'Live with' is a term of bureaucratic art and includes relationships ranging from fraternity to life-after-death. In these, as in other relationships, the Offices are both visible and vulnerable. Some officials seem resigned to play the target in a shooting gallery, suffering for the sins of London and local government, as much as for their own transgressions.

Accountability in the sense of responsibility and responsiveness to the people is a matter for the politicians rather than the officials, and depends on the qualities of the ministers and the majority party. Ministers do react to complaints from the general public, 'taking them up' with appropriate authorities where this seems justified. The whole system is generally deficient in effective complaints procedures, which are of more immediate value to the aggrieved citizen than elections and the like. Hence there is some democratic value in the less publicised operations of the Scottish and Welsh Offices as informal Ombudsmen.

Accountability in the sense of accessibility is clearly enhanced by the existence of the Offices in Edinburgh and Cardiff. But this is a matter of structure and function not simply proximity. The Offices are not accessible as some local government offices are in the towns. But they have opened up a corner of central government to territorial elites and interest groups, breaking the tight hold of the London elites and organisations on the channels of access and pressures. The central elites are extraordinarily powerful in Britain and tightly concentrated in London. Johnson (1977, p. 128) refers to:

> . . . the dominance over a very long period of national political elites and their relatively sharp separation from local politics understood as the maintenance of local positions of political influence. As a result interest and influence do not flow up continuously from the base to the top in British political life. National politics has long been regarded as an altogether grander and more serious affair than local political activity, and more likely to be conducted well if freed from the ties and commitments of

local communities. The social homogeneity of earlier ruling groups, the manner in which national parties evolved, the belief in the negative state held on to for so long, the strength of the national Civil Service and its dislike of any hint of dependence on those who by definition can have only narrow and local perspectives – these are but some of the factors which have conspired to confirm the subordination of local political life to the requirements of government at the centre.

Johnson also refers to the separation of local government elites and national elites, and the comparative importance of the latter. The Welsh and Scottish elites are not separated in this way; and that partial integration, particularly through government channels (Parliament, party, Civil Service, quangos), confers some standing on them. The power of the London elites has not been dissolved but the base of the pyramid of influence has been a little extended. The Scottish and Welsh Offices are not widely accessible, but their existence has made central government a little less inaccessible.

The symbolic values of the territorial Offices elude precise assessment. They provide a national (or sub-metropolitan) constitutional form, distinctive but still integrated within the United Kingdom Government. But they are not widely recognised in this role, and the drama of British politics is often elsewhere. When a former Secretary of State for Wales learned of the overwhelming defeat of the devolution proposals in the referendum, he spoke of 'an elephant sitting on the doorstep'. In a sense, for both Offices there is always an elephant sitting at the front door. It is Whitehall and Westminster, and the commitment of the people to the British Government and Parliament as much as Edinburgh or Cardiff.

The study of these territorial departments leads back to the centre, and shows up the invisible bonds or linkages of the union. These are:

(i) the constitutional centralism built around the Crown-in-Parliament and ministerial responsibility, and paralleled in the organisation of the parties seeking power;
(ii) the financial procedures developed and dominated by the Treasury, and the negotiations related to them;
(iii) the distribution of economic resources in what is a centralised financial system placing a value on uniformity and 'keeping in line', yet confused by a modest commitment to regional economic planning, and decentralisation;
(iv) a system of perpetual consultation, consensual but controlled; central decision-making is softened and civilised by this process, and the whole is suffused with courtesy. It is 'characterised by centralisation,

tempered by kindness' (Bogdanor, 1979, p. 8); but kindness depends on there being some pork to go along with the talk. In a period of cut-back, the emollient effects of kindness are much diminished;

(v) a volatile low-key symbolism, reinforced by occasional crises, royal festivities and sporting events, but now much weakened by an acute shortage of Dunkirks, El Alameins and World Cup victories; such symbolism is more British in form and significance, than Scottish or Welsh.

VII   CONCLUSION

'What the Scottish Office most needed after 1939 was imaginative leadership. . . . The Scottish people needed to be convinced that the creation of St. Andrew's House was not a Tory attempt to stifle Home Rule sentiment and to secure effective Whitehall control over Scotland . . .' (Hanham, 1969, p. 68). Professor Hanham's conclusion is beguiling; but this review of the two territorial Offices does not suggest that imaginative leadership is either likely, or appropriate, given the political conditions and the constitutional scheme of things.

It is not clear that 'most Scots were (or are) by preference Home Rulers', and certain that most Welshmen are not. British government is fundamentally centralised, if not wholly Anglicised; there is not an adequate base of popular support for strong government in Edinburgh or Cardiff. Besides, imaginative leadership is better at raising expectations than in satisfying them. What leadership there is might be better directed not at dramatic political ends, but towards the development of the modest advantages for the United Kingdom as a whole of territorial administration as represented by the Scottish and Welsh Offices.

REFERENCES

Bogdanor, V. (1979) *Devolution* (London: Oxford University Press).

Central Policy Review Staff (1977) *Relations between Central Government and Local Authorities* (London: HMSO).

Commission on the Constitution (1970) *Minutes of Evidence*, Wales and Scotland (London: HMSO).

Crossman, R. H. S. (1976, 1977) *The Diaries of a Cabinet Minister*, vols 2 and 3 (London: Hamish Hamilton and Jonathan Cape).

Hanham, H. J. (1969) 'The Development of the Scottish Office', in Wolfe,

J. N. (ed.) (1969) *Government and Nationalism in Scotland* (Edinburgh: Edinburgh University Press).

Heald, D. (1980) *Territorial Equity and Public Finances: Concepts and Confusion* (Glasgow: University of Strathclyde Studies in Public Policy, No. 75).

H. M. Treasury (1979) *Needs Assessment Study* (London: H. M. Treasury).

Johnson, N. (1977) *In Search of the Constitution* (Oxford: Pergamon).

Keating, M. J. (1976) 'Administrative Devolution in Practice: the Secretary of State for Scotland and the Scottish Office', *Public Administration*, vol. 54 (Summer) pp. 133–45.

Kellas, J. G. (1975) *The Scottish Political System* (Cambridge: Cambridge University Press).

Layfield Report (1976) *Committee of Inquiry into Local Government Finance*, Cmnd. 6433 (London: HMSO).

Mayhew, D. (1974) *Congress: the Electoral Connection* (New Haven, Conn.: Yale University Press).

Midwinter, A. (1979) *The Scottish Office and Local Authority Financial Planning*, paper presented to a Political Studies Association conference on Comparative Local Government, University of Strathclyde, Glasgow, March.

Milne, D. (1957) *The Scottish Office* (London: Allen & Unwin).

Pottinger, G. (1979) *The Secretaries of State for Scotland* (Edinburgh: Scottish Academic Press).

Select Committee on Scottish Affairs, *Scottish Aspects of the 1980–84 Public Expenditure White Paper: Minutes of Evidence*, 7 July 1980. HC 689 (Session 1979/80 (London: HMSO).

Stewart, J. D. (1977) 'Have the Scots a Lesson to Teach?', *Municipal and Public Services Journal*, 19 Jan.

2 The Regional Dimension of Industrial Policy

BRIAN W. HOGWOOD

'The first point is that it is an inescapable fact that life in the UK is complicated, whether in Scotland or anywhere else, and that is not something which results from inward investment but in the way we have decided to organise our society. Everybody at one time or another probably needs some help through it.'

(Ken Binning, Under Secretary, Department of Industry, in evidence to the Committee on Scottish Affairs, 19 March 1980)

I INTRODUCTION

The United Kingdom is conventionally viewed as highly centralised for political decision-making about economic and industrial matters. However, different territories within the UK have different structures involved to varying degrees in industrial policy and there are differences between regions in the responsibilities of the regional units. There has never been a uniform pattern of administration of economic and industrial policy throughout the United Kingdom within its present boundaries. The administration of industry policy in Northern Ireland has been sufficiently different to merit separate examination later in the chapter. More recently in Great Britain, there have been a number of interesting changes in the administration of regional policy in Scotland, Wales and in the English regions.

We can distinguish the existence of four industrial and regional policy subsystems within the United Kingdom. Each of these subsystems is worth studying in its own right and not simply as 'deviations' from an English norm. The use of the term subsystems to characterise Scotland, Wales, England and Northern Ireland implies the existence of system-wide features and integrating characteristics for the system as a whole. However, the pattern is not a neat one, with system-wide features being the responsibility of the centre, and subsystem-specific ones being the responsibility of regional units. Both functional and territorial criteria are employed in allocating industrial and regional policy functions. Some functions are allocated to bodies with British-wide responsibilities and others to bodies responsible for the whole of one of the subsystems, such as Scotland; within each subsystem we find further functional and territorial allocations. Tension frequently exists between organisations as a result of these competing principles of allocation.

While coverage of some policy instruments may be defined in spatial terms, these spatial terms do not necessarily coincide with the boundaries of the regions for which regional units are responsible. For example, the various levels of assisted area in Great Britain do not coincide with the regional offices of the Department of Industry. Despite the attempts since the mid-1960s and earlier to standardise administrative regions, no government department (including the Department of Industry) uses all the standard regions as the basis of its regional organisation (see Hogwood and Lindley, 1980).

It is not possible to draw a neat line between regional policy and industrial policy. Centrally-determined industrial policies defined on the basis of sectors such as ship-building or car assembly may also be spatially skewed in their distribution, because the spatial distribution of the firms in the industry is uneven, or because policies are targeted in a spatially discriminatory way, or for both these reasons. There are now a considerable number of government agencies with overlapping functional and territorial jurisdictions. Accordingly, this chapter will be concerned not simply with describing regional policy structures, but with analysing industrial policy processes in practice.

To compare the degree to which industrial policy functions are exercised by the regional units, it is necessary to use a fairly precise terminology. In this chapter, the term 'deconcentrated' refers to administrative units which form part of a Whitehall department and are responsible for aspects of a policy in part of the UK. The extent of deconcentration can vary from routine administration of standard rules with approval needed from the centre for all decisions, to an element of discretion even in large cases. 'Decentralised' refers to administrative units within a department which is responsible to Westminster for a part of the UK (e.g. the Scottish Office). 'Devolved' refers to administrative units responsible to a local legislature for a particular part of the UK, subject to the removal of these powers by Westminster.

The degree to which deconcentration, decentralisation or devolution involve a meaningful exercise of discretion depends upon the instruments chosen to deliver particular industrial and regional policies. A system of allowances against company taxation will imply a centralised system. A system relying heavily on negative controls, such as Industrial Development Certificates, cannot involve a high degree of discretion in individual regions, because the policy is cross-regional in intent. Automatic grants by definition involve no discretion, so that it makes little difference in policy terms whether Regional Development Grants are administered in Scotland by the Department of Industry, as at present, or by the Scottish Economic Planning Department, as recommended by the House of Commons Committee on Scottish Affairs (HC 769-I, 1979–80, pp. 33–4). The changing importance of individual policy instruments affects the extent of discretionary elements in the system. Thus, the degree of regional discretion in industrial and regional policy is related to the selection of policy instruments.

II DECONCENTRATION WITHOUT DISCRETION IN GREAT BRITAIN TO 1970

The centralist climate of British government was clearly reflected in the foundations of regional policy. Prior to 1966 the stick part of regional policy, that is the regulation of industrial location through industrial development certificates (IDCs), was administered by the Board of Trade, and the carrot was administered partly by the Board of Trade and partly by the Inland Revenue. In the 1950s and the first half of the 1960s, financial assistance was mainly in the form of depreciation allowances and investment allowances administered by the Inland Revenue, without any special staffing structure to deal specifically with investment allowances. Under the Local Employment Acts of 1960 and 1963, selective assistance could be made available, and was administered through the regional offices of the Board of Trade, with approval from the centre being required in all cases.

Following the election of the 1964 Labour government, the 1966 Industrial Development Act provided for investment grants for the whole of Great Britain, but with higher rates applying in the newly designated development areas. There was therefore a need for machinery to cover the whole country and not just the development areas. The investment grant system was administered by five investment grant offices situated in Glasgow, Cardiff, Billingham, Bootle and Southend, with a total staff of 1000. The reasons for deconcentrating the administration of the scheme on a regional basis were: conformity with the government's dispersal policy, a strong preference expressed by industry for local decisions, and administrative convenience in determining eligibility and carrying out subsequent monitoring (Field and Hills, 1976, p. 5). However, because of the need for consistent treatment throughout Great Britain, there had to be frequent inter-office consultations. The investment grant division at departmental headquarters in London provided policy direction and gave guidance to the regional offices on procedures for dealing with applications. These were supplemented by instructions on particular matters raised by individual cases, and there was a continuing need for difficult cases to be submitted to headquarters.

The selective assistance available under the Local Employment Acts of 1960 and 1963 was modified by the Industrial Development Act 1966 and the Local Employment Act 1972. The selective assistance available under these Acts took the form of loans on favourable terms, building grants, removal grants and operational grants. In contrast to investment grants, these were normally negotiated case by case and linked to the provision of new employment, or in some cases to the preservation of existing employment. The grants were standardised by statute or administrative decisions, but loans were more flexible. The administrative machinery for processing this assistance consisted of the departmental headquarters in London (initially the Board of Trade and later the Ministry of Technology), the departmental regional offices, and an advisory committee (Field and Hills, 1976, pp. 7–11). The regional offices were not authorised to approve assistance even for small sums. Both the investment grant offices and the regional offices dealing with selective assistance were limited to application processing and could therefore be described as deconcentrated units without discretion.

Another form of spatially discriminatory assistance introduced in the late 1960s was the regional employment premium (REP), which was payable on the basis of employees in development areas subject to Selective Employment Tax. Applications for REP were processed by twenty-two local offices of the Department of Employment. Although SET was abolished in 1973, the conditions governing eligibility still applied until REP itself was abolished at the beginning of 1977, and the administrative arrangements still reflected REP's origins. Thus, the arrangements were carried out by the Department of Employment rather than the Department of Industry.

In addition to these carrots, the stick of IDC control continued to exist. Distribution-of-industry functions remained with the Board of Trade until October 1969, when they were transferred to the Ministry of Technology. The discretion of controllers at the Board of Trade was, in part, expressed in terms of the size of factory or factory extension for which they could decide to issue IDCs. However, regional discretion was exercised strictly in accordance with centrally-determined policy. The large majority of industrial development applications were dealt with by regional controllers. Regional controllers in the Midlands, South-west England and Wales interviewed by Cross (1970, p. 440) did not feel that they could or should exercise a wider range of discretion. It was felt that industry would view unfavourably the inconsistencies of treatment which a wider range of discretion at regional level would entail. This illustrates a paradoxical view of territorial justice: that spatially discriminatory policies should be determined and administered in such a way as to ensure equality or consistency of treatment.

The period of the 1964–70 Labour government saw the establishment of institutions concerned with 'regional planning'. Regional Economic Planning Boards (REPBs) were composed of the regional officers of the departments dealing with aspects of regional planning, and Regional Economic Planning Councils (REPCs), which were abolished by the Conservative government in 1979, were appointed by the Secretary of State for Economic Affairs (see Lindley, 1982; Watson, 1975; Wright and Young, 1975). The establishment of the regional economic planning machinery and of a stronger regional policy in the mid-1960s reflected a renewed interest in the regional dimension of the British economy. The Regional Economic Planning Councils provided an additional channel for the articulation of regional demands. However, the lines of communication and decision-making were essentially vertical between the relevant regional offices and their Whitehall headquarters, rather than horizontal within the 'planning' machinery at regional level. There was thus a minimal impact of 'regional economic planning' on the actual administration of regional policy.

Until the early 1970s, the system of administration of industrial and regional policy was essentially Whitehall-focussed, and uniform throughout Great Britain, though there were distinctive lobbying activities relating to Scotland and, to a lesser extent, Wales. There was some deconcentration of administration, but this was for the administrative convenience of the centre, and was not designed to provide a regional focus for policy-making or discretion in administration.

III DECONCENTRATION WITH DISCRETION:
THE EVOLUTION OF THE ENGLISH SUBSYSTEM

In 1970 the incoming Conservative government abolished investment grants, replacing them by a system of tax allowances, but there continued to be a need for administrative arrangements to process grants for contracts already signed. In 1972 the Heath government, as part of its now more interventionist approach, introduced regional development grants and a system of selective financial assistance wider than the old Local Employment Act measures.

The 1972 initiatives resulted in two quite distinct types of regions in England as far as the administration of regional policy is concerned: (1) those with substantial assisted areas within their boundaries, for which regional offices exercise discretion on regional selective assistance; and (2) those without large assisted areas, which do not require special aid machinery. A distinction also has to be made between the offices which administer regional development grants in specified assisted areas, and the Department of Industry regional offices, which have some discretion in allocating selective assistance in their region.

Because the regional development grants are payable only in assisted areas, there is a need for grant offices only at Billingham, Bootle, Cardiff and Glasgow. As with investment grants, there is a policy division at the Whitehall headquarters of the Department of Industry (DoI). Because of the limited geographical coverage and the relative simplicity of the regional development grant system, the number of staff involved was cut considerably as the old investment grant system was wound up. The four regional development grant offices administer the grants under policy instructions prepared in London. The grants are automatic rather than selective, and while the department does have some discretion in determining the eligibility of applicants and assets and in imposing conditions, any problems about eligibility are referred to London. Little significant regional variation results from this discretion. Regional variations in outcome reflect variations in application rates, rather than differences in criteria used by the regional development grant offices, which are not strictly regional offices in the sense of covering continuous geographical areas.

The most interesting administrative innovations were those concerned with selective financial assistance under Section 7 of the Industry Act 1972. Within guidelines laid down by Whitehall headquarters in consultation with the Treasury, regional offices of the Department of Trade and Industry in the North-west, Northern and Yorkshire and Humberside regions (and in Scotland and Wales) were given authority to approve assistance in individual cases, initially of up to £0.5 million in loans, and by 1976 of up to £2 million. Table 2.1 indicates for each English region the maximum grant each regional office could authorise in 1980, and the maximum size of project each regional office could appraise. This represents a considerable increase in delegated authority since the introduction of the 1972 Industry Act.

The offices with substantial assisted areas were strengthened by the

TABLE 2.1 Delegated authority of DoI regional offices in Section 7 cases (1980)

Regions	Maximum grant regional office can authorise	Maximum size of project regional office can appraise
Northern North-west Yorkshire and Humberside	£2,000,000	£10,000,000
South-west East Midlands	£500,000	£2,500,000
West Midlands	£50,000	£250,000

Source: HC 772 (1979–80) p. 43.

appointment of Regional Directors at Under-Secretary level, and Regional Industrial Directors recruited from the private sector to help advise on industrial development and to appraise development projects put forward for selective assistance. When an application is received, the detailed work on it is done by a team under the Regional Industrial Director. After this examination, on all but clear-cut cases the Regional Director and the Industrial Director submit a joint application to non-statutory advisory bodies called Regional Industrial Development Boards. In the event of disagreement between the two directors, the matter would be referred to London. The approval of the RIDBs is not mandatory for assistance to be paid, but their view is invariably accepted (Field and Hills, 1976, p. 12).

The regional offices also examine applications for assistance beyond their delegated power (the limits of which are shown in Table 2.1) and they submit a report and recommendations on the case to London headquarters. In such cases the Industrial Development Advisory Board is usually but not always consulted, and there have been cases where the minister has rejected the IDAB's advice. The London headquarters also deals with cases outside the normal guidelines for Section 7 assistance, and with projects which are part of the overall plan of a larger company (HC 600-II, 1977–8, Q. 194). The proportion of assistance which falls outside the normal guidelines varies considerably from year to year; in the year ended March 1976 it amounted to £25.2 million out of a total of £75.5 million, while in the year ended March 1980 there was no assistance outside the guidelines.

Thus, regional offices in regions with substantial assisted areas do have substantial autonomy in practice, though this is limited by the effect of the administrative guidelines. Effectively they take certain decisions about Section 7 assistance. This is monitored by London headquarters who review decisions above the £2 million limit and are consulted about precedent-making cases. Regional offices are not given set budgets, nor has there been an effective budget limit for England as a whole (though the situation may change as a result of the tighter criteria for assistance announced in June 1979). Accordingly, no application has been turned away by regional offices because of a shortage of funds. At least until the late 1970s, even if the forecast limit had been exceeded it would have been expected that extra funds would be made available. Only if there were an investment boom would it be expected that the Treasury would start to put the squeeze on.

Regional offices in English assisted areas also effectively administer Section 8 selective assistance (i.e. non-regional assistance). The regional offices act as 'brokers', indicating to inquiring firms what the best source of assistance is. For example, they might point to Section 8 assistance where projects are capital-intensive, since Section 7 has a cost per job limit. Formal decisions on Section 8 assistance are taken at headquarters. In non-assisted regions the situation is rather different, since they lack the same administrative structure to analyse selective assistance questions as the assisted area regions. Accordingly, more Section 8 assistance is dealt with at headquarters for non-assisted regions.

In addition to these application processing and 'brokerage' roles, regional offices also have 'promotional', 'steering' and 'monitoring' roles. The official DoI approach is to encourage a promotional role for its regional offices, though regional offices vary in the extent to which they play an activist role (see HC 600-II, 1977– 8; Young, 1982).

Regional offices also play a part in steering industry within and between regions. Historically, as we have seen, regional offices have played a role in administering the 'stick' part of location policy, IDC control. The role of offices in regions without assisted areas was essentially the negative one of refusing IDCs for projects which could be located in assisted areas. This emphasised the centralist role of such offices; they were acting against what might be perceived as the interests of their region. However, the 1970s saw a considerable decline in the significance of IDC control, reflecting a concern to secure industrial expansion almost anywhere during a period of recession. From 1972, IDCs were not required in development areas, but this simply removed a routine processing function, since they were automatically available in these areas. More significant was the decreased rigidity with which IDC control was applied in the non-assisted areas. By 1978, the DoI was almost trying to 'give away' IDCs (see HC 600-II, 1977– 8, Q. 141–2). Regional offices also steer industry within their regions. For example, though all large inward investment cases from abroad are processed at headquarters, the regional offices do have a role in showing intending investors around potential sites within their region. Some regional offices take a more directive role in this than others.

After assistance has been given, regional offices monitor firms, and, indeed, this is one of the main 'administrative convenience' reasons for the existence of regional offices. The degree of monitoring varies according to the case, with straightforward cases getting only statistical reviews and more difficult cases involving regular visits by regional officials (HC 600-II, 1977–8, Q. 111).

Although there are no regional development agencies in England corresponding to the Scottish and Welsh Development Agencies set up in 1975 and 1976, the National Enterprise Board (NEB) set up two regional boards in 1977 in the North and North-west regions. These regional boards were given delegated authority to approve new investments of up to £500,000; they also make recommendations to the NEB on investments above that figure, and generally advise the NEB on matters of importance within their regions. Occasionally, companies just over the borders of these regions are handled from Liverpool or Newcastle rather than London, for reasons of administrative convenience. At the same time, a number of firms which are major NEB investments, such as BL, have important plants in the North or North-west regions, and these are handled from headquarters. The potential for overlap between the NEB and Section 7 assistance is reduced by the fact that the latter is mostly in the form of grants and occasionally soft loans, whereas the NEB is mainly concerned with equity investment.

Factory construction within the English assisted areas is undertaken by the English Industrial Estates Corporation on behalf of the DoI and the Development Commission; elsewhere in England Factory construction is undertaken by the Council for Small Industries in Rural Areas (CoSIRA) on behalf of the Development Commission. The Development Commission prefers to operate by securing consensus for its plans for both the Department of Industry and the Department of the Environment. CoSIRA also provides soft loans for building, plant and equipment, and working capital to small businesses in rural areas. Help is focussed on the Development Commission's Special Investment Areas, the government's assisted areas, and other rural areas identified by CoSIRA's Small Industries Committee as requiring special attention. Applications for loans are vetted by local loan panels before being forwarded to headquarters in Salisbury. CoSIRA's work underwent considerable expansion in the late 1970s; for example, its budget for loans almost quadrupled in five years to £3.1 million in 1978–9 (see HC 97, 1974–5; HC 395, 1979–80).

There is one aspect of regional policy administration where there is a considerable local role in the establishment of institutions; the formation of industrial development associations (IDAs). Before the 1960s, a number of regional councils or associations had been established to promote industrial expansion through the cooperative effort of local authorities, and in some cases also involving employers' organisations, trade unions and statutory agencies (see Smith, 1964, pp. 78– 85). Naturally, the IDAs in areas with high unemployment, such as the North-east and the North-west, were more concerned with the attraction of new industry to the region, while those elsewhere were more concerned with relieving congestion and finding land to accommodate expansion. In addition, the IDAs have also carried out research into the problems of their area, have acted as a channel for pressure in consultations with central government, and have been the forum for cooperation between local authorities involved in development designed to affect regional prosperity. The renewed interest in regional matters in the mid-1960s helped to rejuvenate the IDAs, and government departments had to take more notice of IDA activity during the second half of the 1960s (Wright and Young, 1975, p. 238).

Central government gave grants in 1979 totalling around £750,000 to four of the current IDAs: the North of England Development Council (NEDC), the Yorkshire and Humberside Development Association, the North-West Industrial Development Association (NWIDA), and the Devon and Cornwall Development Bureau. These coincided almost exactly with the areas in England designated as assisted areas up to 1980. The allocation of these grants gives central government a legitimate interest in scrutinising the operation of the IDAs. In 1979 the Department of Industry commissioned Coopers and Lybrand Associates to undertake a review of the four IDAs receiving government grants. After receiving their (unpublished) report, which contained criticism of the amount of money spent by the IDAs relative to the jobs they created, the government announced in March 1980 that government funds for the four agencies were to be cut by 14 per cent. The associations are discovering that the price of receiving government grants is a degree of answerability for their activities.

England now has a system of administering regional and industrial policy which differs from that in all other parts of the United Kingdom. Within England there is no uniform system of administering regional and industrial policy, but there is a distinction between the four regions which have substantial assisted areas and those which do not. For the most part, this system was not designed to meet specifically English needs but emerged largely as a consequence of the special Scottish and Welsh arrangements discussed in the next two sections. England is the only one of the four nations of the UK which lacks industrial policy organisations defined in terms of the nation as a whole; it is largely administered through organisations which have some functions in other parts of the UK (though often different from those they exercise in England), and it is geographically subdivided for administrative purposes by those organisations in a variety of ways. We have the paradox that England is the only part of the United Kingdom for which special national arrangements have not been developed; it therefore has its own distinctive system by default.

IV   DECENTRALISATION TO SCOTLAND

The arrangements in Scotland and Wales in the mid-1960s differed from those in England in significant ways. There was already a certain amount of decentralisation (as opposed to deconcentration) which enabled more effective coordination to take place within each country. The Scottish Office had responsibility for land-use functions, and in 1962 it was reorganised and a new Scottish Development Department was made responsible for all physical planning functions. The Secretary of State for Scotland was also given the responsibility for drawing up and implementing regional plans, though without any extra executive functions for implementation. The Secretary of State had a general responsibility to 'oversee' the Scottish economy, though again without control over the policies which most affected it. The Scottish Office played a leading role in promoting interest in regional policy by British government in the early 1960s.

The establishment of a Scottish Economic Planning Board in 1965 was preceded by the establishment in January 1963 of a Scottish Development Group to help produce a plan for Central Scotland. The Scottish Development Group was a committee, chaired by the Scottish Development Department, with senior representatives from all interested departments. When the Scottish Economic Planning Board (SEPB) was set up in parellel with the REPBs in England, it was chaired by an assistant under-secretary at the Scottish Office rather than by a regional official of the DEA as in England. However, as in the English regions, the regional controllers of the London departments concerned with trade and industry still looked to Whitehall, and the financial implications of the proposals were worked out between the GB department and the Treasury in London (Wright and Young, 1975, p. 241). The Scottish Economic Planning Council (SEPC) was chaired by the Secretary of State for Scotland. In December 1970 its name was changed to the Scottish Economic Council (SEC), emphasising its purely advisory rather than planning role. Another distinctive feature of economic planning in Scotland was the establishment in 1965 of the Highlands and Islands Development Board (HIDB), responsible to the

Secretary of State for Scotland, to deal with matters relevant to the development of the Highlands.

Even before the allocation of regional selective assistance functions to the Scottish and Welsh Offices in 1975, they were involved in inter-departmental bargaining about industrial policy. The Board of Trade did not have to consult the Scottish Office on a day-to-day basis on the location of industry in Scotland in the 1960s, though it did discuss major problems. The Secretary of State also lobbied fairly effectively for cabinet decisions favourable to Scotland in industrial matters (see Kellas, 1975, p. 47).

The system of deconcentrated administration of regional industrial assistance described in the last section remains in England, but in July 1975 the administration of selective regional assistance in Scotland and Wales was transferred from the Department of Industry to the Scottish and Welsh Offices. In addition, a Scottish Development Agency (SDA), responsible to the Scottish Office, was set up in December 1975 and a Welsh Development Agency (WDA), responsible to the Welsh Office, was set up in January 1976. The agencies were given responsibilities for industrial investment, industrial promotion, factory construction and management, and environmental improvements. In Scotland these new responsibilities came under the Scottish Economic Planning Department (SEPD) created within the Scottish Office in 1973. The non-statutory RIDBs for Scotland and Wales were replaced by statutory Scottish and Welsh Industrial Development Advisory Boards. Responsibility for non-selective assistance remains with the Department of Industry, which is also responsible for sectoral selective assistance, though it makes use of the SEPD as an agent for administering selective assistance, and consults the SEPD about proposed schemes.

Power to administer selective regional assistance is delegated by the Treasury to the Welsh Office Industry Department (WOID), the SEPD and the Department of Industry on an equal footing. In 1980 this allowed each department to authorise and pay assistance in the form of grants or loans of up to £5 million where projects were considered to create or safeguard manufacturing employment, or up to £2 million in rescue cases (HC 731-II, 1979–80, p. 529). The administrative guidelines on selective assistance, to which all the departments have to conform, act as a force making for uniform treatment.

To use its own term, the Department of Industry is the 'lead department' on all matters of policy. It provides advice on the interpretation of the guidelines for administering selective regional assistance agreed with the Treasury. The Department of Industry also has responsibility for ensuring reasonable consistency of treatment of individual cases by SEPD, WOID and its own English regional offices, and for the general promotion of publicity material about regional selective assistance. The Department of Industry retains responsibility for non-selective assistance, non-regional selective assistance and, of course, the IDC policy.

The concept of 'lead department' means that the Department of Industry takes responsibility for *negotiating* changes on policy, including modifications to the guidelines, in consultation with SEPD and WOID. Thus, the territorial departments were closely involved in the negotiations leading to the changes in regional policy announced in July 1979. This involvement in political bargaining about policy also extends to non-selective regional assistance. George Younger, the Secretary of State for Scotland at that time, is credited with persuading Sir Keith Joseph, the Secretary of State for Industry, not to cut Regional Development Grants for development areas from 20 per cent to 10 per cent, but to limit the cut to 15 per cent.

The Scottish Office has its own budget for selective regional assistance and does not require approval for individual cases from the Department of Industry. Thus, where a Scottish concern makes an application to the Scottish Office, the Scottish Office does not have to refer it to London. However, where there is a matter of special interest or difficulty, the Scottish Office would normally consult the Department of Industry on an informal basis. This was seen by the senior civil servants at the Scottish Economic Planning Department as 'part of the normal process of keeping in line' (HC 104, 1975–6, p. 440). For example, where the Scottish Office gets an application from a firm in an industry in which there was an interest on a United Kingdom basis, it would find out the Department of Industry policy towards that industry, and what information was available about market prospects. The present decentralised arrangements for the administration of regional selective assistance rely to a considerable extent on voluntary coordination and compliance with British-wide policy on assistance to particular industries.

Since firms or plants are part of an industrial sector as well as located in a region, the need for inter-departmental coordination arises when important industrial firms have plants in both England and Scotland. Where the firm is a large one the responsibility will lie with the Secretary of State for Industry, though there will be consultation between him and the Secretary of State for Scotland (HC 104, 1975–6, p. 440).

The Secretary of State's continuing responsibility for the general oversight of the Scottish economy remains of great importance in the determination of industrial policy affecting Scotland, and his membership of the Cabinet is of crucial importance in enabling him to exercise this responsibility. This can perhaps best be illustrated by the role of the Scottish Office in the Government's rescue of Chrysler UK at the end of 1975.

Scottish Office ministers and officials were involved in discussions about Chrysler from the beginning, and were able to point out the consequences of the closure of the Linwood plant near Glasgow (see HC 104, 1975–6). The Secretary of State for Scotland and his allies in the Cabinet were able to secure government assistance for rescuing Chrysler against the opposition of the Secretary of State for Industry, despite the fact that this went against the logic of the recently launched 'industrial strategy'. Although one of the most spectacular cases in recent years, the Chrysler affair is not the only such example. In cases of selective industrial assistance where there is a major Scottish component, there is a close liaison between the Industry Department and the Scottish Office, with Scottish Office officials sometimes attending meetings on these subjects.

Within the SEPD responsibility for the sponsorship of the SDA, i.e. supervision of guidelines, manpower and finance, lies not with the section dealing with Section 7 selective regional assistance, but with the Regional Development and Manpower section. The SDA is keen on keeping separate its 'sponsoring' relationship with the SEPD and its 'casework' role, that is, discussion about investment and assistance to individual firms. The SDA has to conform to guidelines laid down by the Scottish Office, but the SDA was actively involved in the discussions which produced the original guidelines.

Communication between the SEPD and the SDA is close and frequent at both formal and informal levels. Contact takes place daily at all levels and on a wide variety of subjects (HC 769-II, 1979–80, p. 191). Regular case meetings on industrial promotion on a weekly basis were instituted from 1979 to 1980. Details of new cases of possible investment are copied between the two organisations and often form the basis for the case meetings. The formal arrangements provide a framework for the frequent informal contact and a means of ensuring that important matters are not overlooked. The decision about which of the two organisations should take the lead role is usually determined according to the origin of the enquiry; for example, where a prospective investor emerges through the consular service of the Foreign and Commonwealth Office or the Invest in Britain Bureau at the DoI, an SEPD official acts as team leader. The two organisations were actively pursuing better coordination, but in the SDA's view in May 1980, 'we have not yet reached an ideal state of affairs' (HC 769-II, 1979–80, p. 191).

In drawing up a financial package for incoming firms, the SDA's view is that cooperation 'is more difficult and remains a matter of concern'. The problem arises because of government policy that selective assistance should be negotiated with individual companies and that only government departments rather than agencies such as the SDA can conduct such negotiations;

the SEPD has tried to get round this problem to some extent by providing the SDA with examples of assistance based on anonymous real cases.

The SDA's promotional role has led to one of the most open examples of inter-organisational conflict in British regional and industrial policy. During the first two years of the SDA's existence, it paid the Scottish Council (Development and Industry) to continue its previous promotional activity. By early 1979, the SDA was itself ready to take promotional initiatives, and set up its own offices in New York and San Francisco. These arrangements resulted in friction between the SDA, the Foreign and Commonwealth Office and the Invest in Britain Bureau within the Department of Industry, with the FCO expressing surprise that the SDA had decided to set up a New York office without consultation (HC 769-II, 1979–80, Q. 211). For its part, the SDA was clearly dissatisfied that it had little direct link with the IBB, which chanelled its information to the SEPD, and the desire to short-circuit the FCO–IBB–SEPD link was important in the SDA's decision to establish its own offices (see HC 769-II, 1979–80, pp. 44–51). This issue provides a neat illustration of the complex allocation of industrial policy functions in Scotland by the early 1980s. A mixture of functional and territorial criteria are used, and tension can develop from efforts to integrate along either of the two dimensions.

Problems of coordinating promotional effort at UK level tend to be replicated within each nation and region because local authorities and new towns are entitled to launch their own promotional efforts. (Northern Ireland is an exception because of the minimal functions of its local authorities.) The SDA has actively sought to reduce pestering of potential investors by a large number of Scottish authorities and the resulting confusion which can arise. It has tried to do this both by formal coordinating mechanisms, such as a Development Consultative Committee and a Regional Development Officers' Liaison Committee, and by including individual authorities in its own promotional initiatives (see HC 769-II, 1979–80, p. 38; HC 769-I, 1979–80, pp. 28–32).

The SDA is sometimes incorrectly referred to as the Scottish equivalent of the NEB. Apart from the fact that the SDA has environmental, factory building, rural development and small firm functions which the NEB does not have, and has not been landed with a large inheritance of lame-duck firms as the NEB was, the NEB has responsibilities throughout the United Kingdom. Thus, Scottish plants of British Leyland come under the NEB rather than the SDA. Clearly, there is a potential for overlap in the investment functions of the two bodies. There are both formal and informal relationships between the two bodies on both a bilateral and multilateral basis. There is a formal six-monthly meeting of representatives from the

NEB, the SDA, and the Welsh and Northern Ireland development agencies to discuss matters of mutual interest, procedures to be followed, criteria for investment, etc. Apart from this, there are continuing contacts between the SDA and the NEB on their respective functions. The SDA is supposed to contact the NEB if any issue comes up in which the NEB has an interest in a UK sectoral sense, and the NEB is supposed to contact the SDA if it or any of its companies proposes to make an investment or closure in Scotland.

The split between the roles of the NEB and the SDA is not simply one of size of investment. The SDA has undertaken investments which are at least as large as those which can be expected from the NEB. Nevertheless, it remains true that the SDA might not have resources to deal with a really large firm, or such firms may be involved in a matter of UK industrial policy. A rough guideline is that a purely Scottish firm is likely to be a matter for the SDA rather than the NEB. However, this is not an absolute rule. For example, in 1979 the NEB made an investment in an Aberdeen-based firm involved in underwater engineering.

The Highlands and Islands Development Board was not abolished when the SDA was established. The functions of the two agencies overlap in the HIDB's area, though they are not identical. The HIDB is able to provide financial assistance to firms in which they are involved, whereas the SDA is restricted to subscribing equity and making loans at a rate related to commercial terms. However, the SDA is expected to tackle larger cases than the HIDB. Shortly after the SDA was established, agreement was reached with the HIDB on a number of principles on which to operate in terms of day-to-day administration of functions where there was a potential overlap (see HC 647-III, 1977–8, p. 1189). These principles are that small companies within the HIDB area go to the HIDB for assistance, while larger ones are looked at by the SDA in cooperation with the HIDB; that the SDA takes the lead in dealing with the Scottish-wide companies; and that the HIDB retains its own factory building operations. So far, the SDA and the HIDB consider that these arrangements have worked well. The processes of consultation and cooperation are reinforced by the fact that the Chairman of the HIDB is also a member of the SDA board.

The distinctive Scottish arrangements for industrial and regional policy which evolved by 1980 do not constitute a neat package of clearly-defined 'industrial powers', but provide Scottish roles of varying degrees of autonomy within a network extending throughout the United Kingdom. There is no neat package of 'Scottish industrial powers' which could be easily transferred to a devolved Scottish Assembly, a point often overlooked in the devolution debate. Such a transfer would involve changes in the British framework.

V DECENTRALISATION TO WALES

Although the Welsh Office has a much briefer history than the Scottish
Office, the arrangements for both the Welsh Office and British departments
operating in Wales in 1965–8 were similar to those in Scotland. In Wales,
the Board of Trade Office had more freedom than English regional offices to
deal directly with approaches of a political nature, for example by MPs,
which in England would have been referred to the Minister's private office in
London (Cross, 1970, p. 439). As in Scotland, the regional controllers of
GB departments looked mainly to London for guidance (Rowlands, 1972;
Randall, 1972). In April 1969, the Welsh Economic Planning Council
(WEPC) was replaced by a Welsh Council, which, in addition to the
functions of an economic planning council, watched over a number of Welsh
bodies concerned with such matters as tourism and the arts.

Close contact between the Economic Planning Group in the Welsh Office
and the Welsh regional office of the Department of Industry was the norm
before the industry department came under the Welsh Office; they both
regarded themselves as part of a 'Welsh policy community'. The senior
official of the Welsh regional office of the Department of Industry tended to
regard himself as the Welsh voice in the British Department of Industry. The
task of integrating the industry department into the Welsh Office in 1975 was
made easier by the fact that the head of the department was formerly head of
the Economic Planning Group.

The Welsh Office is a unitary department, unlike the Scottish Office
which is a federal one. Thus, the Economic Planning Group and the Welsh
Office Industry Department (WOID) within the Welsh Office each report
separately to the Permanent Secretary, whereas in the Scottish Office the
SEPD which combines both functions is headed by its own Secretary. The
Economic Planning Group is concerned with briefing the Welsh Secretary on
his economic oversight role, especially on the employment consequences
of various issues. The Group has a particular concern with the coal and steel
industry. The WOID has an industrial steering function; that is, it is
concerned with encouraging the provision of specific jobs. It is also
responsible for the Welsh Development Agency. There is an area of shared
concern between the two groups, but it would normally be expected that any
potential difference between them would be resolved without conflicting
papers being put to a higher level.

As in Scotland, the Welsh Office formally has complete autonomy in
applying Section 7 assistance within Wales; it does not have to consult the
Department of Industry but merely has to inform it after the event. However,
again paralleling the arrangements in Scotland, assistance for a project in

Wales for a firm with British interests, where that plant has implications on a British scale (e.g. British Leyland or the decision by the Ford Motor Company in 1979 to locate a large new plant in South Wales), is a matter for the Department of Industry and the IDAB in London, and not for the Welsh Office and its budget. Naturally, the Welsh Office would be involved in discussions. Purely Welsh firms are a matter for the Welsh Office alone, and Welsh plants of British firms where the projects had no 'British repercussions' would be treated as Welsh firms.

Welsh Office Section 7 assistance is separately budgeted for through the Welsh Office bid in PESC, with the Department of Industry assisting in its preparation. In practice, budgeting was not a constraint on the offering of Section 7 assistance, at least up to the late 1970s. It was assumed that money would have to be made available if it ran out while there were still cases for assistance. Thus, the fact that selective regional assistance is separately budgeted for in Scotland and Wales, but not for each of the English regional offices, seemed to confer neither an advantage or a disadvantage on Scotland and Wales.

The Welsh Office, together with the Scottish Office, has been fully involved in discussions about changes in the assistance guidelines since 1975. Even before they were given Section 7 powers, the Scottish and Welsh Offices were fully involved in the discussions about important industrial policy changes, such as the Industry Act 1972.

As in Scotland, the existence of a separate Welsh voice in Cabinet is important, not simply by the Welsh Secretary actually speaking up in Cabinet, but because the threat or potential threat to take to the Cabinet a matter considered by Welsh officials to be important can make it easier for Welsh civil servants to get their way in inter-departmental discussions. Welsh officials accept that Welsh economic prospects are linked to UK economic prospects, so that they are prepared to forgo some apparent immediate advantage or special treatment for Wales if the policy seems likely to lead to advantage for the British economy as a whole, from which Wales would benefit. The sticking point for the Welsh Office appears to be the maintenance of a regional differential in investment aid. Welsh Office officials take the view that the Welsh Secretary is as good as the Scottish Secretary as a channel for obtaining benefits for Wales. They can instance the location in Wales of the Royal Mint, the Vehicle Licensing Centre, and the Ford plant at Bridgend. They can also point to the fact that, unlike in Scotland, no assisted area was downgraded in Wales before 1979.

When a firm asks the Welsh Office for assistance, the amount that the Welsh Office can offer is limited to a ceiling amount per new job created. If a firm indicates that this is insufficient to induce the proposed investment, the

Welsh Office may suggest that the firm try instead for Section 8 assistance from the Department of Industry. This is particularly likely to be the case (a) if the firm is in a sector covered by the 'industrial strategy', or (b) if the jobs created are relatively few but there are advantages to the Welsh or British economy because a new product or technology is being introduced, or British firms would benefit from the construction of the plant, or there are significant import substitution benefits. The Welsh Office may even act as a strong advocate to the Department of Industry for a particular candidate for selective non-regional assistance. The Welsh Office will, in any case, do the preparatory work, since the Department of Industry no longer has a selective assistance assessment capability in Wales. Decisions about whether to grant Section 8 assistance are, however, for the Department of Industry in London to take.

The relationship between the WDA and the Welsh Office differs somewhat from that between the Scottish Office and the SDA. There is a strong Welsh Office view that the WDA belongs under the WOID rather than the Economic Planning Group. The WOID sees responsibility for WDA as part of its industrial steering role. This can be contrasted with the situation in Scotland where, within the SEPD, responsibility for sponsoring the SDA lies on the economic planning side rather than the regional assistance side. In Scotland the SDA has been anxious not to be seen as part of the Scottish Office's industrial steering or regional assistance functions. In Wales the formal allocation of WDA factory premises remained with the Secretary of State, whereas in Scotland it was from the outset the sole responsibility of the SDA. This was a source of irritation to the WDA (HC 731-II, 1979–80, p. 82). Under new guidelines issued in 1980, allocation was to be solely a matter for the agency, though with a continuing requirement to consult the WOID.

The WDA and the Welsh Office direct clients to each other. The WDA will suggest to someone who needs other forms of assistance that they should apply to the Welsh Office for Section 7 assistance. This is particularly likely if the proposal involves industrial expansion; incoming firms are most likely to be a matter for the Welsh Office in the first place. The WDA itself would not be involved in the negotiations about Section 7 assistance. A package of financing might be arrived at which involved both Section 7 assistance and WDA loans (which, for the purpose of computing total state aid, count as equivalent to funds from private sources).

In this context, good communication and good relations between the Welsh Office and the WDA are clearly important. That there is scope for confusion is illustrated by the initial refusal in the first week of the new 1979 Conservative government of assistance to the Triang toy company, and its subsequent reconsideration a week later. According to one report, the initial refusal was the result of a failure of communication between the Welsh Office and the WDA (*Financial Times*, 16 May 1979). The Economic Planning Group and the economic services section of the WDA look at similar things, but this was not seen as a problem; the two groups keep in touch, and the Welsh Office accepts that the WDA has the right to formulate its own strategy.

In 1977 the Government established a Development Board for Rural Wales (DBRW) which operates in mid-Wales. It replaced the Mid-Wales Development Corporation and the Mid-Wales Industrial Development Association, and took over the operations of the Development Commission and CoSIRA in the area. Unlike the HIDB and the SDA, the development board for part of Wales was set up after the development agency was set up for Wales as a whole. There is overlapping of functions, and consequently a need for arrangements to avoid duplication. The DBRW provides factory space in mid-Wales, but looks to the WDA for land reclamation and industrial investment (see HC 647-iii, 1977–8, p. 1191). For small business development, the DBRW operates in conjuction with the WDA and, in particular, plays a part in arranging loans from the WDA. As with the HIDB and the SDA, coordination between the two bodies is reinforced by the fact that the Chairman of the DBRW is a member of the WDA board. By 1980 the Chairman of the DBRW considered that relations with the WDA were friendly, and they had no complaint about the conduct of the WDA, though 'it would be idle to deny that in the early days there was some sort of rivalry' (HC 731-II, 1979–80, p. 227).

When an issue arises in which the NEB might have an interest, the Welsh Office would not contact the NEB directly, though the WDA would. If, for example, British Leyland were considering the establishment of a new components plant to compete with components currently made in Wales, the WOID would get in touch with the motor vehicle section of the Department of Industry, and ask for reconsideration of the proposal because of the implications for Wales. The Welsh Office is not represented on the NEDC, though it does receive all the NEDC papers, but Welsh Office officials could put a case through the Welsh Secretary to brief Cabinet members on NEDC on the Welsh view.

The large number of organisations involved in industrial and employment policies in Wales requires communication between organisations, and threatens duplication of effort. It also attracts criticism. The Social Services and Employment Sub-Committee of the House of Commons Expenditure Committee drew attention to 'the confusion and waste which seems to us to exist because of the proliferation of agencies engaged in attracting industry to Wales' (HC 647-I, 1977–8, p. 9). The WDA has tried to overcome the proliferation of agencies engaged in industrial promotion by channelling its own overseas industrial promotion efforts through the Development Corporation for Wales and has encouraged other bodies to do the same (HC 647-III, 1977–8, p. 1191).

The issue of industrial promotion has been taken up in Wales, as in Scotland, by the new Select Committee for Welsh Affairs. Unlike Scotland, its focus has been on internal Welsh arrangements rather than the tension between regional and British ones. In particular, concern was expressed by the Committee at the way in which the WDA, unlike the SDA, does not carry out industrial promotion overseas itself, but provides funds for this purpose to the Development Corporation for Wales (HC 731-I, 1979–80, p. xxxvii). While formal arrangements and processes in Wales often echo those in Scotland, there is scope for some distinctiveness in Wales, though the ready availability of the comparison acts as a pressure for conformity.

VI   DEVOLVED INDUSTRIAL POWERS IN NORTHERN IRELAND

In Northern Ireland we find a situation which is different in kind rather than degree from structures for industrial policy in Great Britain. In Great Britain since the war, we find processes of deconcentration and decentralisation. However, in Northern Ireland formal responsibility for determining the policy framework, as well as for implementing industrial policy, rested with the Northern Ireland government until its suspension. Since the suspension of Stormont in 1972 (apart from the brief interlude of the Executive), Northern Ireland functions, including those relating to industrial policy, have come under the Westminster-appointed Secretary of State for Northern Ireland. Whereas in Scotland, Wales and the English regions, industrial functions were being moved along the deconcentration–decentralisation– devolution spectrum, in Northern Ireland they moved in the opposite direction, from being devolved to being decentralised.

The extent to which industrial functions are decentralised in Northern Ireland is much more significant than in the Scottish and Welsh Offices which simply administer GB laws. The formulation of the legislated policy framework remains with the Northern Ireland departments. For example, when REP was abolished in Great Britain at the beginning of 1977, the corresponding Selective Employment Payment was retained in Northern Ireland (though it was abolished in July 1979 when other cuts in Great Britain regional assistance were announced). A new package of assistance specific to Northern Ireland was also announced in August 1977. This separate framework thus provides considerably greater flexibility than the Scottish and Welsh Offices' ability to influence rates of assistance for particular areas within the framework of GB legislation prepared by the Department of Industry, or in exercising regional discretion in approving selective regional assistance.

Northern Ireland has been able to exercise its industrial powers in a way distinct from the policies of the GB industry department. The 1950s were not a 'policy off' period for Northern Ireland as they were for Great Britain. Further aid to industry was provided under the Northern Ireland Industries Development Acts 1966 and 1971 and other Northern Ireland legislation, rather than under the Westminster Acts applying to Great Britain: the Industrial Development Act 1966, the Local Employment Acts and the Industry Act 1972. The operation of the Northern Ireland legislation ensured that the combined incentives to attract industry were (and remain) more generous than those for Great Britain.

In formal terms, the Northern Ireland Parliament had up to 1972 completely devolved discretion in policy formulation for regional assistance in the region. However, we have to consider how far that discretion was exercised in practice. Even in a formal sense, industrial policy was not entirely under the control of the Northern Ireland government. Northern Ireland has benefited, together with the GB assisted areas, in the operation of the IDC system to divert expansion away from the Midlands and South-east of England. Thus, what Northern Ireland officials themselves recognised to be one of the most important industrial policy instruments affecting them depended on the GB department administering it in such a way as to ensure that Northern Ireland received similar treatment to the GB regions (see Commission on the Constitution, 1971).

Further, while Northern Ireland could pass legislation on industrial policy for Northern Ireland, Westminster retained the right to pass legislation applying throughout the United Kingdom. So, for example, the Shipbuilding Industry Act 1967 applied to Northern Ireland as well as to Great Britain. The National Enterprise Board and the sectoral schemes under the 'industrial strategy' also apply to Northern Ireland; the Northern Ireland Department of Commerce (DOC) acts as agent for sectoral schemes in Northern Ireland, since the Department of Industry has no presence there. In practice, although within the discretion of the Department of Commerce, where a case has 'special features', such as the assistance to the controversial De Lorean car firm in Belfast, the decision would be taken at United Kingdom level, and the Secretary of State for Northern Ireland 'may need to consult his colleagues' (HC 769-II, 1979/80, p. 255).

For reasons of convenience to Northern Ireland, the Northern Ireland industrial promotion effort is closely integrated into the UK system. Northern Ireland has two Department of Commerce (DOC) officials in its own Northern Ireland Industrial Development Office in New York, which liaises closely with the British Trade Development Office in New York. Northern Ireland also has its own promotional arrangements in Japan and certain European cities. However, as a result of a review in 1978, it was decided by the DOC in agreement with the GB Department of Industry and the Foreign and Commonwealth Office that officials should be seconded from the DOC to consular posts in the United States. These officers were supposed to have 'an unambiguous responsibility for serving the whole of the UK', and were 'seconded from the DOC in order that the peculiar resistance to the idea of investment in NI might be countered by officers with detailed first hand experience of the area'. By early 1980 there were four such seconded posts, with arrangements made for the secondment of a further two DOC officials. These Northern Ireland arrangements received considerable attention from the Committee on Scottish Affairs in 1980, as a possible model to be copied by Scotland (HC 769-I, 1979/80, p. 26; HC 769-II, 1979/80, pp. 73-87, 234-59). More generally, the DOC works closely with the consular posts, and has an agreement with the Invest in Britain Bureau (IBB) of the Department of Industry.

The crucial issue is the financing of industrial assistance. Unlike the Assembly envisaged in the Scotland Act 1978, the Northern Ireland government did have some limited tax-raising powers of its own. In practice, with a few small exceptions, tax rates for the taxes controlled by Northern Ireland were the same as in the rest of the UK (see Brett, 1970, p. 262). Similarly, the principle of parity in social services between Northern Ireland and Great Britain was established. This desire not to be taxed more or to accept a lower standard of service should not be surprising. The Ministry of Finance had to consult the UK Treasury in advance about any new items of Northern Ireland expenditure other than those concerned with providing parity of services.

Each change in industrial assistance in Northern Ireland had to be negotiated with the UK Treasury. Even when revising rates under existing schemes, e.g. the Capital Grants to Industries Acts, the Northern Ireland government had to make representations to the UK government to be allowed to make the change. Agreement between the two governments did enable Northern Ireland to have a considerable differential over GB development areas in levels of industrial assistance and to exercise greater flexibility in considering individual cases – a flexibility which the Northern Ireland Ministry of Commerce itself regarded as part of the differential (Commission on the Constitution, 1971, p. 90). The existence of the

Northern Ireland Parliament enabled the passage of special Northern Ireland legislation.

However, the increase in assistance to the development areas in Great Britain from the mid-1960s onwards eroded the Northern Ireland differential. Industrial assistance in Northern Ireland became even more flexible than in the past and a differential continued to exist, but the margin of advantage was drastically reduced. As regional programmes became more comprehensive and expensive to maintain, it became more difficult for the Northern Ireland government to persuade the Treasury, particularly in times of economic constraint, that Northern Ireland should be allowed to maintain its differential. The Northern Ireland Ministry of Commerce's own conclusion was that 'the amount of finance available is more important than the relatively minor differences which exist in powers, and that the piper – in this case the British Treasury – largely calls the tune' (Commission on the Constitution, 1970, p. 29).

Problems of civil disorder since 1968 have influenced development proposals. For example, the details of the Northern Ireland Development Programme 1970–5, which were worked out in conjunction with UK government officials and approved by UK government ministers, took account of the difficulties of maintaining an acceptable level of industrial expansion during a period of civil unrest (Commission on the Constitution, 1971, p. 190). In addition, the Westminster government increasingly took an interest in the fate of large firms in Northern Ireland, such as Harland and Wolff, even before the suspension of Stormont in 1972. Fears in Northern Ireland about economic withdrawal being a prelude to political withdrawal mean that decisions about the future of large firms are inevitably highly politicised – over and above the usual concern about the unemployment effects of the closure of large firms.

The abolition of the Northern Ireland Parliament seems to have made remarkably little difference to the industrial policy processes in Northern Ireland, though there would not have been a different framework in the first place in the absence of Stormont. A distinctive Northern Ireland policy framework and a differential over mainland assisted areas remain, and indeed have been subject to continuing development. That this is not simply a result of inertia is underlined by the retention until 1979 of the equivalent of REP in Northern Ireland after its abolition in Great Britain at the beginning of 1977, and the package of new measures announced later that year. The Northern Ireland DOC has not been absorbed into the British Department of Industry. Important decisions remain a matter for discussion initially among the Northern Ireland departments, with discussions between the DOC and the Department of Finance being of greatest significance. Under direct rule, the UK Treasury remains the key Whitehall department whose approval for changes in industrial policy must be sought, though the Department of Industry and the Scottish and Welsh Offices will also be involved.

As with other parts of the UK, Northern Ireland has specialist industrial investment agencies. The Local Enterprise Development Unit (LEDU) is aimed at small local businesses, and gives financial assistance in the form of grants and small loans, and makes available factories and sites. First contact with LEDU by businessmen is with staff at one of four area offices, and eligible projects are then passed on to project teams at Belfast headquarters for analysis. The Northern Ireland Development Agency (NIDA) has a rather different history and different functions from the Scottish and Welsh Development Agencies. In 1976, the NIDA replaced the Northern Ireland Finance Corporation, itself set up only in 1972, which had become involved in a number of problem firms. Interestingly, the initiative for the establishment of NIDA did not come from within Northern Ireland departments, in the usual way, but from Westminster. The NIDA differs from the SDA and the WDA in that it does not have small business, factory building and environmental functions and in that it has a greater role in providing risk capital and assisting problem firms. This role in providing risk capital is illustrated by the NIDA's substantial equity investment in the controversial De Lorean car plant. Where the NIDA is of the opinion that a proposed investment would not meet commercial criteria, it may refer the case, with a recommendation, to the DOC for it to decide on social or political grounds whether it wishes to direct the NIDA to make the investments. In such cases, the NIDA is reimbursed specifically for its involvement. This indicates a different casework relationship between the NIDA and the DOC from that which exists between the SDA and WDA and their sponsoring departments.

There is clearly scope for overlap involving these bodies, both within Northern Ireland and within the UK. The NIDA is required to consult LEDU before assisting a firm falling within the LEDU's remit (i.e. firms whose plans provide for the total employment of less than 50 people). The NIDA has to have the prior approval of the DOC before it acquires or assists any firm located in Great Britain for the purpose of relocating it in Northern Ireland. Because the NEB's remit extends to Northern Ireland, the NIDA is required to hold regular discussions with the NEB to identify areas of common concern, and to inform the NEB of any matters affecting prominent Northern Ireland companies which could have significant consequences for the Northern Ireland industrial sector concerned. The NIDA is expected by the NEB to take the initiative in dealing with companies which are predominantly Northern Ireland based, except where it is felt that wider industrial reorganisation would be dealt with best on a UK basis. The NEB is expected to consult the NIDA before taking action on proposals which affect companies with significant interests in Northern Ireland.

By early 1980 the government had completed a review of the industrial development institutions and incentives in Northern Ireland, and concluded that all existing organisations should continue: 'any gains to be achieved from a more fundamental reorganisation of the institutions were likely to be outweighed by the inevitable loss of momentum which the disruption of change would bring' (HC 769-II, 1979/80, p. 237).

One general implication from Northern Ireland's distinctive experience is that the scope for offering a differential is worth most during a 'policy off' period for other regions, the value of Northern Ireland's differential being severely eroded in the mid-1960s. A second implication is that the existence of formal industrial 'powers' is meaningless unless accompanied by effective access to the finance to enable the exercise of those powers. Thirdly, the more favourable incentives in Northern Ireland were not entirely due to the existence of a devolved assembly – as noted earlier, the incentives have continued after the suspension of Stormont. The more favourable treatment was due largely to the economic and political conditions in Northern Ireland, with the different institutional arrangements enabling a package of different instruments, rather than simply more generous provisions within a GB framework. Finally, from the perspective of industrial policy administrators, there can be advantages in being able to offer a package of assistance and commitments about planning permission and infrastructure.

VII OVERVIEW

Two related features emerge clearly from the developments described in this chapter.

(1) The trend has been towards greater (though still relatively limited) discretion to deconcentrated units in the English assisted areas, and greater decentralisation in Scotland and Wales, whereas Northern Ireland has for the moment moved in the opposite direction, from being devolved to being decentralised (see Figure 2.1).

(2) The pattern of responsibilities for industrial policy has become much more complex; there has not been a general switch from centralised to decentralised or devolved functions, but an extension of policies along the whole spectrum of categories.

Industrial and regional policies are not administered by a monolithic central government department located in London, but by a multiplicity of

REGIONS	DECONCENTRATED	DECENTRALISED	DEVOLVED
English regions with assisted areas	---→ 1972		
Scotland	---→ 1972	---→ 1975	
Wales	---→ 1972	---→ 1975	
N. Ireland			1972 ←---

FIG 2.1   Recent changes in the administration of some regional policy functions

organisations. To some extent, the pattern of industrial policy organisations with overlapping policy jurisdictions reflects the incremental progress of industrial policy initiatives. It is also an inherent consequence of the problem of relating agencies and instruments to their targets. However carefully the government attempts to define the demarcation of responsibilities, there will inevitably be what Hood (1976, chap. 4) calls 'categorisation problems'. Both geographical and functional considerations are used in the formulation and administration of industrial policy. Moreover, within a territory such as Scotland we find both further functional differentiation within Scotland (e.g. between the SEPD and the SDA) and territorial differentiation (e.g. SDA and HIDB). Within Scotland, Wales and England special arrangements have been made for those parts of the country which can loosely be thought of as peripheral.

It is important not to exaggerate the implications of the extent of decentralisation in the early 1980s. The four subsystems are firmly embedded in a Westminster system with a high integrative capacity. The main departments exercising United Kingdom functions are the Department of Industry (both in dealing with cases of UK-wide implications and in its role as the 'lead' department of the four British industry departments), the Foreign and Commonwealth Office in its roles in attracting overseas investment and promoting British exports, and the Treasury in negotiating initial policy with the industry departments and ensuring subsequent territorial even handedness. The Scottish, Welsh and Northern Ireland Offices, inspite of their territorial labels, are also Whitehall Ministries. The Cabinet and its committees also perform an important integrative role, though it would be misleading to describe this as coordination: it is chiefly concerned with conflict resolution when inter-departmental disagreements are not resolved by bilateral negotiation, and with ratification of policies agreed among the four industry departments and the Treasury.

Industry policy has special features, as a policy area, which have implications for the territorial dimension of public policy. It is concerned with certain generalised functions (e.g. inward investment), specific sectors of industry and firms within these sectors (e.g. steel, cars) and, through regional policy, with specific geographical areas. These differing roles have been institutionalised into a large number of different organisations, some with territorial and others with cross-cutting functional responsibilities for industry policy. The relationship between these organisations can be conceived of as an 'industrial policy network'. Clearly this network does not join every industrial policy organisation with every other. Some links may be tenuous, indirect or non-existent: for example, when an issue arises in the Welsh Office relating to the activities of an NEB subsidiary, the Welsh Office would get in touch with the relevant section of the Department of Industry rather than directly with the NEB. Links are often weakest where sectoral and regional concerns cross-cut: for example, links between regional development agencies and 'industrial strategy' organisations such as the NEDC are weak.

Other links are obviously much stronger. Among the strongest links are those between development agencies and their 'sponsoring' departments, since this link is underpinned by the power of the sponsoring department to appoint board members and issue guidelines. This formal bilateral link is supplemented by informal links on an operating basis where both department and agency are involved in supplying funds to industry on a selective basis.

Any set of organisations may be linked to each other in a variety of different ways. For example, the formal and informal links between development agency and sponsoring department will be further supplemented by formal multilateral links in the form of regular meetings of all British development agencies and their sponsoring departments. These in turn will be supplemented by informal contacts between sponsoring departments about their operating practices towards their development agencies.

Formal and informal consultation are the methods of adjusting relationships between industrial policy organisations which are overwhelmingly employed in British industrial and regional policy, though issues do arise, such as the Chrysler rescue, which do lead to political conflict which can only be resolved at Cabinet level (see Hogwood, 1979). Such inter-organisational adjustments are essential to the operation of industrial and regional policy to prevent the needless conflict that would arise if every organisation sought to carry out to the full its jurisdictional remit.

The concept of an industrial policy network can help us to analyse the implications of a new industrial or regional policy instrument, the establishment of a new organisation, or an alteration in political arrangements of the kind involved in devolution. Since there are now a considerable number of organisations with overlapping functional or territorial jurisdictions, adjustments in the policy jurisdiction of one agency or the establishment of a new agency would mean that the industrial policies delivered by that agency would interact with those of other organisations as part of the total pattern of government involvement. That pattern would itself be likely to be altered by the transfer or introduction of functions, since the overall pattern of government involvement in industry is not so much the sum of the effect of all the policy instruments, as a product of the interaction between these policies and the agencies administering them.

The concept of an industrial policy network focusses on the relationships between organisations as unitary bodies. However, for a full understanding of these relationships, particularly the importance of informal consultation, we need an understanding of how members of these organisations interact as individuals. Such informal consultation depends on a high degree of shared purpose, shared background and contacts, and mutual trust. Heclo and Wildavsky (1974) used to great effect the concept of an 'expenditure community', in analysing how public expenditure decisions are made in Whitehall. The idea of an 'industrial policy community' may also be useful in understanding how industrial policy currently operates in the United Kingdom. The industrial policy community is clearly a much more dispersed and fragmented community than the 'village' community described by Heclo and Wildavsky. The officials involved are in widely dispersed locations, but telephone conversations with colleagues play an important part in inter-organisational communication and, to some extent, compensate for the relative lack of face-to-face contact. Interchange of staff and regular formal meetings help to provide the basis for informal contacts. Because of the widespread use of paragovernmental organisations ('quangos'), the officials involved are not all part of a unified staffing structure. However, personnel matters in paragovernmental agencies are dealt with in a similar way to the Civil Service; many of the officials have Civil Service backgrounds, and accountants, economists and industrialists recruited to the agencies are likely to have been part of the 'industrial policy advisory network'. Thus, they know the 'language' of the Civil Service and of government policy. Such a common language is important for communication within an organisation, and it is at least as important for inter-organisational communication.

The industrial policy community is, however, clearly much more fragmented than the Whitehall expenditure community, and much less effective at ensuring consultation and conveying information between organisations. However, it should be remembered that some of this ineffectiveness may be due to the number of organisational upheavals there have been in industrial policy, at both UK and regional level. An official may simply 'forget' to consult a colleague in another interested organisation if such informal contacts are not routine.

In Scotland, Wales and Northern Ireland, members of industrial policy organisations are also part of 'regional' or 'national' 'policy communities'. These communities are broader in scope than, say, the corps of officials employed in the Scottish and Welsh Offices. For example, even when the Scottish Industrial Development Office was part of the Department of Industry before 1975, its officials thought of themselves as being part of a 'Scottish policy community' and regarded themselves as a Scottish voice within the Department of Industry. This sense of being part of a local policy community is reinforced by shared background. At present, this membership of two policy communities presents no severe problems of identity for officials, since both policy communities are ultimately responsible to the same cabinet system.

A number of criteria could in principle be used to evaluate the operation of the system described in this chapter. One relevant criterion is the smoothness of inter-organisational relations. In practice, decisions about changes to the network tend to be taken with little regard for the framework as a whole. This has produced a pattern of considerable complexity, which has, so far, shown a remarkable capacity for avoiding and resolving inter-organisational conflicts.

Ideally, we should try to measure any effect of territorial discretion in terms of regional variations in assistance. However, some reflection will indicate that a simple attribution of regional variations to the exercise of regional discretion could be misleading. In the first place, there are large cases and other applications referred to headquarters of the DoI which reflect central priorities rather than regional discretion. Secondly, variations in application rates arise from two different causes, which are difficult to untangle: autonomously generated applications from firms in the region, and those which have been solicited or encouraged by the regional office. Application rates as recorded will also be affected by the extent of pre-vetting by regional offices to weed out cases which stood no chance of success. Because of the potential for variation in pre-vetting and other factors, we are also unable simply to attribute variations in the success rate of applications to varying use of discretion by regional offices. Thirdly, it is misleading to aggregate total figures of assistance, since these are made up of a mixture of grants, loans and interest relief grants, which can vary over time and between regions. Finally, there is the problem of the basis for comparison. It might seem obvious to use unemployment, or unemployment in development areas within each region. However, we should not assume that uniform exercise of discretion would be directly correlated with unemployment, since the correlation is more with the general state of industry in the region (see HC 600-II, 1977/8, Q. 131–2).

Ideally we should also want to evaluate the employment success of the overall pattern of institutional arrangements described in this chapter, and the contribution made by each organisation and policy instrument. Even though regional policy has been systematically evaluated by economists much more than have most fields of public policy, we are left with limited, tentative and largely dated findings (see Ashcroft, 1978; Moore and Rhodes 1979; Marquand, 1980). Bearing in mind the difficulty of assessing what would have happened in the absence of policy, the various estimates tend to show that regional policy from 1963 did produce a substantial number of jobs in the development areas (about 220,000 in 1963–70). However, it is almost impossible to say whether this represents a substantial increase in net jobs created for the UK as a whole, or merely a diversion from one region to another. Estimates vary from very slight net output gains for the UK economy as a whole, to quite substantial ones. These tentative overall assessments of the effect of regional policy tell us nothing about the contribution made by individual policy instruments or individual organisations.

The economic impact of the mechanisms for delivering industrial and regional policy is only one criterion by which they can be evaluated, and it is not necessarily the most important one for the politicians and officials who operate the system. The establishment of new organisations or the transfer of responsibilities can have important symbolic significance, regardless of any substantive economic impact. The establishment of the Scottish and Welsh Department Agencies and the transfer of responsibility for administering selective regional assistance to the Scottish and Welsh Offices in 1975 can only be fully understood as political actions, with the electoral upsurge of the Scottish National Party very much in mind. More generally, although there are good economic arguments for reducing the current degree of overlap in the industrial policy field, particularly over promotion, the creation and relative emphasis given to the role of specific organisations reflect political as much as economic arguments.

NOTE

I should like to thank all members of government departments and other agencies who provided me with information in interviews and in other ways. Without them this article would not have been possible. All responsibility for matters of fact and interpretation is, however, mine. I should also like to thank all those who have commented on earlier drafts of this and related papers. I should like to thank Michael Littlechild for detailed comments and information, and Harry Mycock for access to material collected for his Ph.D. research. All information not specifically attributed in the text comes from one or more of the above sources.

REFERENCES

Ashcroft, B. (1978) 'The Evaluation of Regional Economic Policy: the Case of the United Kingdom', *Studies in Public Policy*, no. 12, Centre for the Study of Public Policy, University of Strathclyde.

Brett, C. (1970) 'The Lessons of Devolution in Northern Ireland', *Political Quarterly*, vol. 41, pp. 261–80.

Commission on the Constitution (1970) *Written Evidence,* vol. 3, (London: HMSO).

Commission on the Constitution (1971) *Minutes of Evidence*, vol. III: *Northern Ireland* (London: HMSO).

Cross, J. A. (1970) 'The Regional Decentralisation of British Governments', *Public Administration*, vol. 48, pp. 423–41.

Field, G. M. and P. V. Hills (1976) 'The Administration of Industrial Subsidies', in A. Whiting (ed.), *The Economics of Industrial Subsidies* (London: HMSO).

HC 97 (1974–5) *Development Fund Accounts 1973/4* (London: HMSO).

HC 104 (1975–6) *Expenditure Committee (Trade and Industry Sub-Committee): Chrysler UK Ltd: Minutes of Evidence* (London: HMSO).

HC 600-II/28i and ii (1977–8) *Eighth Report from the Expenditure Committee: Selected Public Expenditure Programmes,* Ch. II: 'Regional and Selective Assistance to Industry', (London: HMSO).

HC 647-I (1977–8) *Expenditure Committee (Social Services and Employment Sub-Committee): People and Work: Report* (London: HMSO).

HC 647-III (1977–8) *Expenditure Committee (Social Services and Employment Sub-Committee): People and Work: Evidence* (London: HMSO).

HC 395 (1979–80) *Development Fund Accounts 1978/9* (London: HMSO).

HC 731-I, HC 731-II/485 (1979–80) *First Report from the Committee on Welsh Affairs: the Role of the Welsh Office and Associated Bodies in Developing Employment Opportunities in Wales*, vol. 1: *Report*; vol. 2: *Minutes of Evidence and Appendices* (London: HMSO).

HC 769-I, HC 769-II (1979–80) *Second Report from the Select Committee on Scottish Affairs: Inward Investment*, vol. 1: *Report*; vol. 2: *Minutes of Evidence and Appendices* (London: HMSO).

HC 772 (1979–80) *Industry Act 1972: Annual Report by the Secretaries of State for Industry, Scotland and Wales for the year ended 31 March 1980* (London: HMSO).

Heclo, Hugh and Aaron Wildavsky (1974) *The Private Government of Public Money* (London: Macmillan).

Hogwood, B. W. (1979) 'Analysing Industrial Policy: a Multi-Perspective Approach', *Public Administration Bulletin*, no. 29, April 1979, pp. 18–42.

Hogwood, B. W. and P. Lindley (1980) 'Which English Regions?', *Studies in Public Policy*, no. 50, Centre for the Study of Public Policy, University of Strathclyde.

Hood, C. C. (1976) *The Limits of Administration* (London: John Wiley).

Kellas, J. (1975) *The Scottish Political System*, 2nd edn (Cambridge: Cambridge University Press).

Lindley, P. (1982) 'The Framework of Regional Planning', in B. W. Hogwood and M. Keating (eds), *Regional Government in England* (Oxford: Clarendon Press).

Marquand, J. (1980) 'Measuring the Effects and Costs of Regional Incentives', *Government Economic Service Working Paper No. 32*, Department of Industry.

Moore, B. and J. Rhodes (1979) *The Impact of Regional Policy*, D323, Block 2, Unit 7, Open University Press.

Randall, P. J. (1972) 'Wales in the Structure of Central Government', *Public Administration*, vol. 50, pp. 353–72.

Rowlands, E. (1972) 'The Politics of Regional Administration: the Establishment of the Welsh Office', *Public Administration*, vol. 50, pp. 333–52.

Smith, B. C. (1964) *Regionalism in England*, vol. 1: *Regional Institutions: A Guide* (Acton Society Trust).

Watson, M. (1975) 'The Regional Dimension of Planning', in J. Hayward and M. Watson (eds), *Planning, Politics and Public Policy* (Cambridge: Cambridge University Press) pp. 285–94.

Wright, M. and S. Young (1975) 'Regional Planning in Britain', in J. Hayward and M. Watson (eds), *Planning, Politics and Public Policy* (Cambridge: Cambridge University Press) pp. 237–68.

Young, S. (1982) 'Regional Offices of the Department of the Environment: Their Roles and Influence in the 1970s', in B. W. Hogwood and M. Keating (eds), *Regional Government in England* (Oxford: Clarendon Press).

3 The Welsh Language in the Policy Process

PETER MADGWICK and PHILLIP RAWKINS

I THE DECLINE OF THE WELSH LANGUAGE

At the beginning of the nineteenth century, and perhaps well into it, almost the whole indigenous population of Wales spoke Welsh and a few also spoke English. By 1901 only 50 per cent spoke Welsh, according to the census, and the number of monoglot Welsh speakers had contracted sharply. Subsequently, there has been a steady decline in the proportion of Welsh speakers in Wales, from 37 per cent in 1931 to 26 per cent in 1961, and 21 per cent in 1971. The monoglot Welsh speaker has virtually disappeared.

The principal causes of this transformation of the linguistic character of Wales lie in economic development, government policy and, partly a consequence of these, popular indifference. Industrialisation in the nineteenth century, particularly in the coal-fields of South and North-east Wales, led to massive immigration from England and the depopulation of the Welsh countryside; depression led to emigration from Wales to England and overseas. Government is conducted in the English language. An objective of government policy after 1536 was the Anglicisation of Wales, at least in the negative sense that Wales was administered from London as an undifferentiated extension of England. The Welsh language became a language of the hearth, and not a public language, except in the chapels. In the new Board schools of the late nineteenth century, English was taught as the language of advancement, and the use of Welsh was actively discouraged. The inferior status thus ascribed to the Welsh language was accepted by most Welsh people, and the language itself was weakened by its isolation from administration, commerce and technology.

In the last eighty years, economic change has continued to threaten the language, and the activities of governments and schools have, at best, reflected its decline. However, the indifference or neutrality of these forces, if that be conceded, was quite eclipsed by the destructive power of the rapidly developing mass media, especially television. At the same time, a process of secularisation of society undermined the chapels, which had been the central support of Welsh as a public language. The Welsh language, unlike Irish, has never had a secular stronghold in the pubs and clubs – rather the reverse.

The decline of the language has been uneven. The rural areas of the West and North-west have remained the heartland of Welsh-speaking Wales. In 1971 five of the old counties of this area each had above 60 per cent of Welsh speakers. But the frontier of Anglicisation has crept westwards. No other county has above 30 per cent Welsh-speakers. While the industrial South and North-east of Wales had long been subject to the loss of language, the 1971 census showed the beginnings of a new corridor of Anglicisation in mid-Wales. A narrow coastal strip in the West formed a second frontier of the language, squeezing the heartland from the West (see Bowen and Carter, 1974, 1975).

The situation of the language is inevitably more complex than this brief outline allows. Welsh-speaking is itself an elusive concept, and the census data is necessarily based on rough questions. Most language situations in Wales are mixed, and the mixture varies by area and function.

Within the complexities there are factors which give some strength to the language. Some goodwill towards the language seems to exist, though it is probably neither universal, nor very positive (see Madgwick *et al.*, 1973, pp. 109–10). For most people language must serve daily lives, centred on jobs, family, sport – lives more humdrum than are envisaged in the romantic rhetoric of linguistic nationalism. But Wales has never lacked movements to foster the language (cf. Rawkins, 1975). Since the early 1960s, these have evinced a new vigour and political drive (see Betts, 1976; Stephens, 1979). The Welsh Language Society (Cymdeithas yr Iaith Gymraeg) has been the militant and youthful wing of a more general resurgence of enthusiasm for the language. It has undoubtedly changed the climate of opinion, gaining recognition as well as resentment, and has won some specific advances in the official use of Welsh. In education there has been a renewed emphasis on the teaching of Welsh, both as a medium of instruction and as a second language, and some development of Welsh-medium and nursery schools. Broadcasting in Welsh has increased from the negligible to something like 14 hours altogether each week on television, and 64 on radio. It is accepted policy to extend broadcasting in Welsh. After some vacillation, and in face of widespread protest, the Conservative government reverted to its commitment to establish in Wales a predominantly Welsh-medium fourth television channel.

Despite the greatly improved public facilities for the use and dissemination of the language, the comparative and specialist evidence discourages any objective more ambitious than the preservation of Welsh at its present modest minority level. Professor Lockwood sees no long-term future for Welsh: '. . . No small language has the secret of survival' (as quoted by Betts, 1976, p. 12). Professor Price believes the prospects of Welsh are not as good as those of Faroese or Catalan, but better than most minority languages (Price, 1979, p. 15). The present state of bilingualism in Wales, in which everyone speaks a major language and a fifth of the people also speak a minor language, is seen as inherently unstable and transitional (Fishman, 1970, p. 27). The goal of a completely bilingual Wales, even within a long time-scale, is against the tide of social and economic forces. It seems unlikely that the special circumstances facilitating the restoration of Hebrew in Israel will be recreated in Wales.

Mixed-language situations pose peculiarly difficult political problems. Criteria of convenience and efficiency of communication are overlaid by the historical interpretations and political aspirations of nationalism and counter-nationalism. The rhetoric of freedom and rights dramatises the conflict, but offers no principle by which to resolve it, since there are claims to freedoms and rights on each side. While personal or individual choice cannot be safeguarded, territorial language policies (e.g. the designation of areas by dominant language) involve, in Wales at least, both practical difficulties and serious infringements of individual liberty.

Thus, an education official in Gwynedd, defending his authority's positive policy for the Welsh language referred to the unity of the community as a desirable objective: 'Aims to preserve and foster Welsh and to unify the community must be placed above the success of the individual' (Rawkins, 1979a, pp. 93–4). The priorities set out here are plainly open to disagreement, and they are, in any case in conflict with the full freedom of the individual, as viewed from a liberal perspective. Further, the compulsions of the state in promoting the language are more deliberate, and may well be more absolute and impersonal than the constraints arising from socio-economic conditions. The conflict here is as profound as the conflict between *laissez-faire* liberals and the new collectivists. The 'language freedom' fighters take up a conventional liberal position; the language advocates press for state intervention.

These considerations have consequences for policy-making. They make difficult the achievement of consent for the initiation of policy; and they make for uncertainty in implementation and instability in the maintenance of policy. However, there is scope for policy-making in the elusiveness of the political values at stake. Losses which cannot be measured objectively may well be much exaggerated subjectively and bitterly resented. But there are possibilities of persuasion and bargaining. The game may be presented as not leading unavoidably to clear victory or defeat. The tendency of ethnic conflict to a 'zero-sum' outcome need not apply in linguistic conflict. It follows that a serious language policy – serious in the sense of scope, penetration and firmness – would be marked by sensitivity and flexibility, rather than missionary zeal, and would need to be promoted and defended in the arena of politics.

The consideration of other Western democracies with linguistic cleavages is not encouraging. It indicates that the problems may be aggravated both by neglect and by vigorous and positive action. Delicate steps towards limited objectives are indicated. For Wales such a programme might be:

(a) The maintenance of the Welsh language as a medium appropriate for all areas of public and social life, and the natural and historical language of substantial numbers of Welsh people. The definition of 'substantial' might well be left open, but full bilingualism, involving the mass conversion of non-Welsh speakers, would not stand as an official objective.

(b) The general acceptance of bilingualism, in the restricted sense that some people speak two languages, as the natural and desirable condition of Wales, and with this the acceptance that a modest degree of bilingualism has implications and consequences for all people living in Wales.

(c) The establishment of a framework of institutions and procedures to provide support for the Welsh language, and a maximum of security and freedom for both Welsh speakers and monoglot English speakers.

(d) A degree of territorial and functional differentiation designed to maximise both the efficiency and the acceptability of the policy.

These objectives assume a move away from the concept of universal bilingualism. There are good grounds for this. First, it is a deceptive goal, since universal bilingualism leads in practice to unilingualism, as soon as one language serves the minimal needs of communication. Second, the achievement of full bilingualism is no longer possible in Welsh conditions, given the massive loss of Welsh as a home language, the cultural dominance of English, the continuing mobility of population, and political restraints on coercion; and the struggle against such odds to achieve bilingualism would be debilitating and contentious. Third, the separation of languages leads to more or less peaceful co-existence, while mixing them (the 'compound solution') encourages language shifts, tensions and resentments.

Such precepts do not, of course, meet the claims of a linguistically based nationalism, nor the claims for Welsh as the historic language of Wales. These are legitimate claims, but for their implementation they require the consent of the people of Wales. The government of the language operates within such complex and delicate political considerations.

II THE GOVERNMENT OF THE LANGUAGE

Institutions

Arrangements for the development and application of language policy in Wales are comparatively unsystematic and diffuse. The 'arrangements' are, like much else in British government, mainly the result of reactions to particular problems, and are marked by uncertainty of objectives, and unpredictability in operation. A map or inventory of the government of the language is inevitably no more than an outline.

(a) The framework of law and precept

The Welsh Language Act, 1967, following the Hughes–Parry Report (1965), provided for 'equal validity' for the language in the courts and on official forms. This extended the Welsh Courts Act of 1942, and parallels the principle of the Elections (Welsh Forms) Act of 1964.

Other policies have been established as the government response to the reports of particular government-appointed committees. Thus, the policy on road signs arises from the report of the Bowen Committee (1973). Education has been the subject of several reports, notably in 1927, 1953 and the Gittins Report of 1968, which 'endorsed the principle of a fully bilingual education'. A 'framework of policy' arising in this way tends to be incomplete, ambivalent and insecure.

(b) The institutions of central government

The Welsh Office now has responsibility, in some cases mainly as agent and overseer, for most aspects of policy in Wales. It has a small section within its General Division specifically for the language, but language policy is also dealt with as it arises in education, and other public services. The Welsh Office has some mandatory powers, as over trunk road signs; other largely persuasive powers, as in education; and some exemplary influence. So far, the Permanent Secretary has been a Welsh-speaker, but the government rejected the recommendation of the Hughes–Parry Committee that all departmental heads in Wales should be Welsh-speaking. Of the Secretaries of State, two of five have been Welsh-speakers, and their attitudes to the language have at times reflected most of the more 'reasonable' attitudes to be found among the Welsh people.

Broadcasting poses complex problems for the language and for government. Responsibility for broadcasting in Wales, in so far as the government accepts responsibility at all, rests with the Home Office. But it has been the practice in recent years for the Welsh Office to be involved as a major partner in deliberations concerning Welsh-language broadcasting. Thus the Welsh Office was formally represented on the Home Office Working Party on the Welsh Fourth Channel Television Project. Similarly, during the debate on those clauses of the Broadcasting Bill relating specifically to Wales, the government was represented by both the Home Secretary and a Welsh Office Minister. In education, official and professional views broadly coincided. In broadcasting, by contrast, the interests of the commercial companies and the broadcasting professionals and administrators diverged from the Welsh Office view, and modified official policy. For all that, elite opinion in Wales, channelled through the Welsh Office, has had considerable effect in gaining acceptance in Westminster and Whitehall for the principle of the extension of the number of hours of Welsh language broadcasting, on both radio and television.

In Parliament, the Welsh Grand Committee, which includes all Members of Parliament sitting for Welsh constituencies, has devoted two sessions in the last ten years to the subject of the language. In 1980 the controversy over the fourth channel issue invested the Committee's July sitting with unusual importance. Normally, however, the proceedings of the Grand Committee have had little impact on government policy. The Select Committee on Welsh Affairs started in 1979 is likely to be more significant. In its first year of activity, the Select Committee has shown a remarkable degree of all-party unanimity in focussing on the failure of central government to allow sufficiently for the Welsh dimension in the policy-making process.

(c) Regional and advisory bodies

The Council for the Welsh Language, an appointed body established in 1973, advised the Secretary of State, and urged public and private bodies to foster the language. It was a device characteristic of recent Welsh government, and lapsed in 1978.

The Welsh Council, a nominated advisory council abolished in 1979, avoided pronouncing on the language, perhaps because it was likely to be sharply divided on the subject. Its predecessor, the Council for Wales and Monmouthshire, was less inhibited, and more strongly Welsh in its leanings. It issued a sympathetic report on *The Welsh Language Today* in 1963. There are a dozen or more other public bodies, some with modest funds, which have responsibilities affecting the language; for example, the Arts Council, Books Council, Broadcasting Council and Tourist Board.

(d) The institutions of local government

These include the County and District Councils, and the local authority associations. Of the County Councils, Gwynedd is at present in effect controlled by nationalists, and has the most positive language policy. This reflects (and conceivably only just reflects) an area which is the most intensely Welsh of all, with about two-thirds of its people speaking Welsh. In other ways the reorganisation of local government did not help the language, particularly in Dyfed, where strongly Welsh areas are joined with highly Anglicised areas.

The District Councils, as local planning authorities, are responsible for the vast majority of decisions on planning applications. Some District Councils in Gwynedd are seeking to use their limited powers to restrict the availability of cottages as second homes. Following the lead of two of its constituent authorities, Anglesey and Caernarfon, the county of Gwynedd has sought to incorporate language considerations into its county structure plan.

Among the Welsh local authority associations, the Welsh Joint Education Committee has been an active promoter of the efficient teaching of Welsh in schools.

(e) Dominant groups

It is arguable that the government of Wales is characteristically elitist and accords substantial influence to comparatively small groups, a high proportion of which are Welsh-speaking. In this way Wales has acquired two overlapping establishments. The evidence is inevitably difficult to assemble. Partly, the role accorded to elites is a matter of culture, and relates to the old chapel tradition of respectability and the dominance of ministers and deacons. The absence, in local government in many parts of Wales, of competitive two-party politics encourages the rise of the small dominant group. The modern political history of Wales could be written in terms of a succession of elites: first Conservative, then Liberal, now Labour, with Plaid Cymru alone struggling for representative mass politics (though probably destined, were it ever successful, to degenerate rapidly into a remote establishment itself).

Then there is the plethora of advisory bodies, which bulk large in a small country, and draw heavily on a comparatively thin line of appropriate individuals, the shadowy Welsh equivalent of the 'great and the good'.

(f) Language groups

These include bodies with avowed linguistic aims, for example Urdd Gobaith Cymru (the Welsh youth movement – literally, 'the League of Wales' Hope'), the Royal National Eisteddfod and UCAC (Undeb Cened-laethol Athrawon Cymru: the National Association of Teachers of Wales), along with Mudiad Ysgolion Meithrin (the National Association of Welsh-medium Nursery Schools and Playgroups). These have as a principal or major objective the preservation and promotion of the language. There are other bodies which pursue linguistic ends amidst other purposes, notably some religious and educational associations. In addition there are a number of bodies which contain a natural majority of, or which have been captured by, language enthusiasts; for example, the Guild of Graduates of the University of Wales, and from time to time, the Court of the University of Wales. Also prominent are language-based organisations like the Welsh Language Society and Adfer, which resort to direct action. (For an annotated inventory of Welsh-language organisations see Jones, 1979.)

The groups which arise from time to time to promote language freedom (that is the rights of monoglot English speakers) are usually short-lived, because they lack the deep commitment of the Welsh language movement, because they do not feel the sharp insecurities of the threatened Welsh-speaker, because they are appeased with modest concessions, or perhaps because they are soon persuaded of the error of their stance; or because they sense that the English language needs no protection in Wales.

(g) The political parties

Driven by the tides of enthusiasm and nationalism in the 1970s all the parties had formally adopted programmes to support the language. But, in practice, there have been hesitancies and ambiguities. Even Plaid Cymru has been reluctant to commit itself to firm and detailed proposals (see Betts, 1976, Ch. 13). Political parties rarely say anything against the language, yet do not do a great deal to advance it. Mealy-mouthed evasiveness seems to be characteristic of the government of the language; in the long run this discourages the making of appropriate policies, and is unhelpful to both sides in the conflict.

Functions

The government of the language may also be analysed by function or linguistic domain.

(a) Government and public service

The principle of equal validity means that within limits public services (forms, correspondence and counter services) are available in either language. Some local authorities now transact business and keep records in Welsh. Gwynedd and Dyfed County Councils use simultaneous translation equipment. In the courts, a defendant may choose to speak Welsh only. All road direction signs will eventually be bilingual but not warning signs. English will be placed on top for reasons of safety, except where a local option has been insisted on, as in Gwynedd. This is symbolic bilingualism or environmental bilingualism, according to one's position on the language issue.

Some general limitations arise from a shortage of funds and of Welsh language facilities. It is comparatively easy and economical to issue bilingual forms, more difficult in some areas to guarantee counter service in Welsh. The cost of converting road signs throughout Wales has risen steeply and implementation of a uniform policy is likely to be long delayed.

(b) Education

This is largely in the hands of the local authorities, although finance and the influence that goes with it are still finally determined by central government. The major issues are the extension of Welsh teaching facilities in every grade from nursery to higher education, the provision of Welsh-medium schools, especially in Anglicised areas, and the degree of compulsion in the teaching of Welsh, especially to children from non-Welsh-speaking homes.

(c) The media

The press is in private hands and is largely English in language and style. Some subsidy has been arranged recently for a Welsh language newspaper, and two or three periodicals are already subsidised. But commercial considerations mainly apply and there is little scope for government intervention. Broadcasting, on the other hand, ultimately depends on government for its statutory structure and finance. It has been the subject of acute political pressures.

Broadcasting is in the hands of the BBC, Harlech Television, the IBA and the Broadcasting Council for Wales. When the government's plans for the new fourth television channel are implemented, a significant change in the pattern will occur. Despite obvious misgivings about a drastic departure from established practice, among both Whitehall and broadcasting executives, the government has moved to establish a separate Welsh authority to supervise Welsh language broadcasting, whether originating from the BBC or from Harlech.

Following extensive consultations, and the deliberations of four government commissions of enquiry, by 1979 there was widespread if not unanimous agreement that the fourth channel in Wales should become primarily a vehicle for broadcasts in the Welsh language. The proposition was accepted by both the Labour government of the time and the Conservative opposition. However, once returned to office, the Conservatives reversed their position. Careful study of the implications of concentrating Welsh language broadcasts from both the BBC and Harlech on the fourth channel led them to regard their earlier commitment as unwise. As the Welsh Secretary explained, the government was concerned about costs and the loss to Welsh viewers of the UK-wide fourth channel service, as well as the loss of casual Welsh viewing of interspersed programmes. Hence it was decided that 'the best way to make early progress was by requiring the ITV and the BBC to provide additional Welsh language programmes on their own channels . . .' (as quoted in *Western Mail*, 20 August 1980). It appears that the pressure from commercial broadcasting circles may have been a significant factor in causing the government to reconsider (see the letter from the Managing Director of HTV to the Editor of *The Times*, 19 August 1980).

The government's 'U-turn' provoked a storm of criticism. The Welsh Language Society resumed an earlier campaign of property damage directed at broadcasting installations in England and Wales; Plaid Cymru encouraged its members to refuse to renew their television licences until justice was done. Finally, Gwynfor Evans, the party's president, gave notice of his intention to begin a Gandhi-style fast until death unless the government kept its earlier promise.

Among elites too moderate opinion opposed the government decision. The Commons debate on arrangements for the utilisation of the new channel in Wales (*Parl. Debates*, 24 June 1980, cols 384– 93) demonstrated a quite unusual unanimity among a majority of Welsh MPs, English-speaking and Welsh-speaking, in opposition to the government's change of mind. A notable contributor to the Lords second-reading debate on the Broadcasting Bill was Lord Annan (Chairman of the Committee on Broadcasting, 1974), who argued that the government's decision suggested that concern over financial considerations had taken precedence 'over what I think is political and cultural good sense' (*Western Mail*, 26 July 1980).

Both the Home Secretary and the Secretary of State for Wales expressed the government's determination to resist the growing volume of criticism of its policy. However, over the summer of 1980, a series of minor concessions were made, along with a number of conciliatory speeches. Finally, in September, the government acknowledged its unwillingness to defy Welsh opinion any further, and reversed its policy for a second time. The decision came a week after the Home Secretary, William Whitelaw, had received a delegation of Welsh notables: Lord Cledwyn, a former Labour Minister, the Archbishop of Wales, and the former Permanent Under-Secretary of the Welsh Office. Also, it came three weeks before Gwynfor Evans was to commence his fast.

One consequence of this conclusion to the fourth channel controversy will be the establishment of a Welsh institution with responsibility for coordination and overseeing of broadcasting. This administrative innovation runs against the traditional separation of government from direct overseeing of the media. Further, the arrangement to combine on one channel BBC and HTV programmes in the Welsh language runs against the conventional separation of public and private broadcasting.

A special difficulty of the broadcasting situation is that Wales has, by general standards, a small Welsh-speaking audience of half-a-million at most, and cannot draw on the programme resources of another country, as is the case in Switzerland or Quebec for example. There are financial problems since commercial profitability is impossible, and the requirement for government subsidy might be judged excessive in terms of money, and uneconomical in relation to the population served. According to a recent BBC estimate, each additional hour of television in the Welsh language will cost an extra £1 million annually. The government's current proposals indicate a target of 21–2 hours per week; the language lobby has proposed 25 hours as a more satisfactory figure. Altogether, the Fourth Channel episode showed that the heavy financial costs of Welsh language broadcasting were partly offset by the political costs of frustrating Welsh demands.

(d) Commerce

The private sector is still comparatively untouched by language pressures. Small firms usually arise from and adapt to the locality. The larger businesses directed from Cardiff, or with head offices in England and elsewhere, tend to ignore the Welsh language, but recently some banks, building societies and stores have made voluntary changes, for example displaying bilingual signs, providing bilingual cheque books, and seeking bilingual counter staff. The larger stores like Woolworth, Boots and W. H. Smith have made modest moves in this direction and are now being urged by the Welsh Language Society to adopt bilingual signs and labelling. The test of profitability is a hard one for the language and some would argue also inappropriate.

(e) Employment

In the real world, people compete for jobs and marriage partners. The competition for marriage partners is not unaffected by language, and mixed marriages are a serious threat to Welsh-speaking within a family. Sex, even more than commercial life, is beyond the writ of the legislators, and so perhaps is the strongest agent of secularisation. The competition for jobs on the other hand is continuous, and is subject to some measure of public control.

Generally there is remarkably little systematic categorisation of jobs by language requirement, but the Welsh Office, some local authorities and the BBC reserve some posts for bilinguals. Except in the county of Gwynedd, and more widely in the education service, the number of such jobs is quite small, though in some cases significant among the higher posts. The BBC is a frequent target of criticism for showing a bias towards Welsh speakers, but partly the critics fail to understand that BBC Wales is responsible for only a small part of the total output of the BBC in Wales, which is predominantly in English, by non-Welsh-speaking people employed in London (with many Welshmen among them).

III LANGUAGE POLICY AND EDUCATION: A CASE-STUDY

The education system is a special object in the struggle for influence over language policy: other groups too would reform society through the schools. Education is a favourite arena for amateur democrats. The harassed teacher in the classroom has borne with fortitude the inability to meet the expectations pressed by clients, while coping with the immediate demands of children and their parents. Thus teachers may recognise more than others that the schoolchildren of Wales are the ultimate arbiters of the language policies laid down by education authorities, and the authorities may discover that their writ runs against formidable obstacles of inertia and hostility.

Education is the most highly sensitive of the state 'welfare' services. It takes up a substantial part of children's lives; it aims to train and influence them in a far-reaching and profound manner; the special expertise of teachers is open to challenge (the universal experience of education confers a sense of universal competence); and the dual relationships of teacher–child, parent–teacher gives some (still largely unexploited) advantage to the parent. The schools may belong to the local education authorities or the teachers, but the child surely belongs to the parents, or to himself. Language in education raises the most difficult problems for citizen and policy-maker alike. In other fields the individual is left with a large area of choice. Except in broadcasting, the 'unwanted' language can be discarded with little loss. This is not always the case in schools. The 'unwanted' language may be a compulsory element in the curriculum, and the distribution of the two languages may tend towards a total pattern of education leaning to one or the other.

Initially, the powers of the Secretary of State for Wales were limited in education to exercising 'oversight within Wales of the execution of national policy by the Department of Education and Science'. In 1970 the Conservative government transferred the direct responsibility for primary and secondary education from the Department of Education and Science to the Welsh Office. Finally, in 1977, the responsibility for further education was devolved to Cardiff, leaving only the University of Wales under the DES.

In education, as in other matters, the Welsh Office pursues policies common to England and Wales. The initiative and the power rest with the 'parent' ministry in London. However, the Welsh Office is consulted by Whitehall at all stages in the formulation of policy, and in the resolution of conflicts arising in implementation. It has, further, a special role in matters in which Welsh interests are unique or plainly diverge from English conditions. Among these the Welsh language is pre-eminent. This was evident, for example, in the discussion on the question of a core curriculum, which has followed the publication of a Green Paper. The Welsh Office has directed that consideration be given to Welsh, in addition to the subjects currently under consideration by educators in England (English, Mathematics and Religious Education).

The powers of the Secretary of State for Wales in education are derived from the Education Act of 1944, and by subsequent amendments. Section 1 of the Act stipulates that in the fields of primary, secondary and further education, the Secretary of State is required:

To promote the education of the people [of Wales] and the progressive development of institutions devoted to that purpose, and to secure the effective execution by local authorities, under his control and direction, of the national policy for providing a varied and comprehensive educational service in every area.

However, Section 23 of the Education Act stipulates that the local authority is responsible for the actual process of education. Thus, while central government determines policy (and provides finance), a good deal of influence in the day-to-day running of the system, rests on the localities. Like the Secretary of State for Education in England, the Welsh Secretary has the general power to intervene only when and where he may determine that the local education authority is acting 'unreasonably'.

The character of central–local relations in education is further compli-cated by the convention that school governors and headteachers are given wide discretionary powers with regard to school organisation and cur-riculum. In appointing staff, whatever the local procedures, the advice of the headteacher is likely to carry great weight; and teachers themselves very much wish to maintain the relative autonomy of educators as the principal decision-makers in curriculum matters.

In education, the principal initiatives of the Secretary of State for Wales have been on matters relating to the Welsh language; but these have necessarily been advisory, and hortatory. Given the political delicacy of the language issue, as well as the understandable resistance on the part of the local education authorities to what may appear to be additional intrusions into their jurisdiction, there is little scope for the imposition of central authority. Much depends on the informal influence of education department officials and members of the Welsh Inspectorate. The encouragement, advice and prodding of the Welsh education department has been a significant factor in creating a willingness on the part of local authorities to make provision for Welsh-medium education, and for the teaching of Welsh as a second language. However, it remains for the local authority, and not for the education department, to take action.

The room for initiative on the part of the local authority is covered by Section 76 of the 1944 Education Act: 'So far as is compatible with the provision of efficient instruction and training and the avoidance of unreasonable public expenditure, pupils are to be educated in accordance with the wishes of their parents.' This provision has been most generally utilised for the provision of denominational schools, distinguished from the conventional local authority schools by the place of religion in the life of the school (Regan, 1977, pp. 42–6). However, the same section of the Act may be taken to apply to the development of facilities for Welsh-medium instruction. In the 1940s a number of local authorities, responding to public interest, and motivated by a belief in the importance of the language, moved to establish Ysgolion Gymraeg (Welsh Schools) at a primary level. Such institutions catered for a minority of parents, living in predominantly English-speaking areas, seeking Welsh-medium education for their children. In the 1960s and 1970s, some local authorities acted more vigorously in this field and the number of such schools has increased substantially.

Conflict over the language in education has occurred in most areas of Wales, and in both urban and rural settings. The major specific catalysts to conflict are decisions concerning the designation of bilingual schools (or failure to make such decisions). Bilingual schools tend, in practice, to emphasise the Welsh language and are unofficially regarded as Welsh schools. In North and West Wales, such schools exist only in areas where Welsh-speakers are already in a minority position, or where the proportion of the population able to speak Welsh is in rapid decline. The most straightforward examples are Bangor, Aberystwyth and Carmarthen.

Demands from Welsh-speakers for bilingual schools to protect their language may be met by resistance from English-speakers, objecting to disturbance of established schools, changes in accommodation and travel arrangements, and the division of the existing community on linguistic grounds. There may also be objection to the reduction of the range of subjects, teachers and facilities in the smaller schools. Hence English-speakers may feel that the quality of education offered to their children suffers as a result of concessions to Welsh-speakers on what they regard as non-educational grounds.

The Welsh schools movement is comparatively vigorous; the proportion of pupils wishing to obtain entry to bilingual secondary schools has been increasing rapidly, though the actual number of bilingual schools is quite small (just under 5 per cent of the secondary schools). To the people of the towns of south-east and north-east Wales, the language appears to be gaining in status and support. In Cardiff, the capital city of Wales, where bilingual schools were initially the preserve of the Welsh-speaking professional middle class, the pupils are now increasingly from working-class and English-speaking homes. The growing proportion of English-speaking, working-class children is even more marked in the bilingual schools of Mid-Glamorgan. The motives of parents are admittedly mixed. Small schools, aiming at high academic standards, may look like an acceptable escape from the local comprehensive. But the effect on the Welsh language is positive; for once it is associated with educational privilege and social advancement.

Whenever the linguistic status of a school changes, conflict is likely to develop. The scarcity of resources, together with declining enrolments, make it unlikely that the local authority would obtain the necessary permission from the Welsh Office to build a new school to accommodate separate bilingual facilities. The alternative is to reorganise the use of existing school buildings and to reassign children in order to release an existing school to serve a new purpose. Strong attachment to neighbourhood in south-east Wales inevitably produces strong parental reaction against a decision to close a local school and to move its pupils elsewhere, even where this may be accomplished with a minimum of inconvenience. Once again, a situation develops where Welsh-speakers, or those who wish their children to become fluent in Welsh, may be perceived as a privileged minority, who gain at the expense of the locality, which loses its school. The prominence in the Welsh schools movement in Cardiff of local notables leads to a suspicion that decisions seen to favour the language have been produced by pressure exercised behind closed doors.

Political partisanship may also complicate the situation. Where Plaid Cymru has been relatively strong at a local level, as is the case in a number of areas of Mid-Glamorgan, tensions between a Labour-dominated local authority and the nationalist opposition may increase the political loading of educational decision-making. In some cases, Welsh schools have been regarded as seminaries for nationalists. Language policy in the schools is necessarily involved in the political tensions of contemporary Wales.

Polarisation occurs most frequently in small urban centres in strongly Welsh-speaking areas. In educational and administrative centres such as Bangor, Aberystwyth or Carmarthen, the involvement of prominent nationalists in campaigns for bilingual schools is balanced by the mobilis- ation of English-speaking academics and professionals in defence of the linguistic rights of the English-speaker. While the English-speakers may well be the dominant group in their professions, they perceive themselves as part of a political minority in matters of local decision-making. Similarly, advocates of the language, even in Gwynedd and Dyfed, see themselves as an embattled minority in Wales, fighting a last-ditch struggle on behalf of a threatened language. Hence there exists the classic double-minority situ- ation.

Problems also arise in the Welsh-speaking, but sparsely-populated rural areas of Wales, where a parallel system of linguistically streamed schools might be desirable; but limited facilities, distances and the scattered distribution of population may make such a policy difficult to operate. Hence conflict may emerge between Welsh-speakers, teachers and parents, who wish to see more time and attention devoted to Welsh-medium instruction, and an articulate English-speaking minority, who may argue that their children will be placed at a disadvantage if there is more Welsh in the curriculum.

In these smaller communities, linguistic conflicts may be reinforced by class and ethnic divisions. This is likely to occur where the leaders of the opposition to an extension of bilingual education are, or are perceived to be, prosperous English 'immigrants', and where the language advocates are led by those associated with Plaid Cymru or the Welsh Language Society. The latter see themselves as representing the interest of the local community, which is both poor and deeply Welsh. Each group may suspect that the other has undue influence with the local authority and its officials. For the most part, such conflicts are local and temporary. However, the growing anxiety of many Welsh-speakers, together with the indifference of the majority, increase the potential for a broadening and politicisation of linguistic divisions.

The implementation of language policy has given rise to greatest controversy in the county of Gwynedd. One factor which distinguishes Gwynedd from Dyfed is the concentration in the former county of a substantial and well-established Welsh-speaking professional class. It may be conjectured that the creation of the new authority provided an opportunity for this group to extend and strengthen its local political control. The Gwynedd platform has enabled the group to state its goals and policies and to strive to achieve them with a new self-confidence. The controversies which have emerged are similar in kind to those which have taken shape in Dyfed. However, the solid commitment to the policy of the majority of councillors and officials has led them to view each challenge as but one battle in a long war, rather than as a local and temporary problem to be solved as quietly as possible. Hence, in Gwynedd, the language issue in the schools has been bitterly contested and has attracted substantial national publicity.

There have been a number of allegations of linguistic discrimination against non-Welsh-speaking children in Gwynedd's schools. In a speech made in the course of the committee stage of the Wales Bill, in March 1978, Neil Kinnock went so far as to suggest that there was evidence of 'linguistic racialism' in certain schools in Merioneth (*Guardian*, 7 April 1978). He went on to claim that nationalists were undertaking 'warfare against children not capable of defending themselves' (as quoted in *Western Mail*, 6 July 1978). The allegations were subsequently examined in detail and refuted by Gwynedd County Council, following investigations by the Inspectorate. The findings were endorsed by the Welsh Office. However, the evident solidarity of the opposition to the Kinnock allegations served only to deepen the suspicions held by many English-speaking parents that a conspiracy was afoot. It may be concluded that fears and suspicions are an almost invariable outcome of the authority's policy.

In the Anglicised areas such as Holyhead and Llandudno, where only 25 per cent and 56 per cent, respectively, of primary school children speak Welsh, most of the instruction, in the majority of schools, is in English. However, as an aspect of teaching Welsh as a second language, Welsh is used together with English in such activities as physical education and arts and crafts. There are *no* totally English-medium primary schools in Gwynedd. In Bangor, where 30 per cent of primary school pupils are Welsh-speaking, since local government reorganisation every primary school head master has retired. The new appointees tend to be enthusiastic supporters of the language policy, whereas their predecessors were, at best, lukewarm on the question of language in the curriculum. In consequence, protest has developed, particularly in Bangor and Llandudno, as English-speakers have come to feel that their children are being denied their right to a strictly English-medium education. In discussing the Aberystwyth situation some years earlier, it was concluded that the political question raised for English-speakers is 'the extent to which people living in a Welsh county may be permitted to disagree about Welshness' (Madgwick *et al.*, 1973, p. 120). Within that problem lies another, now emphasised by the shifting of educational powers to the new large counties since 1974: what territory should properly be used to determine linguistic character? – nation, county, district, town or neighbourhood? The answer is necessarily a statement of political preference.

The evidence suggests that, so far, Gwynedd has received a generally sympathetic hearing from the Welsh Office in questions relating to the interpretation of what is meant by acting 'unreasonably' with respect to the implementation of educational policy and responsiveness to parental demands. A senior Inspector has pointed out (in an interview with one of the authors in July 1978) that in any area of Wales where Welsh-speakers are a majority or a significant element in the population, the school 'should take account of the linguistic character of its area'. Thus, the Secretary of State decided to uphold Gwynedd County Council's policy to make Welsh (or Welsh studies) compulsory up to the age of 16 – against the wishes of a substantial minority of parents in Llandudno and Bangor, represented by the pressure group 'Parents for Optional Welsh'. A spokesman for the Welsh Office, explaining the decision, declared that the county had acted within the law, and added: 'as an authority they have a responsibility for social cohesion within their community, in the light of which there are advantages in having a language policy which is basically similar throughout the county' (as quoted in *Western Mail*, 11 October 1979). He concluded that while the authority was expected to take into account the views of parents who did not wish their children to take Welsh or Welsh studies, it was also entitled to weigh such views against the broader 'social cohesion' or 'character of the community' argument.

In the schools in which parents resisted the extension of Welsh language teaching, the education authority offered pupils the alternative of Welsh studies, although it was not clear what would constitute that subject. Hence the Council could not be accused of imposing compulsory Welsh on the children of those who did not want it. In providing an alternative to Welsh, the Council has stepped back from a situation in which the Secretary of State would have had little choice, even in terms of the ambiguous provisions of the existing law, but to rule against the county. As he himself stated some months later in a speech delivered, appropriately enough, to representatives of Gwynedd Council in April 1980: 'it is not only wrong in principle, but also positively harmful to the cause of the Welsh language and bilingual education to seek to disregard the views of parents about the teaching of Welsh to their children.'

Both language advocates and resisters had some reason to feel that they had won something. The Secretary of State had made it clear enough that living in Wales might mean that a child would not necessarily be able to obtain an education exactly equivalent to that available in England. On the other hand, he had avoided committing himself to the proposition that Welsh should necessarily take its place in the core curriculum, even in Gwynedd.

In refusing to come down in favour of either the proponents of the extension of Welsh-language education or the defenders of freedom of choice in the curriculum, the Secretary of State has perhaps taken the wisest short-term political course. The Minister appears to be seeking to discover variable-sum aspects of what is normally a zero-sum game, avoiding the political consequences of a winner-takes-all outcome. Where the advocates of the 'collective rights' of Welsh-speakers clash with English-speaking defenders of 'individual rights', the Secretary of State is under strong pressure to find a middle position. Each set of principles has been recognised by government as a legitimate basis for intervention in education and in other fields. The choice is not between self-evident good and obvious evil.

IV THE CHARACTERISTICS OF POLICY-MAKING FOR THE WELSH LANGUAGE

The passionate concern of a minority

The language issue is characterised by high sensitivity but low salience. It is a central issue but for much of the time hardly visible. While a few people have very intense feelings towards it (for or against), for most people the language is not a part of their daily anxieties or delights: they speak it or do not speak it, and they bear it vague goodwill. However, the sensitivity of the issue means that unconcern and goodwill can quickly change to insecurity and hostility. This is evident in comparatively low support for Plaid Cymru and expressions of hostility towards that party related to a (sometimes confused) association of the party and the language. The massive rejection of the proposed Assembly for Wales in the referendum of 1979 may also be explained partly by the mobilisation of language insecurity.

While language politics is thus a minority pursuit, it is conducted in a debate engaged in with great passion and intensity, and with a strong sense of self-righteousness. The high rhetoric of language politics does something, no doubt, to counter inertia with enthusiasm. But its overall effect is to raise the costs of policy-making, by raising expectations on one side, hostility on the other, and insecurity on both.

Language politics is directed at government actions, and displays high, possibly excessive, expectations of governments in general and education in particular. The language issue has taken a form characteristic of the politics of the post-war period; inter-group competition is conducted as competitive demands for government favours, preferences and policies. Both language advocates and resisters conduct their battles through the government, each choosing the territorial unit – locality, Wales, or the United Kingdom – which suits best their view of the issue. Both sides in language disputes switch from central direction to local option and back, according to their perception of advantage in policy output.

The climate of opinion

The struggle to create a favourable climate of opinion was won in the 1960s and 1970s by the language advocates. 'Climate' is a usefully vague term and is useful because it is accurate. But if it is to figure in the serious analysis of policy-making, some definition is required. It includes two sets of assumptions – those of persons engaged in or influential in policy-making, and those of more widespread, or 'popular' opinion, in practice, the opinions of concerned people. The former is likely to be positive, and the latter largely negative. Thus the relation of policy to this climate is roughly: the assumptions of influentials about what is necessary to be done modified by the assumptions of concerned people about what should not be done.

In the creation of the favourable climate of the 1960s and 1970s, two factors stand out: Saunders Lewis's BBC Wales radio lecture of 1962 and the Gittins Report (1968) on *Primary Education in Wales*. Saunders Lewis argued that the language '. . . will cease to exist as a living language towards the beginning of the twenty-first century'. But it could be saved if people refused to deal in the English language with local and central government. He added: 'I do not deny that there would be a period of hate and persecution and strife. . . . Success can only come through revolutionary methods. . . . The language is more important than self-government' (Lewis, 1971, p. 16). The exhortation to disruption was explicit: 'Go to it in earnest and without wavering to make it impossible to conduct . . . government business . . .', so explicit, indeed, that only the status of the talk as an Annual Lecture by a Distinguished Speaker saved the BBC from embarrassment. The lecture itself might soon have been forgotten, but it sparked the formation of the Welsh Language Society, a society of young activists dedicated to saving the language by militant campaigns of protest, agitation and civil disobedience.

The language movement was itself related to the widespread radical political activity of the 1960s associated with the protests of youth and of oppressed minorities, especially the blacks in the USA. The militant tactics of the Welsh Language Society antagonised non-Welsh and moderate Welsh opinion, and in the long term may have damaged the cause it fought for. But it hardened loyalties among the well-disposed minority, and appears to have played a significant role in the wider politicisation of the Welsh-speaking population in the 1970s. It also jogged the conscience and attitudes of the Welsh cultural establishment. In this way, there developed an inclination for action rather than passive sympathy. While many people supported its objectives but deplored its methods, all could recognise its success in shifting the inertia of government (see Davies, 1979, pp. 266–86; Rawkins, 1979b, pp. 440–57; Williams, 1977, pp. 426–55).

The times were changing. Saunders Lewis' lecture was given in 1962. The Welsh Language Society was established the following year. In July 1966, Gwynfor Evans, President of Plaid Cymru, won the Carmarthen seat in a historic by-election. The following year the Central Advisory Council for Education (Wales) published the Report it had been preparing since 1964. The Report endorsed the principle of a fully bilingual education. It had a notable place in the development of opinion, for it reflected and extended the climate, establishing it as an elite consensus of sufficient weight (certainly) and breadth (less certainly) to guide and legitimise policy.

The boldness and unexpectedness of the case made by Gittins can be understood by reference to the incredulous reaction of one of only two 'outsiders' (both Welshmen and professors, but not working in Wales) on the committee. Professor David Marsh wrote in a Minority Report:

... I was surprised to find that at the first meetings of the Council the Welsh Language was clearly seen to be of crucial importance to our deliberations on primary education. . . . Having heard, read and carefully considered the extreme view of those who fervently hope that Welsh will one day be the predominant language, I can only say that their arguments were to me unconvincing, their aims impracticable of attainment, and that if their aims were achieved it would be disastrous not only for education but for the whole of the future development of Wales.

... Reluctantly I have come to the conclusion that it is primarily for sentimental reasons that so much emphasis has been laid on the Welsh language in our report, and I find myself unable to accept these reasons as sufficiently valid to impose on children in Wales the burden of learning a language which has no real value outside Wales.

(Gittins Report, 1968, pp. 555–6).

Professor Marsh's trenchant criticisms of the Report's approach to the Welsh language, rational and realistic though they might have been, disappeared without trace in the heady climate of those times.

The Gittins Report has had an appreciable influence on the place of the Welsh language in the schools of Wales. In 1969 the Secretary of State for Education welcomed the Report and specifically endorsed the principle of bilingual education. He called on local authorities to review their language policies, which he expected would be 'clearly stated', 'well-understood in the schools', and 'sufficiently flexible to meet the varying linguistic "needs" '. He 'hoped' that the wishes of parents in each neighbourhood would be taken into account (Rawkins, 1979a, pp. 42–3). By the conventions of official communication, this was a pressing invitation to initiate, strengthen or extend programmes of Welsh teaching. Thus, through official endorsement, the Gittins Report had an influence quite unusual for such documents and comparable with the Robbins Report on Higher Education. It contributed substantially to the establishment of 'the informal legitimacy of bilingualism' (Rawkins, 1979a, p. 106).

The influence of elite opinion depended on the access of the elite to educational policy-making. Many of the elite (including members of the Gittins Committee) were, in fact, already directly involved in education policy-making as professionals, councillors and committee men. They had the power. All they needed was concertation and the absence of a contrary opinion among the concerned public. Popular opinion seems to have ranged from goodwill towards the language to indifference. The goodwill tended to be cost free: it weakened if costs such as learning the language or displacing other subjects were involved. On the other hand, the indifference lacked hostility. A comparatively small minority showed hostility to the language, balancing the small minority who showed fervour and zeal in its cause. However, opinion on the language tends to instability. In particular, the cost-free goodwill can be turned quickly into insecurity and suspicion. This seems to have happened during the devolution referendum campaign, when such insecurities were exploited by opponents of the Assembly. By the end of the 1970s the climate seemed to have changed. By contrast with Gittins, the Report of the Council for the Welsh Language (1978) met with a limited response among policy-makers, and little public recognition.

Militancy and resistance

The transformation of the 'climate of opinion' underlies the comparative success of the militant tactics of the language movement in the 1960s and 1970s. The Welsh Language Society had been avowedly responsible for most of the militancy – defacing or removing English signs, refusing to buy car and television licences, and pay subsequent fines, damaging broadcasting equipment, breaking up exhibition displays, 'sit-ins', occupations and old-fashioned marches and demonstrations. The Society drew strength and support from the temper of the times, and the belated discovery in the 1960s that mass disobedience is difficult to prevent or punish. Drawing on young people, especially students, it has never lacked supporters with time to spare and little to lose by engaging in militant tactics. The tactics of the Society have carefully avoided violence against persons. Altogether more than five hundred members of the Society have spent short terms in prison since the mid-1960s. They have been chided rather gently for their methods by more elderly and established sympathisers, but their objectives and courage were applauded. In this way elite language advocates succeeded in encouraging the Society's militant tactics, without being openly associated with them. The Society developed its philosophy and strategy with great deliberation, and its tactics were carefully controlled. In that respect it differs from the undisciplined mobs ('rent-a-crowd') evident in some industrial picketing and race disturbances of the time. It was also distinct from occasional violent protest activity of other groups and individuals in Wales, notably the 1979–80 campaign of setting fire to holiday cottages.

The Society's kind of militancy appeared to win significant gains for the language, particularly in matters like signs, forms, car licence discs and higher education through the medium of Welsh. The costs (except for road signs) were comparatively low, and the costs in coercing non-Welsh speakers were negligible. There is a case for concluding that the tactics of militancy scored dramatic success: but the conclusion requires qualification.

First, the successes lay in comparatively cost-free matters, which are not of great significance to the survival of the Welsh language. In any case the so-called 'environmental bilingualism' of official signs and forms is partly offset by the daubings of the protesters. Second, the most significant advances made by the Welsh language lay in education, and were due to the work of the elites, and the educationists, and the transformation of the climate of opinion. The same is largely true in broadcasting. Such pressures were sharpened by Gwynfor Evans' dramatic threat to starve to death; but were, if anything, reduced by interference with broadcasting stations by protesters.

Thus, militancy has paid; but it has been most profitable when it has reflected a favourable climate of opinion and elite pressures. Governments have adopted policies for which they had no enthusiasm, but also no hostility. Concession to militancy is not the most noble and rational form of policy-making; it may be realistic, and, in that way, effective, and even wise. But justice requires that governments do not regard the extent of militancy as the only measure of grievance. Realism suggests that governments, in Wales as elsewhere, have responded to cries of pain and anger more often than to mute suffering. This conclusion is not wholly to the credit of governments.

Resistance movements, that is movements to resist particular measures of language promotion, differ from these militant campaigns. They are movements of parents resisting a new measure of language policy in the schools, e.g. the extent of compulsory Welsh in Cardiganshire and Gwynedd or the redesignation of schools in South Glamorgan. Their motives and objectives are mainly educational, though these are inevitably associated with attitudes to the Welsh language. These attitudes range from negative goodwill to hostility. A parent may see Welsh as displacing a subject in the curriculum more highly valued by himself (undeniably true since this is a subjective judgement), or more broadly as an irrelevant subject, carrying with it cultural and political objectives which he does not share.

Resisters are usually comparatively well-educated, middle-class people, good at running meetings and writing minutes and letters, the kind of middle-class protester familiar in airport resistance and similar movements. They are rarely Welsh-speakers, but not all are English immigrants. In Cardiganshire, 'the BAs, Honours Welsh, and a few BDs, of the Welsh Language Society face the PhDs of the Cardiganshire Education Campaign in a comparatively sophisticated argument, which must largely pass over the heads of the loyal Welshmen of the farming and lower manual working class' (Madgwick *et al.*, 1973, p. 111). The highly educated are the initiators and leaders of protest. Their supporters are more widely representative. In South Wales, resisters may be less English and less middle class, reflecting the secular Labour-voting Welshness of that area.

Resistance movements occur sporadically, do not normally engage in militant tactics, and fade away after a few years. Work and family responsibilities displace protest activity in their scale of social priorities (in contrast with student members of the Welsh Language Society). Their record has been much less successful than the militant language-promotion movements. They are appeased by modest concessions, or, more likely, by persuasion and discussion; their children move on or out of school; and they feel less threatened than the Welsh speakers. They are likely to be denounced fiercely as 'anti-Welsh', a term which seems to carry in Wales the racist implications of 'anti-semitic', and the moral overtones of 'anti-Christ'.

The 'anti-Welsh' Welshman is indeed an interesting phenomenon in the rhetoric of language politics in particular, and Welsh politics in general, and is of some significance in the making of policy. The currency of the term shows the intensity of the historical struggle to assert Welsh values and a Welsh national identity. The anger with which the term is used suggests a sensitivity to the threats to 'Welshness' from immigrant Englishmen and renegade Welshmen. A particular target is the historic tendency of political Welshmen to seek their future in London.

In policy-making the term, with all its implications, acts as a way of defining the philosophical and moral parameters of the debate, emphasising the Welsh values, excluding the 'secular' values. This is an effective strategy for a policy debate which is determined, more than British issues, by the shape and substance of the climate of opinion, as perceived by the policy-makers. The term is not of course employed deliberately, as part of a strategy of persuasion. But if a market research firm were to devise a strategy for the Welsh language, they might well see potential in fixing such an attractively deleterious pejorative label on the opposition. Welshmen labelled in this way – Abse, Kinnock, Bevan and George Thomas in his political days – have a hard time fighting back. They may find their arguments already discounted. The victory of those who had been called anti-Welsh in the devolution referendum was particularly sweet – and significant of the potential of the people's voice to transform the set of assumptions which make up the climate of opinion.

The institutional framework

Language policy is made in an 'arms-length' relationship. London keeps its distance but does not let go. The universities offer a non-territorial example of the same kind of relationship. In practice, administration, including minor policy-making as well as execution/implementation, is devolved; finance is not. Influence is thus extended to territorial elites and interest groups; rather less to the territorial cadres of the centralised parties.

Two consequences follow. First, the issue tends to be depoliticised. This means it is removed from immediate central government concern and from direct party conflict, and very largely from public political processes. Second, language policy falls into the three-tier relationships of local government, Welsh Office and Whitehall (involving the processes of supplication, consultation and control into which Wales is fitted). For language policy, these relationships have worked in a special way. The Welsh Office (and in particular John Morris as Secretary of State from 1974 to 1979) has been able to influence policy to an unusual extent.

In particular his personal support for bilingual education had provided an important stimulus to educators, officials and language pressure-groups. The appointment of a less sympathetic minister, less willing to devote his time to considering how he might best employ his resources to assist the language, or to oblige his officials to give the language in education priority consideration, would certainly have slowed the flow of developments.   (Rawkins, 1979a, p. 46)

The Conservative Secretary of State, Nicholas Edwards, has followed in the path established by his predecessor. Significantly, prior to the Secretary of State's Gwynedd Speech of April 1980, which contained the announcement of a series of new initiatives and increased spending on the language, a Welsh Office Minister, Wyn Roberts, had held extensive consultations with a wide range of organisations with an interest in the language. Another significant departure was the decision to begin a new policy regime in 1981–2, with the stipulation in the Welsh Public Expenditure Programme of an identifiable item devoted to support for the Welsh language. In the first year, government spending will total £1.5 million (including £0.5 million for specific grant assistance to bilingual education). Finally, since the change of government, the status of the Language Unit within the General Division of the Welsh Office seems assured. This appears to be a consequence of the need to fill the vacuum which had emerged with the winding-up of the Council for the Welsh Language.

In the most significant field, education, language policy has been subject to a special form of the three-tier relationship described above. Britain's system for the government of education is highly decentralised. What goes on in schools (which is after all the major part of educational policy) is determined by headmasters, teachers and pupils, professional associations, local education authorities, governing bodies and parent–teacher associations. These are roughly in descending order of power. For language policy, however, there has been a tendency to reassert the power of the education authorities and the Welsh Office. John Morris, as Secretary of State, pressed hard for the institution of specific grants for Welsh language instruction (Rawkins, 1979a, pp. 45–6). This was against the conventions of educational finance and was resisted by local authorities, and local authority and professional associations. The Secretary for Education was, herself, interested in specific grants for in-service training. In the event, the Cabinet approved provision for specific grants, but only with regard to bilingual education, in the Education Bill of 1979, which lapsed with the fall of the Labour government. The provision was subsequently adopted by the Conservatives in its Education Act of 1980.

The episode is one more illustration of the ambivalence of decentralists when faced with a policy preference likely to be favoured by central but not local government. This ambivalence also operates in the opposite way. The next issue of this kind is the core curriculum, which might in Wales include a knowledge of the Welsh language. Broadly, Welsh decentralists will support standards imposed centrally (whether from London or Cardiff) and British centralists will favour local option.

The political parties have had very little impact on language policies. There are several explanations. The most obvious is that political parties never do have much influence on policy of any kind, and especially policies that are outside the main stream of politics. Second, the two major parties are centralised. Third, the Welsh organisations of the two parties were slow to develop policies on the language, for a mixture of reasons: political calculation (language policies lose votes), traditional subordination and modesty, and simple lack of awareness of language as an issue. In this respect, the territorial organisations of the political parties have proved to be of little account in this policy process.

At parliamentary level, the Welsh language has arisen as an issue from time to time in recent years, especially in the period following the February 1974 General Election. The language has found its support in occasional, *ad hoc* coalitions of MPs, with a few maverick Labour and Liberal MPs joining with Plaid Cymru in supporting amendments to proposed legislation, or in simply seeking to draw attention to the condition of the language. In the debate of June 1980 on the Broadcasting Bill, a Conservative, Geraint Morgan, moved an amendment against his party's policy on the fourth television channel.

In local government, parties have had rather more impact. In Gwynedd.

Plaid Cymru has been particularly successful in pushing policy in the direction it favoured, while the Conservatives have consistently opposed them. In Dyfed and Mid-Glamorgan, the Labour party has at times intervened to slow down the growth of bilingual education or to modify its character. In Mid-Glamorgan, Labour has favoured the principle of the Welsh unit, attached to a conventional primary school, over a separate Welsh-medium institution. In South Glamorgan, the creation of an all-party (Labour and Conservative) working-party on bilingual education in 1974 was significant in freeing the issue from party competition. The bipartisan policy survived a change of party control, and has continued to the present time (see Rawkins, 1979a, pp. 57–63).

The territorial elites

By contrast with parties, territorial elites have been remarkably influential. While it is difficult to prove that there is a Welsh elite, there is a fair amount of evidence of the influence of a comparatively small number of people. A few are entirely outside the government, but must hold public positions of some sort, in local government, and public corporations, on advisory bodies, in political parties and the educational system. The term 'establishment' may be justified though here it plainly does not connote a formal structure of influence. The clearest evidence of elite access to influence is in the membership of the advisory committees appointed by government – the Bowen committee on road signs, the Gittins committee on education, the Royal Commission on the Constitution, and the Welsh Language Council. The latter body could almost have conducted its meetings in Welsh; the Gittins committee was about two-thirds Welsh-speaking. None of this is improper, or even politically miscalculated. But it does seem to have accorded Welsh language advocates (and, in the case of Kilbrandon, Welsh nationhood advocates) a voice beyond its proportions in the population, though conceivably no more than its due share in the historic entity of Wales. If the establishment interpretation is correct, then the peculiar representative character of these bodies was not due to a conspiracy by the elites, or calculation or obtuseness on the part of the government; it happened 'naturally', because it was in accord with the nature of the political system.

The consequences of elite influence should not be exaggerated. Elites have had opportunities to make public pronouncements, and private access to policy-makers. They have been able to shape the climate of opinion, but their specific influence on policy has been limited by the nature of the policies and of the policy process, and of public opinion. When elite recommendations ran beyond the limits of popular support, as in the case of the Council for the Welsh Language, then there was little response. There is, quite simply, no one lever of power in the system, open to the control of the elites, or, indeed, any other group. Hence policy-making for the language has been diffuse. variable and uncertain, and there has not been a great deal of policy-making at all.

Two views of language policy

(a) The view from London: the limits of policy

Seen from London, the Welsh language looks like an issue for low cost, low benefit policy-making. Language policy will cost a little money, but not much. Apart from finance, it carries no threat to other policies. There are modest ideological gains, in that a government should properly be seen to support a minority culture. The costs in support are very low and putative, compared with the benefits of earning the favour of the elites, and, with luck, the pacification of the militants. There appear to be neither gains nor losses within the government party. Two considerations arising from an analysis of costs and benefits tend to hold governments back from heavy commitment to language policy. One is the possibility of arousing hostility among the normally indifferent public. The second is doubt about the effectiveness of a policy aimed at restoration of the language.

If calculations of this kind make sense for the London government, then language policy may be predicted to: (i) reduce salience of the issue and gain time; (ii) show concern, and concede to elite and militant pressures, trying to hold a balance; (iii) eschew decisive action, and regard action as a temporary modification of a pattern of inactivity.

It follows that policy will have some of the inconsistencies criticised by Birch (below). Short-term reactions will disturb a modest long-term strategy which does not accord the language high priority. Thus the policy will not satisfy language advocates. Likewise, those who see language as a source of conflict cannot expect a consistent approach, and neither side in the conflict can expect steady support.

This analysis is applicable to similar issues which are in the perspective of central government, marginal, low cost, low benefit policy opportunities. The conclusions of the analysis are not intended so much as a criticism, still less a denunciation, of government, but as a statement about the reality of policy-making. Governments, like doctors, suffer from massive limitations. Doctors can diagnose and mend broken limbs but cannot cure bad temper or cancer. Governments can rebuild roads or schools, but they cannot do much about defects of human nature, the consequences of history or terminal disease. The prime element in the making of policy for the language, and most other issues, is an acceptance of the limitations of policy.

(b) A view from Wales: inadequate to the needs of the language

In the eyes of concerned Welsh-speakers (a minority in Wales), the system of policy-making described lacks coherence, consistency, openness, defined objectives and a clear sense of scope and limitations.

(i)   There is no openly-avowed and clearly-defined set of institutions and procedures for the development of language policy and the management of conflict. The arrangements are not fully a part of public politics, but are rather partly private and 'under the counter'. They tend to lack system, coherence and consistency.

(ii) There is no consistent and avowed range of objectives, but rather a melange of alternative aims, lying between the extremes of Welsh and English unilingualism, and related to the imprecise and partly self-deceptive use of the central term in the debate, 'bilingualism'.

(iii) There is no articulated agreement over the extent or limits of government power in language policy, nor a full understanding of the nature and limits of governmental power over language use.

There are, broadly, two views about this policy-making system. It may be chaotic and ineffective, or pluralistic; negligent of the critical condition of the language, or properly concerned for consensus. In the first, the inconsistency and unpredictability are seen as serious defects. Anthony Birch has given one view of the consequences:

> . . . first, to provide opportunities for defenders of the language to propose reforms; secondly, to accept most of these proposals in principle and thus raise expectations; thirdly, to allow (or encourage) officials and local authorities to drag their feet in the implementation of the proposals, thus creating anomalies and grievances; and, finally, to make various concessions, not in a spirit of generosity or conviction but grudgingly and with bad grace.   (Birch, 1977, p.147)

It has been argued that open discussion of the language question would help both the resolution of conflict and the restoration of the language. Thus the establishment of a Welsh Assembly would have been to the advantage of both Welsh speakers and monoglot English speakers (P. J. Madgwick, as quoted in Osmond, 1977, p. 267; see also Rawkins, 1979a, pp. 100–8).

The alternative view is that it is just these possibilities of conflict which require depoliticisation, pluralism, and behind-the-scenes accommodation.

Caution, flexibility, ambiguity, variability in implementation, advance – and retreat – by stealth are all essential if public indifference is not to be converted to hostility. This view stops just short of the principle that ineffectiveness of policy is the price of consent.

V THE WELSH LANGUAGE AND THE GOVERNMENT OF THE UNITED KINGDOM

A study of the Welsh language in the policy process raises the question of whether the Welsh political system is designed to work and move. The process appears characterised by uneven relationships involving an establishment urged on by enthusiasts and militants, working with institutions they cannot control. If the Welsh institutions are used too brutally, resistance builds up in the centrally-focussed political system. In that way, both the referendum and the argument between Neil Kinnock, MP, and Gwynedd County Council (see above, p. 83, and Rawkins, 1979a, pp. 77–84) look like paradigms of the Welsh political system, a dialogue of the deaf, or rather communication between people inhabiting different universes.

A view of a political system designed not to function fits language policy-making better than other policy areas. For a sensitive issue, the system fragments and legitimacy declines. But even in other policy areas there are great difficulties in achieving serious political objectives. The Welsh political system is like an early steam engine. Leather, wood and iron, and a great deal of human effort, are joined together to make the great wheel go round. Whether it drives anything but itself is not clear.

If this be so, the consequences for the Welsh language are clear. The restoration of the language may require constitutional change on a scale beyond the objectives of most cultural nationalists, and far beyond the wishes of the popular majority. Cultural integrity requires constitutional disintegration. Language and the nature of the state are related. This was the conclusion of one of the first serious students of politics to consider the Welsh Question, Henry VIII.

It is evident that language is a potential source of conflict in Wales. Language policy-making raises a question of wider significance for the relation between politicisation and conflict management. Policy-making for the language is very largely depoliticised, that is, removed from the arena of public political contestation between the parties. There are some advantages in this. British politics are adversary in style and majoritarian in outcome. Power-sharing works only where party majorities cannot be built. Minorities, it is assumed, will seek their interests within a larger group.

However, the chances for the language issue are that this process will not take place, or that if it did, the open contest over language matters would exacerbate tensions and expose the minority to swings of fortune and further insecurity. Better, it may be thought, the less dramatic but more dependable protection afforded by non-partisan government action.

The advantages of depoliticisation are evident in this case, and there are indeed grounds for doubting the benefits of the normal kind of party contestation for other policy issues. However, there is more to be said for public political competition. It makes people aware of the issue, and it mobilises support, while risking the mobilisation of opposition. It provides an opportunity for achieving a form of consent, which is the only basis on which substantial and controversial policy can be pursued. In the present system, the Welsh language lacks that basis, and the policies pursued to promote it are necessarily, and properly, somewhat half-hearted. This is not a defect of the political system, but rather its special merit. The Heath Robinson system of government described is extra good at adaptability, contrivance, elastoplast and improvisation. The British constitution will surely survive; whether the Welsh language will is less certain.

REFERENCES

Betts, C. (1976) *Culture in Crisis: the Future of the Welsh Language* (Upton, Wirral: Ffynnon Press).

Birch, A. (1977) *Political Integration and Disintegration in the British Isles* (London: Allen & Unwin).

Bowen, E. G. and Carter, H. (1974) 'Preliminary Observations on the Distribution of the Welsh Language at the 1971 Census', *Geographical Journal*.

Bowen, E. G. and Carter, H. (1975) 'Distribution of the Welsh Language in 1971: an Analysis', *Geography*, 60.

Council for Wales and Monmouthshire (1968) *The Welsh Language Today* (London: HMSO, Cmnd. 2198).

Davies, C. (1979) 'Cymdeithas Yr Iaith Gymraeg', in Stephens (1979).

Fishman, J. A. (1970) *Sociolinguistics: A Brief Introduction* (Rowley, Mass.: Newbury House, 1970).

Gittins Report (1968) *Primary Education in Wales* (London: Department of Education and Science).

Jones, D. G. (1979) 'The Welsh Language Movement', in Stephens (1979).

Lewis, Saunders (1971) 'The Fate of the Language', *Planet*, 4, pp. 13–27.

Madgwick, P.J., with Non Griffiths and Valerie Walker (1973) *The Politics of Rural Wales* (London: Hutchinson).

Osmond, J. (1977) *Creative conflict: the Politics of Welsh Devolution* (Llandysul: Gomer Press).

Price, G. (1979) 'Minority Languages in Western Europe', in Stephens (1979).

Rawkins, P. M. (1975) 'Minority Nationalism and the Advanced Industrial State: a Case-Study of Contemporary Wales', Ph.D. dissertation (Toronto: University of Toronto).

Rawkins, P.M. (1979a) 'The Implementation of Language Policy in the Schools of Wales', *Studies in Public Policy*, no. 40.

Rawkins, P. M. (1979b) 'An Approach to the Political Sociology of the Welsh Nationalist Movement', *Political Studies*, xxvii, pp. 440–57.

Regan, D. (1977) *Local Government and Education* (London: Allen & Unwin).

Stephens, M. (ed). (1979) *The Welsh Language Today* (Llandysul: Gomer Press).

Welsh Office (1980) *Welsh in the School Curriculum*.

Williams, C. H. (1977) 'Non-violence and the Development of the Welsh Language Society', *Welsh History Review*, 8, pp. 426–55.

4 Is the United Kingdom a State? Northern Ireland as a Test Case*

RICHARD ROSE

Neither the 'state' nor the 'United Kingdom' are terms commonly or carefully used in contemporary British politics. In Maitland's judgment, the explanation was that the state is 'a person whose personality our law does not formally or explicitly recognise' (Marshall, 1971, p. 12). So careful a scholar of modern English history as G. Kitson Clark (1959, p. 551) can casually assert that defining the state 'is relatively easy'. The definition he gives – 'The *State* is the Community organized for the purposes of *government*' – begs more questions than it answers. This implies that the United Kingdom is a single community, embracing both Northern Ireland Protestants and Catholics, or that the United Kingdom is not a state.[1] Loose contemporary use of the term justifies the conclusion of Peter Nettl's (1968, p. 551) polycultural review that the idea of the state is a variable not a constant, because of the relative 'statelessness' of British and American non-thinking about the subject.

The oldest and most familiar way to describe the central political authority of the United Kingdom is to speak of the Crown, a portmanteau term symbolising 'the sum total of governmental powers and synonymous with the Executive' (Wade and Bradley, 1970, p. 171). The very vagueness of the concept can be useful because it can accommodate many different political outlooks. It is also devoid of any territorial modifier. Historically, the

* This paper is a product of research into the Political Structure of the United Kingdom, financed by Social Science Research Council grant HR/4689. It should be particularly noted that the views expressed here are solely the responsibility of the author. In view of the nature of the subject, it would not be appropriate to acknowledge by name the individuals who commented constructively on an earlier draft.

domain of the Crown once referred to less than the United Kingdom and in the days of Empire, much more. In effect, the Crown is a concept of 'indefinite domain' (Rose, 1980a, pp. 131ff).

In the absence of a written constitution in the United Kingdom, there is no organic act that defines the state. There is no way to know whether any particular action by government may be constitutional, except by ordinary political controversy, albeit about issues affecting constituent elements of government. Nor is there any means of resolving conflicts claimed to be about constitutional issues, except by ordinary votes in Parliament. One consequence of this is that there is no provision for amending a constitution with the explicit consent of those affected; for example, the decision whether to hold a referendum is a decision for Parliament. Equally important, there is no 'buffer' institution – like a Supreme Court or a federal Second Chamber – to which one group of disputants can appeal in defence of claimed 'rights' (cf. Rose, 1976a). Garvin (1980, p. 309) argues: 'Northern Ireland exhibits a pathological version of a set of general constitutional difficulties. . . . There is no constitution at all if the term constitution is taken to mean a series of entrenched prohibitions of injunctions on governmental action.' In the absence of a written constitution, setting out the status of the two historic kingdoms, one principality and one province, 'No one knows what the relationships of these entities to the central government really are, or are supposed to be.'

Contemporary students of politics in England normally refer to 'the government' as the central political institution of society. This term, however, confuses two different political phenomena: the elected and partisan 'government of the day', and the 'established and persisting institutions of a regime'. Confusion is also created by functionalist American social scientists, who use the term 'political system' to blur distinctions between legal authorities and other influences upon political behaviour.[2] Marxists are guilty of reducing institutions of government to dependencies of economic institutions in society, and neo-Marxists tend, like American functionalists, to globalise the idea of the state, treating it as if it were a portmanteau synonym for political power (cf. Jessop, 1977).

Confusion is further compounded because of the absence of any agreed geographical modifier for the state at issue here. The terms 'British' and 'English' are used interchangeably to describe the government of the United Kingdom. There is no adjective derived from the United Kingdom itself, nor is the United Kingdom normally considered a historic community or *Volk* as in a 'nation-state'. The norm is to follow A. L. Lowell's (1912, p. 137) practice of excluding 'the peculiar institutions of Scotland and Ireland . . . except so far as they affect the central government'. Given inconsistencies in the very structure of government and social differences between Scotland, Wales, Northern Ireland and the home counties of United Kingdom government, it is reasonable 'to talk about British government and English society' (Rose, 1980b, p. 51).

The absence of an English concern with the state is explained by Barker (1977, p. 3) as the result of a 'particular historical experience. . . . The people of Britain have never experienced the alien and occupying presence of a Bismarckian state in all or any of its simplicity.' Such a statement is true of England *vis-a-vis* the experience of *étatiste* lands in Continental Europe. But it is not true for all parts of the United Kingdom. The story of the Crown in Ireland is a record of centuries of efforts by the Crown to assert authority there. Indigenous inhabitants could see a British (if not Bismarckian) state clearly enough to rebel against it, and in 1921 to repudiate its authority in most of Ireland. Today, Northern Ireland is a reminder of the different experiences of government within the United Kingdom; it is the remnant of centuries of challenge to the authority of the Crown.

Whether the United Kingdom exists as a state today is an important question. The question is not usually asked in England; the fundamentals of political authority are so taken for granted that it may be ignored. But in Northern Ireland, subjects of Westminster can hardly talk about any other political issue. Given that both England and Northern Ireland are areas meant to be part of the same state, the difference should be reconciled. It could be argued that questions about the existence of the state are artificial, the consequence of applying alien conceptions to English experience. Conceivably, the United Kingdom might be said to exist for some purposes, but not for others, that is, the United Kingdom may be only partially, intermittently or in some respects, a state.

The purpose of this chapter is to test, carefully and systematically, whether the United Kingdom has the defining attributes of a state. The first section specifies a definition of the state, and discusses its relevance in United Kingdom circumstances. The next three sections consider how the dynamics of Northern Ireland politics have eroded the state known in law as the United Kingdom of Great Britain and Northern Ireland. The concluding section considers the implications of recognising that the United Kingdom is a problematic state.

I THE DEFINING ATTRIBUTES OF THE MODERN STATE

Integrity is essential for a modern state. In international relations, a state's integrity is represented by its claim to be the irreducible unit with which other governments must treat about its citizens. Nor can it allow the integrity of its territory to be impaired by civil or military agents of other states. Within its territorial realm, a modern state can accept social diversity to the extent of being 'multi-national'.[3] But its citizens remain subject to its constitutional authority, and 'no subject is its equal' or can claim exemption (Poggi, 1978, p. 117). Notwithstanding many differences in the institutions and purposes of modern states, a state must insist upon the integrity of two defining attributes – territorial boundaries and effective force – or fail in the claim to be a state (Watkins, 1967, p. 155).

Clearly defined *territorial boundaries* are a *sine qua non* of a modern state. Within given boundaries a state's claim to authority is meant to be exclusive and pre-eminent. When its territory is contested by competing armies, as in war-time, there is no state, only a battlefield on which armies determine which state will prevail. In many parts of the Third World, the definition of clearly demarcated boundaries, where once tribes roamed at will, has been a necessary first step toward modern statehood. So too has been the ending of exceptional status for foreign nationals within a territory, like the 'capitulations' common in late 19th century China.

The territorial dimension is important within a state in delimiting government's authority over people within given boundaries. Where a modern state exists, its authority is meant to take precedence against other institutions of society; the precedence of a church, say, is the sign of a pre-modern state. In a federal system, government may differ in different parts of the territory. Within the United Kingdom, laws sometimes vary between Scotland, Wales, Northern Ireland and England. For example, four different sets of licensing laws govern the sale of drink in the United Kingdom. Different government departments deal with local government, depending upon the part of the United Kingdom in which they are situated: the Department of Environment, the Scottish Office, the Welsh Office or the Northern Ireland Office. Reciprocally, the absence of a territorial base precludes Pakistani immigrants scattered throughout Britain from demanding their own government Minister.

A reasonably *effective claim to a nationwide monopoly of organised force* is a second *sine qua non* attribute of a modern state. Many contemporary political scientists mention in passing the control of force as a necessary attribute of a state. The criterion is central in such continental writers as Carl Schmitt, who held, 'effectiveness, not legality, is what counts' (see Poggi, 1978, pp. 5ff). If the monopoly of force is breached by external occupying forces (as in the Second World War) or by treaties requiring the demilitarisation of an area (e.g. the Rhineland in Weimar Germany), then a state's integrity is negated or impaired. A rebellion also can undermine this integrity, if alternative organisations effectively compete with the security forces of the state for *de facto* control within a portion of the state's territory. This happened, for example, in Ireland from 1912 to 1921; the conflict was only resolved in Southern Ireland by the withdrawal of British forces. The resulting 26-county Irish Free State was then challenged by anti-Treaty Sinn Fein forces that rejected its acceptance of partition. The new government established a monopoly of force by winning a bloody civil war, thus making the Free State a state in fact as well as in name.

Whereas the rule of law is at the forefront of English politics, the force of law has recurringly been important in the Irish part of the United Kingdom. In Ireland there was a history of rural disorder that was difficult to control, as at Donnybrook Fair; equally, there was a history of organised challenges to the forces of the state. Ireland remained under the Crown for centuries because the Crown was prepared to use force to prevent or subdue rebellion. Whereas nationalist historians may criticise the Royal Irish Constabulary for repressing the populace, Unionists would criticise it, or the government directing it from Dublin Castle and Westminster, for failing to repress rebellion (cf. Bowden, 1977).

To speak of the political authority of a state, that is, the relationship between government and the population from which it seeks obedience and allegiance, by itself tells nothing. A Government's authority may be fully legitimate or discredited, or a state may exist because of coercion or voluntary acceptance of its authority.[4] The character of a state's authority depends upon the degree of compliance it secures from intended subjects within its territory, and the nature of its support from subjects.

A government must secure compliance with basic political laws especially laws intended to secure public order. Basic political laws are only a small portion of the totality of laws promulgated in the name of authority. They are laws which, if broken, will result in a 'crime against the state' and not just an 'anti-social' act, like a motoring offence or conventional armed robbery. The government determines whether a law is central to political authority; it must take into account both the intent of those violating the law, and the probability of successfully enforcing laws that it says are 'basic'. For example, Westminster did not introduce conscription into Northern Ireland in the Second World War for fear it would undermine its authority there, as the introduction of conscription did in Southern Ireland in the First World War. In Northern Ireland, the display of particular colours of cloth has been defined as politically subversive under the Flags and Emblems (Display) Act (NI) 1954, and wearing IRA-type apparel can also be a political crime under Westminster's Prevention of Terrorism Act, 1974, Section 2, subs 1 (Calvert, 1968, Ch. 20). In any country, breaches of public order are evidence of non-compliance if (and only if) the breaches are committed by groups intending to challenge the authority of government. This distinguishes violence between police and football enthusiasts ('hooliganism') from the same level of violence between police and supporters of Sinn Fein.

The failure of a government to secure compliance with its basic political laws is *prima facie* evidence that it lacks the effective moral and physical force to secure its will. If challenges to authority are organised, this is a further indication that authority has lost its monopoly of force. Non-compliance with laws may also be evidence that borders are readily permeated, a particularly important point when internal dissidents are aligned with an external power, a phenomenon characterising not only the Middle East today but also Northern Ireland.

A government can secure voluntary or involuntary compliance with its basic laws. The advantages of voluntary consent are practical as well as moral. Subjects who give diffuse support to government will be predisposed to accept voluntarily its claims upon them, without requiring coercion or material incentives. It is more economical of a government's resources if its citizens voluntarily do the things that government regards as most important. It is also more effective if citizens themselves are motivated to do what government wants. In England, voluntary support for the regime is evidenced in many ways, such as the nearly unanimous vote for pro-regime parties at general elections, and rejection of anti-regime candidates nominated by the Communist Party and the Workers Revolutionary Party, as well as 'ultra-loyal' National Front candidates. Public disorder is an uncommon political phenomenon, and the political intelligence sections of the police are primarily concerned with 'alien' groups, such as Middle Eastern terrorists, or IRA sympathisers, and, in Scotland and Wales, the furthermost fringe of nationalism.

Where voluntary support for a system of government is lacking, then politicians have two broad choices: to rely upon coercion to secure their basic political aims, or to reduce their demands for mass compliance. Resort to coercion or the threat of coercion is a familiar means of securing compliance in Eastern Europe, and recalcitrant parts of the Soviet Union. In Britain, government has the technology but not the political values to govern by the systematic invocation of coercion. The 'on again, off again' use of conciliation *and* coercion in 19th century Ireland provides an historical example of this.

The authority of government can take many different forms besides full legitimacy (that is, diffuse support and popular compliance) conventionally assumed by Anglo-American politicians (Rose, 1971a, pp. 31ff). In fact, most 20th century political authorities have not been fully legitimate. The largest single category belong to the historic past, repudiated regimes failing of support and compliance. In some cases, the state itself ceased to exist (e.g. Austria–Hungary and the Ottoman Empire); in others, the state remains though regimes change (e.g. France from the Third to the Fifth republics). Isolated regimes, that is, authorities with high support and low compliance, are inconsistent with a modern state. But coercive regimes, securing high compliance with low support, are a familiar part of the modern world from Prague eastwards.

Whether the United Kingdom is regarded as fully legitimate depends upon the empirical focus. If England is used to characterise the United Kingdom as a whole, then it can be said to be fully legitimate. But England is *not* the whole of the United Kingdom; to act as if it were violates the integrity of the state. If Great Britain is the focus, full support is challenged only by Scottish and Welsh Nationalists, and compliance only by a very small group of Welsh language protesters organised in Cymdeithas. When Northern Ireland is recognised to be part of the United Kingdom, the claim to full legitimacy fails, because of the palpable absence of full support for Westminster and the flouting of basic political laws there. Moreover, as subsequent sections will demonstrate, the Westminster government has been much less willing (and successful) in defending itself against challenges to its authority in Northern Ireland than have authorities in the Fifth French Republic, West Germany or Italy.

To determine whether the United Kingdom is a state requires a bifocal perspective. Attention must be given to actions both at Westminster[5] and in Northern Ireland. The people of Northern Ireland cannot be excluded from the United Kingdom without doing violence to constitutional facts. At a minimum, Ulster people are expected to be compliant or coerced subjects. Equally, Westminster cannot be excluded from the government of Northern Ireland, except by a secession or rebellion that would break up the present territory of the United Kingdom.

To test Northern Ireland's place within the United Kingdom, the following three sections examine the territorial integrity, the monopoly of force, and the perceived authority of this part of the United Kingdom in three very different circumstances: when Ulster's position was generally taken for granted in the steady-state United Kingdom; when Westminster sought to reconstruct authority in Northern Ireland from 1968 to 1974; and during the operation of temporary direct rule since. The conclusion considers the implications for the rest of the United Kingdom of governing without a state in Northern Ireland.

II NORTHERN IRELAND IN THE STEADY-STATE
UNITED KINGDOM

From this side of the great political fault line of 1968, it is usually forgotten how Northern Ireland used to be governed when it was not in the headlines. The answer is: as an accepted and more or less peaceful part of the United Kingdom, albeit a part that had its own local peculiarities and distinctive opposition. None of these features detracted from its claim to be an integral part of the United Kingdom, or the claim that the United Kingdom was a conventional state.

Northern Ireland was created by force and the threat of force, against the wishes of political leaders in Belfast, London and Dublin. Ulster Protestants had no wish to see any change in the United Kingdom of Great Britain and the whole of Ireland, but were even more adamant that they would not become part of a home rule or independent Ireland separate from Westminster. From 1912 onwards, Ulster Protestants organised military forces to support this view (Stewart, 1967) and, through the sympathies of Conservative and Unionist politicians such as Bonar Law, himself an Ulster Scot, had a strong voice in Westminster too. In 1920, Westminster enacted a bill that promised two parliaments in Ireland, one in the North and one in the South, and a Council of Ireland composed of representatives of each, with provision for an eventual union of the two Irish Parliaments. A Northern Ireland Parliament was established under the Act, but in the South, five years of rebellion culminated in the establishment in 1921 of a 26-county Irish Free State, a dominion nominally under the Crown. The Northern Ireland Parliament, one result of 'the imperial government's anxiety to extricate itself from Ireland' (Buckland, 1979, p. 2), came into effect for the predominantly Protestant parts of Ulster. The forces to defend the new Northern Ireland government were primarily indigenous Ulster Protestants and the opponents were Ulster Catholics. By 1924, years of violence reached their symbolic conclusion with the lifting of the curfew in Belfast.

From the foundation of the Northern Ireland Parliament in 1921 (colloquially known as Stormont, after the Belfast site it chose), the boundaries of the western-most part of the United Kingdom have always been clear if not consensual. A Boundary Commission was established following the Anglo–Irish Treaty to review the possibility of altering the border to follow political and religious loyalties. Such a task was, and is impossible (see Rose and McAllister, 1975). The Commission never published an official report. In 1925 the Irish Free State government in Dublin recognised the existing boundary *de facto*. But Dublin has never recognised this boundary of the United Kingdom *de jure*. The 1937 Irish

Constitution, in Article 2, declares: 'the national territory consists of the whole island of Ireland, its lands and the territorial seas'. The claim is also supported by a substantial proportion of the minority Catholic community in Northern Ireland.

The Stormont government demonstrated an effective monopoly of force for four decades after the cessation of hostilities in the early 1920s. It did this first of all by 'de-militarising' the various armed groups of defenders that had been created as 'home guard' units in support of but outside official armed forces (Farrell, 1978). The Ulster B Special Constabulary became the official part-time auxiliary force for the Royal Ulster Constabulary, and both were under control of the Stormont-based Ministry of Home Affairs. The B Specials were exclusively Protestant, and the RUC overwhelmingly Protestant. Both were armed as well as uniformed forces (Clark, 1967; Hezlet, 1972).

The sporadic outbreaks of violence from the 1920s to 1962 demonstrated Stormont's effective force. Stormont did not seek or claim the full moral support of the Catholic community; sometimes mutual enmity was emphasised. What Stormont could claim was effectiveness in defending itself against outbreaks of violence, and maintaining public order when challenged (cf. Mansergh, 1936; Barritt and Carter, 1962; Farrell, 1976). In the Second World War, when the Irish Free State was neutral and there were fears of the IRA deciding 'England's difficulty is Ireland's opportunity', the RUC interned several hundred people and successfully maintained the peace. In 1956, the Irish Republican Army launched what it regarded as a major offensive against the continued existence of Northern Ireland, with armed attacks upon political and military installations. In response, the RUC interned several hundred people in the period 1957–60, and mounted an armed defence of the regime until 1962, when the IRA formally announced the end of the campaign, after 19 people had been killed (Bell, 1970; Coogan, 1980).

Within Northern Ireland, the population divided along religious lines about support for the United Kingdom. The Protestant two-thirds voted overwhelmingly for the Unionists and other parties emphasising loyalty to the United Kingdom. Catholics voted overwhelmingly for Nationalists, who refused until 1965 to take the title of Loyal Opposition as a way of asserting their loyalty to a 32-county Ireland (Rose, 1971a, Chs 3, 6). Unlike local government ballots, where in some areas Catholics could expect to be in a majority in the population (and sometimes a majority in the local council), in voting for Stormont Protestants were an assured majority under any electoral system used, and even more under the first-past-the-post electoral system used in Northern Ireland's Westminster constituencies. Divisions about political authority were stable. Unionists made it clear that their first (and perhaps only) agreed aim was to maintain the United Kingdom (cf. the motto of William of Orange, *Je maintiendrai*).

Northern Ireland's government was not questioned by Westminster, nor was it much talked about. The creation of a Northern Ireland Parliament was welcomed as a means of getting Irish business out of the House of Commons. In 1923, the Speaker of the House of Commons established a convention that matters should not be raised there that were within the responsibility of the Stormont government. This convention was strictly adhered to for more than four decades (Calvert, 1968, Ch. 6). In the Second World War, the strategic position of Northern Ireland, offering harbours to guard Britain's Western approaches, gave the Northern Ireland government a distinctive role in defence of the United Kingdom, different from that of the neutral 26-county Irish government in Dublin (Blake, 1956). Consequent to Ireland becoming a Republic outside the Commonwealth in 1949, the Labour government brought in a Government of Ireland Act which declared:

> Northern Ireland remains part of His Majesty's dominions and of the United Kingdom and it is hereby affirmed that in no event will Northern Ireland or any part thereof cease to be part of His Majesty's dominions and of the United Kingdom without consent of the Parliament of Northern Ireland.

The willingness of Parliament to avoid any show of interest in the Province was confirmed as late as 1962, when a minor amendment of Stormont's powers was passed without dissent (see House of Commons, *Debates*, vol. 658, the Northern Ireland Act, col. 821, 1 May 1962).

In everyday matters of government, particularly after 1945, the Northern Ireland government normally sought to follow Westminster policy on a step-by-step basis, especially in welfare state legislation. This meant that the British Treasury, as the source of Ulster's revenue, provided money to meet Ulster's needs, even when this was more than could be raised from local resources. The nexus between policy and finance meant that there was continuous, close and quiet contact between Northern Ireland civil departments and their Westminster counterparts, to ensure that the Province was not moving 'out of step'. This contact was paralleled on the political side by occasional meetings between 'Imperial' (as they were known in Belfast) and Stormont Ministers. On both sides of the Irish Sea it was accepted that Stormont's legislation and administration did not need to be identical with that of Westminster. This was most notably the case in home affairs. To argue otherwise would be to deny the administrative case for devolution.

Neither civil servants nor ministers publicly declared up to the mid-1960s that they considered Stormont to be departing, in any fundamental or unacceptable manner, from Westminster's basic standards (see, for example, Lawrence, 1965; Green, 1979; Oliver, 1978a).

In the mid-1960s the United Kingdom was a state. The boundaries established by the 1921 Anglo–Irish Treaty had persisted for more than a generation; the defence forces of Stormont had demonstrated the ability to defend the state against attack at its most vulnerable points. At Westminster successive Labour as well as Conservative governments had publicly affirmed their endorsement of the status quo. Terence O'Neill, installed as Northern Ireland Prime Minister in 1963, set out to demonstrate that Northern Ireland was not only a part of the United Kingdom, but also a place where 'normal' politics (that is, concern about the economy) could dominate public affairs. By securing an official visit to Stormont by the Republic of Ireland's Taoiseach, Sean Lemass, O'Neill hoped to demonstrate that the integrity of the western-most border of the United Kingdom was also accepted by the historic British enemy in Ireland.

III ATTEMPTING TO RECONSTRUCT THE UNITED KINGDOM

The 1968 civil rights campaign raised novel questions about Northern Ireland's position in the United Kingdom. While lasting only a matter of months, it launched an avalanche of events, culminating in Westminster's suspension of Stormont, and attempts to reconstruct the institutions of governance there.

Within Northern Ireland, the 1968 civil rights campaign challenged the legitimacy of Stormont, but not in the conventional Republican way. Instead, civil rights demonstrators claimed what were regarded as 'normal' British rights, such as 'one person, one vote, one value'. They also attacked housing conditions and unemployment levels that were deemed bad by British standards. Although many of the founding members of the Northern Ireland Civil Rights Association had Republican sympathies (Deutsch and Magowan, 1973, p. 154), the demonstrators did not campaign against the border and used 'protest' demonstrations rather than traditional IRA violence to call attention to their demands. In the absence of any justiciable (that is, legally enforceable) rights, civil rights demonstrators could not be encouraged to move from the streets to the courts, as American blacks had done (Rose, 1976a). Civil rights marches, especially in defiance of Ministry of Home Affairs bans, demonstrated publicly the refusal of thousands of Catholics to comply with Stormont's basic political laws. The presence at demonstrations of people with Republican backgrounds or affiliations was carefully noted by Ulster Protestants.

Westminster's interest in Northern Ireland had already been stimulated by the election to Parliament in 1966 of Gerry Fitt, standing in West Belfast, under the label of Republican Labour. Labour MPs ignored the Republican label and came to regard him as 'one of ours', that is, a working-class politician representing an urban area where economic problems were especially bad, and facing an unsympathetic and inadequate Stormont administration. The founding of the Campaign for Democracy in Ulster brought together a group of Labour MPs to press the Labour government for change in Northern Ireland. The *Sunday Times* (3 July 1966) described Northern Ireland as 'John Bull's Political Slum'. Under the weight of the pressure of events in Ulster, the Speaker's Convention prohibiting discussion of important Northern Ireland questions was abandoned (P. Rose, 1970).

The Northern Ireland civil rights campaign raised a banner evoking media attention and sympathy on a worldwide basis, starting with the televising of the RUC use of batons and water-cannons to break up a civil rights march in Londonderry on 5 October 1968. The evident abnormality of conditions in Northern Ireland was taken by the media and by MPs to show the need to 'normalise' Northern Ireland, that is, to make it meet the standards applied elsewhere in the United Kingdom (see, for example, *Sunday Times*, Insight, 1972; cf. the accounts of those involved in Van Voris, 1975). Subsequent to internment in 1971, the opposite conclusion was drawn: abnormal conditions justified using abnormal or irregular means of governance. The belief that Ulster politicians were 'just like us' reached its climax with the parliamentary reception of Bernadette Devlin in April 1969, who was elected by voters who had endorsed convicted Sinn Fein felons 14 years earlier. James Callaghan, speaking as Home Secretary, praised her 'very great brilliance', and MPs wished her welcome to a good career at Westminster (House of Commons, *Debates*, vol. 782, col. 318, 20 April 1969).[6]

The Unionist government of Terence O'Neill was also vulnerable to attack from loyalists within. Critics charged that O'Neill's 'normalisation' measures were a sign of weakness that had encouraged civil rights demands and demonstrations. The Stormont government was also vulnerable to loyalist attacks. This was demonstrated by Ulster Volunteer Force killings in 1966, by Protestant mobilisation under Dr Ian Paisley's leadership for counter-demonstration in 1968–9, and by a Protestant-inspired bombing of Belfast's water supplies at Dunadry in April 1969, intended to discredit the O'Neill government's claim to maintain public order. Disheartened by failure to secure backing by a firm majority of Ulster voters or Unionist MPs in a test election of February 1969, Terence O'Neill resigned office in April 1969, and removed to a banking post in London (cf. Cameron, 1969; O'Neill, 1972; Faulkner, 1978).

Whereas Westminster was ultimately responsible for Northern Ireland, the immediate power of government, including the maintenance of public order, was in the hands of Stormont. The Labour government at Westminster was out of sympathy with the Stormont government; this reflected differences between electorates in the two unequal parts of the United Kingdom. There was, however, no way to adjudicate the differences between them. Whilst the power of the purse was in London, the power to carry out policies, especially on security, was in the hands of Stormont and of elected local authorities. Loyalist opposition to change meant that the Northern Ireland government was cross-pressured by Westminster and its own supporters. The ultimate sanction of Westminster – the power to abolish the Stormont government – was likened by one responsible Labour Minister to 'dropping an H-bomb', an action that could be used only in extreme circumstances, creating as many problems as it could possibly resolve (Rose, 1971b).

Labour and Conservative governments pursued two diverging goals: not to become entangled in the affairs of the Stormont government, yet to press Stormont for reforms that would make it more readily acceptable (or, at least, defensible) at Westminster. Neither the Prime Minister, Harold Wilson, nor the Home Secretary, James Callaghan, liked the way the Unionists had governed from Stormont, but they did not wish to take on the job themselves. The Home Office, nominally responsible for overseeing, had only one senior official concerned about Northern Ireland – plus the Channel Islands, the Isle of Man, and the Charity Commission. The Labour government concentrated on urging the Unionists to speed up the tempo of reforms; privately it threatened unspecified difficulties if this was not done, while publicly defending Unionist efforts. On the eve of the 1969 summer marching season, James Callaghan (1973, p. 15) described the mood thus: 'We were debating whether we should intervene, but hoping and praying that we would not have to. The advice that came to me from all sides was on no account to get sucked into the Irish bog.'

'*C' est le premier pas qui coute.*' That was the private comment of Denis Healey upon the decision to send British troops into action in Northern Ireland when public disorder erupted there in August 1969, and the RUC was exhausted (Callaghan, 1973, p. 21). The Prime Minister, Harold Wilson (1974, p.871), explained that the troubles of Ulster were not troubles 'on our doorstep . . . it is in our house'. The troops were sent in to defend the civil power – that is, the Stormont government – a point not lost upon Catholics. The Downing Street Declaration issued in mid-August 1969, following a meeting between the Prime Ministers of Great Britain and of Northern Ireland, started by re-affirming Northern Ireland's place within the United Kingdom, and that its domestic affairs were primarily the responsibility of Stormont. But the communique also emphasised Westminster's belief that a reformed Stormont was more readily acceptable in Northern Ireland, and also defensible at Westminster. The Home Secretary went to Northern Ireland to confirm details, and British civil servants followed to advise their Northern Ireland counterparts about drafting legislation meant to remove anomalies in British eyes (e.g. the retention of an out-of-date local government electoral franchise), and make Northern Ireland institutions more acceptable to Westminster. By 1971, Stormont ministers claimed that more changes had been introduced in three years than in the previous 47 of Stormont's existence (Government of Northern Ireland, 1971; cf. *Commentary*, 1971). In his memoirs, James Callaghan (1973, p. 169) described this as 'a good record'.

The reformist policy of Westminster very heavily discounted the risk of a challenge to its monopoly of force. In October 1969, the Hunt Report on the police declared:

> It should not be inferred, from this assessment of the possible threat from terrorism, that terrorist attacks are likely. Indeed everyone hopes that the reforms already in hand and those still being planned will, by removing the causes of discontent, make it less likely that in the future extremists will be able to provoke disorder and so bring about the conditions in which terrorism can be effective. Moreover, a realistic assessment of the capacity of the IRA to mount serious terrorist attacks would probably not rate it very high, particularly as the Government of the Irish Republic has stated publicly that it is opposed to the use of force on the border. (Hunt, 1969, para. 27)

This convenient hope (cf. Coogan, 1980; Burton, 1978; Flackes, 1980, pp. 210–12) was not borne out. By the time of disorganised street rioting and communal killings in August 1969, the civil rights movement had already disintegrated. The challenge to Stormont reverted to the physical force tradition. Spurred by the wish of Catholics to secure their armed self-defence in the face of RUC partisanship during Protestant–Catholic confrontations, the Provisional and Official Irish Republican Army groups began organising forces in Catholic communities. Recruits were plentiful. In 1970, house searches by the Army and RUC in Catholic areas found hundreds of firearms, thousands of rounds of ammunition, and hundreds of pounds of explosives; 25 people were killed in political violence that year.

The high point of commitment to defending authority in Northern Ireland with the full force of the British Army was the introduction of internment on 9 August 1971. But internment turned what had heretofore been sniping between the IRA and the British Army into a fully-fledged shooting war. IRA recruitment rose, and Catholic civilians hardened in opposition to the Stormont regime. It also generated pressure on the government of the Republic of Ireland to become involved in the affairs of Northern Ireland. The events of 'Bloody Sunday', 30 January 1972, when British Army paratroopers shot 13 people dead at a demonstration in Londonderry, resulted in unfavourable world publicity for Westminster's actions. The Prime Minister, Edward Heath, decided to treat Northern Ireland as 'the most important matter of the moment' and, in the revealing words of his political secretary, to go 'back to first principles on Ireland' (Hurd, 1979, p. 102).

Since reform from within the Province was proving unsuccessful, reconstruction from without was regarded as the alternative. In March 1972, the Heath government decided to take full responsibility from Stormont for security; the consequence was the resignation of the Unionist government. In default of any Stormont majority for Westminster's unilateral action, this meant the abolition of the Stormont Parliament, initially described as its suspension. The prompt Protestant reaction in Belfast was a two-day strike, involving an estimated 190,000 workers, and a rally at Stormont attended by an estimated 100,000 Protestants protesting against what had happened to an authority to which they were 'ultra-loyal' (Kelly, 1972). In three days Parliament approved the Northern Ireland Temporary Provisions Bill, 1972, authorising 'temporary' direct rule. The authority formerly held by Stormont was vested, by an annually-renewable Act of Parliament, in the Secretary of State for Northern Ireland. In place of Stormont MPs acting in ways accountable to a Northern Ireland electorate, there was a British Secretary of State for Northern Ireland, accountable to the Westminster Parliament. A small number of Whitehall civil servants were stationed in Belfast; the bulk of the work of this ministry remained in the hands of the Northern Ireland Civil Service (cf. Windlesham, 1973; Oliver, 1978b, p. 13; Birrell and Murie, 1980).

Formally, the suspension of Stormont strengthened the central authority of the United Kingdom. Westminster was now the sole, as well as the supreme, constitutional authority for the United Kingdom of Great Britain and of Northern Ireland. The logic of suspension was that Westminster would use its superior authority to engage in a complete reconstruction of the government of Northern Ireland. If force could not maintain the authority of the United Kingdom in the Province, then political engineering was expected to remove Catholic causes of grievances. This would re-establish the state's monopoly of force by undermining the will behind its challengers.

But the challenge to the state became greater, as 'no go' areas were established by armed Republican groups. In the first full year of direct rule, the number of political deaths rose from 243 to 464, and the number of reported shooting incidents from 2,837 to 11,574. Moreover, the violence became triangular, as armed Protestant groups actively engaged in conflict with Republican groups, and the Army ran the risk of being caught in the middle or, even more embarrassing for an authority expected to have a monopoly of force, of being left on the sidelines as local armed forces fought each other (Dillon and Lehane, 1973).

The border with the Irish Republic became more porous, politically as well as militarily. Cross-border movement by Republican groups became common. The Fianna Fail government was divided about what to do, a division made public in 1970 when a senior minister, Charles Haughey, and a Secret Service man were accused of illegally importing arms for the use of Republican forces; a jury did not convict after a very well publicised trial (cf. Kelly, 1971; MacIntyre, 1971; Browne, 1980). Yet the Irish government also wished to retain sufficient goodwill in London to influence policy there (Peck, 1978). After suspension, it publicly proclaimed that the political solution to the vacuum of authority in Northern Ireland would come from steps toward a united Ireland, rather than by strengthening Westminster's authority in what Dublin regarded as its six 'lost' counties.

The positive object of suspension – guaranteeing the state of the United Kingdom by reconstructing in Northern Ireland a government acceptable to Westminster – has so far proven outside the power of the Westminster government. The starting point was, in the words of the then Home Secretary, Reginald Maudling (1978, p. 185), 'that the Westminster pattern of democracy, which suits us so well, is not easily exportable' The reference to 'exportability' implies that Northern Ireland is an 'alien' land and not an integral part of the United Kingdom. What Northern Ireland needed was easily stated in the abstract: a system of government commanding widespread support from both Protestant and Catholic communities. Instead of removing practices anomalous by Westminster standards, the government sought to introduce new anomalies.

Initially, Westminster was most concerned with the political response of the Catholic community, because of the desire to cut the ground out from under the IRA. To appeal to the principal elected representatives of that community, the Social Democratic and Labour Party, and also the government of the Republic, which provided a redoubt for Republicans, Westminster announced that any constitutional settlement must have an 'undefined Irish dimension' (*The Future of Northern Ireland*, 1972, paras 76–8). In place of the conventional Westminster 'winner-take-all' system, which had excluded the Catholic minority from office because of their minority vote, a 'power-sharing' government would guarantee Catholics a permanent role in determining and executing policies. This could generate the positive Catholic support and compliance necessary to secure the state, and end Catholic support or tolerance for groups challenging Westminster's monopoly of force.

Protestants were troubled (Nelson, 1980). Commitment to illegal Protestant paramilitary forces was strengthened by Westminster's discussion of their part of the United Kingdom with the Republic. Protestants had already been made anxious by the abolition of Stormont, the sole lawful guarantee under the 1949 Ireland Act that their constitutional status would not be altered without their consent. In an attempt to assuage Protestant anxieties that Westminster was not 'soft on the border', Parliament authorised a Border poll on 8 March 1973, which offered voters two alternatives:

	by total electorate
Do you want Northern Ireland to remain part of the United Kingdom?	57.5%
Do you want Northern Ireland to be joined with the Republic of Ireland outside the United Kingdom?	0.6%
Abstentions and spoiled ballots	41.9%

The result showed that there was virtual unanimity among the Protestant community in Northern Ireland in favour of the status quo. The deliberate and massive Catholic abstention (in a place where turnouts of up to 90 per cent could be achieved in close contests) showed that the Catholic community was unwilling to give positive support to a place in the United Kingdom.

The 1973 Northern Ireland Constitution Act authorised a form of power-sharing government that differed emphatically from the Westminster model applied in the old Stormont. The differences included election of an Assembly by proportional representation, and installation of an Executive only after the Northern Ireland Secretary was satisfied that the Executive had broad support among both Protestants and Catholics. The launching of the Executive was also made conditional by Westminster upon the Unionist leader, Brian Faulkner, accepting the establishment of a Council of Ireland, at a December 1973 'summit' conference at Sunningdale, Berkshire, involving the Republic of Ireland government as well as the United Kingdom government, and the SDLP and the Unionist parties. Faulkner was installed as Head of the new Executive – and promptly deposed as leader of the Ulster Unionists.[7]

Westminster's attempt to reconstruct the United Kingdom by reconstructing the government of Northern Ireland collapsed in May 1974 in the face of the Ulster Workers Council strike. The strike – the first successful challenge of its kind to an elected government in the United Kingdom – was called to protest against the creation of a power-sharing executive committed to a Council of Ireland. The UWC demanded an immediate general election to see whether or not the Executive represented a majority of Ulster opinion. The premise of the strikers – that it did not – was shared by Brian Faulkner, his SDLP colleagues and the Northern Ireland Office. The results of the February 1974 Westminster general election justified this view (Rose, 1976b, p. 30).

The Ulster Workers Council strike did more than demonstrate that Westminster lacked a monopoly of force. More than 400 dead from the introduction of direct rule to May 1974 was evidence enough of that. The strike showed that the Westminster government lacked the understanding, the will or the means to defend a government that it had created. Harold Wilson poured scorn on the strikers, as spongers 'who are systematically breaking the law and intimidating the people of Northern Ireland – their fellow citizens and our fellow citizens within the United Kingdom' (Fisk, 1975, p. 253). But he was unwilling to order the British Army to act in defence of the law. Nor was the British Army wanting to confront the strikers in a test of power. One reason was: 'The Army did not trust the political judgment of the British ministers at Stormont' (Fisk, 1975, p. 240; see also Flackes, 1980, p. 202; Evelegh, 1978; McKittcrick, 1980). When Faulkner saw that Westminster would not attempt to defend the government it had sired, he resigned, and Northern Ireland returned to 'temporary' direct rule.

Any doubt about Westminster's incapacity to reconstruct the United Kingdom was removed by the Constitutional Convention called in 1975 (Rose, 1976b). The Convention was asked to consider 'what provision for the government of Northern Ireland is likely to command the most widespread acceptance throughout the community'. The proportional representation ballot returned a majority- of candidates from the United Ulster Unionist Council (UUUC), committed to the rejection of power-sharing endorsed by Westminster. The Convention Report, approved by a vote of 42 to 31, reflected the UUUC's wish for a British-style majority rule Parliament. It was rejected by Westminster. The Convention was dissolved in March 1976. Westminster's hopes for reconstructing authority had thus failed, for power-sharing requires the support of a majority of the majority, as well as a majority of the minority.

IV   GOVERNING WITHOUT A STATE

In formal terms, the government of Northern Ireland since suspension appears to resemble the government of Great Britain, because it is carried out by Cabinet departments. The principal responsible ministry, the Northern Ireland Office, is nominally parallel with the Scottish Office and the Welsh Office, a ministry with delimited territorial responsibilities within a formally unitary state.

In practice, the Northern Ireland Office (NIO) is distinctive, in that it acts as the Secretary of State's advisor and as a Ministry of Home Affairs. Departments of the old Northern Ireland government continued in being as administrative divisions under the Secretary of State for Northern Ireland, complete with permanent secretaries for finance, commerce, agriculture, education, environment, health and social services. The great bulk of administration remains in the hands of the Northern Ireland Civil Service, which constitutes 98 per cent of NIO staff in the Province. The great difference is that Northern Ireland administrators now work to the direction of Westminster ministers, rather than locally-elected Stormont ministers. In Westminster terms, this is not distinctive, for neither Scottish nor Welsh affairs are administered by ministers accountable to a Scottish or Welsh assembly. What is different is that the Northern Ireland Office ministers have never represented an Ulster constituency, or even a party with an MP in Northern Ireland, whereas the Scottish and Welsh Offices are directed by ministers from Scotland and Wales, and speak for parties fighting and winning seats there.

Superficially, government in Northern Ireland today may appear to be like 'normal' politics in Scotland and Wales. But such a judgement is inadequate for government must also cope with 'real' politics in Ulster terms. Doing this is a joint responsibility of several Westminster departments, each with a distinctive departmental perspective. The Ministry of Defence is much involved in the day-to-day affairs of the Province, because of its security responsibilities. The Foreign Office, with its own Republic of Ireland Department, is intimately concerned with Northern Ireland through issues raised by the Irish government in Dublin (cf. Peck, 1978; and Enoch Powell, statement in *The Times,* 4 January 1980). Because the Ministry of Defence and the Foreign Office are important in Whitehall, the Northern Ireland

Office cannot necessarily be sure of committing the whole of the United Kingdom government by its initiatives – as demonstrated by the absence of Ministry of Defence support for the NIO-sponsored Assembly during the 1974 Ulster Workers Council strike. It is indicative of the 'war footing' of Northern Ireland that the Treasury, usually *primus inter pares* in major inter-departmental matters, has had a confined role in Northern Ireland, accepting bills incurred by civil and military policy in a setting where the principal costs are measured in lives lost.

Officials and ministers in each of the three disparate departments most concerned with Northern Ireland are likely to have different and distinctive priorities. The Northern Ireland Office has administrative and political responsibilities; Defence, primarily security concerns; and the Foreign Office, responsibility for relations with the Republic of Ireland and other foreign nations concerned with this aspect of United Kingdom affairs.

When Northern Ireland problems approach crisis, a Cabinet committee under the Prime Minister may assume direction of policy. For example, Cabinet committees were created in 1969 to review the prospect of sending in troops, and in 1980 to review alternative recommendations for ending direct rule. In 1973, Edward Heath played an active role in the Sunningdale negotiations; in May 1974, Harold Wilson made a Prime Ministerial broadcast about 'spongers' in Northern Ireland; and Mrs Thatcher stimulated the unsuccessful 1979–80 inter-party talks on devolving governmental powers.

Even though Westminster carries out a variety of administrative tasks within Northern Ireland, this is not proof that the United Kingdom is a state. For this to be the case, Westminster must assert an effective monopoly of organised force, and protect the territorial boundaries of the United Kingdom. It must also maintain the integrity of the United Kingdom, and not treat Northern Ireland as if it were an alien land or a colony, rather than an integral part of the United Kingdom. On all three of these criteria, Westminster fails.

The failure of Westminister's claim to monopolise force has been evident since August 1971, when the introduction of internment revealed (contrary to Second World War and 1956–62 experience) that within Northern Ireland there were now IRA forces capable of carrying on a lengthy and sustained guerrilla war. Since that date, at least *nine* different forces have been active within Northern Ireland, most of which are independent of government. Moreover, the Westminster government has held discussions and negotiations with illegal forces, thus granting them political recognition as a *de facto* part of the politics of Northern Ireland.

The Crown maintains four different forces in Northern Ireland. Only one of these, the British Army, is an 'all-United Kingdom' force, staffed by soldiers recruited in conventional ways, and ready for posting anywhere at the direction of the Ministry of Defence. Depending upon the military situation, the Army has anything from 6,000 to 20,000 men on active duty in the Province; the total has been nearer the lower end of the range since 1976. In addition, the Army is supported by a locally raised and armed auxiliary force, the Ulster Defence Regiment (UDR) with 8,500 members; a full-time Royal Ulster Constabulary (RUC) of 6,500, also recruited locally; and an RUC Reserve of about 4,500 persons.

Two-thirds or more of Crown forces in Northern Ireland are Ulstermen and women serving full-or part-time in the UDR, the RUC or the RUC Reserve. Unlike conventional British soldiers, these mobilised Ulstermen have a permanent commitment to their Province, as citizens as well as security forces. In default of Catholic recruits, Ulster people in security forces are overwhelmingly Protestant, and therefore politically opposed to a United Ireland. Their readiness to defend Northern Ireland is not a temporary assignment, but a communal commitment, and some pay with their lives. Since 1975, the number of people from Ulster security forces killed each year has normally been greater than the number of British soldiers killed; 169 UDR, RUC and RUC Reserve dead compared to 122 British soldiers from 1975 to 19 October 1981. Past history suggests that some members of these forces would not be reliable agents of Westminster should Westminster appear to endorse measures perceived as leading to a United Ireland.

Most armed organisations in Northern Ireland today are *illegal*. The Irish Republican cause has at least three distinctive and at times openly conflicting military standard-bearers: the Official IRA (which declared a cease-fire in 1972); the Provisional IRA (which has been the principal active proponent of Irish unity by physical force since its organisation in December 1969); and the Irish National Liberation Army (a small but active splinter group from the Official IRA, aligned with the Irish Republican Socialist Party). Republican military forces direct their violence not only at British soldiers and Ulster defence forces, but also attack targets in the Protestant community, and, occasionally, each other.

Protestant paramilitary forces lack the traditional military organisation and discipline of Republican forces, since for two generations Protestants were almost exclusively organised under Stormont's authority. Since suspension, Protestants have also organised in defence of what is called the Loyalist cause; technically, they are 'ultra' loyal, that is, prepared to take measures to defend Northern Ireland *as they see it,* even if actions are not constitutionally authorised (Nelson, 1980). The Loyalist cause has at least two main bodies: the Ulster Defence Association, a loosely-linked group of local 'defenders', and the Ulster Volunteer Force, the name usually used to describe militant Protestants prepared to carry out armed attacks against Catholics, especially those suspected of Republican attachments. As convictions of a number of UDR and RUC Reserve men show, some Crown forces are also prepared to carry their defence of Ulster beyond the bounds authorised by the Crown.

Since 1969 Westminster has recurringly given evidence of not even seeking to claim an effective monopoly of force in the Province. British officials have time and again negotiated with groups representing or acting as intermediaries for 'extra-legal' or illegal military forces. The pattern of negotiations has shifted from public and well-publicised efforts by British military officers to talk down barricades erected in Catholic quarters of Belfast in 1969, to more or less secret or unacknowledged talks. The purpose of talks with representatives of illegal armed groups has been to advance Westminster's broad political policies; the significance here is that they give *de facto* official recognition to the absence of a necessary attribute of the state in Northern Ireland.

The IRA (and, to a much lesser extent, Protestants) have always sought recognition that they are an army with political aims. After a hunger strike by Republican prisoners in the spring of 1972, the Northern Ireland Office granted 'political prisoner' status to persons serving long sentences for offences related to the troubles. Such prisoners were exempt from work, and other standard features of a criminal prisoner's routine. More than 1500 special category prisoners were incarcerated, including a number of loyalists. Subsequent to the Gardiner Committee (1975) Report on terrorism, no new prisoners were admitted to that status for crimes committed after 1 March 1976, and William Whitelaw subsequently admitted that the political recognition originally given to the IRA had been a mistake. Removal of this status led Republican prisoners to go 'on the blanket' – refusing to wear prison uniform – and to go on a major hunger strike in 1980, terminated by a compromise that refused political recognition (Coogan, 1980).

'Backstairs' negotiations were initiated in 1969 with the establishment of the office of UKREP (United Kingdom Representative in Northern Ireland) to provide a flow of political information to London independent of Stormont. By definition, this meant talking to opposition politicians. The office of UKREP was also the recognised channel for British discussions with leaders of armed groups euphemistically known as 'para' military organisations. The listening post was normally staffed by a Foreign Office official; the fiirst incumbent, Sir Oliver Wright, had previously worked at 10 Downing Street. One holder of the post, Sir Howard Smith, subsequently became head of MI5. With the suspension of Stormont, British ministers and home civil servants were able to deal directly with party political people in Ulster, but UKREP continued in being until 1977.

Negotiations between British officials and illegal or extra-legal organisations resulted in the temporary IRA cease-fire of May–July 1972 (still observed by the Official IRA); it quickly broke down on the Provisional IRA side in a dispute about Belfast housing. In 1974, the Ulster Volunteer Force was 'de-proscribed', in the hope that it would become an electoral rather than paramilitary group. The UVF was 're-proscribed' in October 1975, after an admission that it had been responsible for most of the violence in which a dozen people died. In December 1974, talks initiated by Protestant clergymen with Provisional Republicans at Feakle, Country Clare, were followed by a cease-fire, and British government recognition of Provisional Sinn Fein incident centres. Provisional Sinn Fein claimed to be a political party and therefore different from the Provisional IRA, but, as the former British Ambassador to Dublin put it (Peck, 1978, p. 20): 'In practice, nobody was fooled by the switching of civilian hats and military caps'. The cease-fire broke down as death tolls rose, and the government closed the incident centres in November 1975.

Upon occasion, senior Westminster politicians have met IRA leaders for discussions. In July 1972, the Northern Ireland Secretary, William Whitelaw, met Sean MacStiofain, head of the Provisional Army Council, as the culmination of truce negotiations with UKREP officials. In 1971 and 1972, Harold Wilson, then leader of the Opposition, twice met with Provisional IRA leaders, once in London and once in Dublin (to the anger of the Dublin government, which rightly regards the IRA as subversive of *its* authority). At each meeting, IRA officials repeated their demands for the Westminster government to leave Northern Ireland (MacStiofain, 1975, Ch. 16; Haines, 1977, Ch. 6; Flackes, 1980, pp. 57–9; Coogan, 1980, Ch. 4).

In addition to the inability to maintain an effective monopoly of force, Westminster has also been ambiguous about defending the territorial integrity of the United Kingdom as far as Northern Ireland is concerned. This is a second important derogation from the claim that the United Kingdom is a state. The stated position of the Westminster government is that Northern Ireland should remain a part of the United Kingdom as long as a majority of its people wish to do so. In other words, *the right to unilateral secession from the United Kingdom is given to one portion of it.* Moreover, the institutional machinery to give effect to withdrawal (if a majority wished to do so) is provided by the 1973 Border Poll Act, which stipulates that there may be a vote on the border once every ten years.

In practical terms, the border between Northern Ireland and the Republic is virtually 'wide open'; there is an easy movement back and forth of people with business and friends on both sides of the border, as well as ready transit by IRA units. The British Army and the RUC maintain some patrols on the border, but these are intermittent and ineffective, by comparison, say, with patrols on the much longer border separating West and East Germany. There is no political will at Westminster to invest the effort required to make the border secure, or to face criticisms from those dedicated to the principle of abolishing the border between Northern Ireland and the Republic.

The lack of boundaries is also evidenced in the status conferred upon citizens of the Irish Republic. Even though Ireland became independent in 1921, and left the Commonwealth in 1949, Irish citizens continue to enjoy the right to unlimited entry to Great Britain, and, once in Britain, enjoy the same rights as British subjects. When Westminster enacted the Ireland Act in 1949, consequent to Ireland leaving the Commonwealth, Section 2 declared: 'Notwithstanding that the Republic of Ireland is not part of His Majesty's Dominions, the Republic of Ireland is not a foreign country for the purposes of any law in force in any part of the United Kingdom.' (The opposite is not true for British subjects moving to the Republic.) A member of Parliament or a Privy Councillor does not need to be a British subject, and several MPs are Irish citizens and travel on passports of the Republic of Ireland. The same is true of a number of leading SDLP politicians. The 'fuzzy' boundaries are illustrated in the extreme case of the 1975 Devolution White Paper, which proposed that the only qualification for membership of the Scottish or Welsh Assembly, besides attaining the age of 21, would be that a person is 'a British subject or a citizen of the Republic of Ireland' (*Our Changing Democracy*, 1975, p. 61).

The conditional nature of the Westminster government's commitment to its western-most border of the United Kingdom is in marked contrast with the unconditional claims of the Irish government, and of the Social Democratic and Labour Party of Northern Ireland, to abolish the border. The Republic of Ireland's claim to incorporate Northern Ireland within its own territory is laid down in Article 2 of its Constitution. The tactics used to advance (or ignore) this claim to Irish unity have varied through the years; the consistency of the objective is indubitable.[8] From a Dublin perspective, Irish unity is a legitimate aspiration or even a constitutional obligation; the obstacle is the Westminster government's conditional guarantee of Northern Ireland's continued membership in the United Kingdom. In the blunt words of the 1979 Westminster election manifesto of the SDLP: 'The question is not *whether* Britain should disengage from Ireland, but *when* and *in what circumstances*' (SDLP, 1979, p. 8; italics as in the original).

Notwithstanding the mutually exclusive claims to Northern Ireland of the

Westminster and Dublin governments, Westminster has always been ready to engage in a dialogue with Dublin about Northern Ireland. In preparing for the ill-fated power-sharing Executive, the British government sought to institutionalise an Irish dimension in the affairs of a part of the United Kingdom, with a Council of Ireland concerned with cross-border or 'intra-Irish' affairs. British military intelligence has a different view of the Irish dimension. 'The Republic provides many of the facilities of the classic safe haven so essential to any successful terrorist movement. And, it will probably continue to do so for the foreseeable future' (Walker, 1979, p. 13) The readiness of Westminster to listen to Irish demands for British territory is a continuing source of anxiety to Ulster Protestants, especially since the abolition of Stormont, which by statute had the right to veto any proposal to alter the border. The asymmetry of outlooks is also illustrated by the Republic's refusal to extradite to Northern Ireland persons accused of violent crimes, as long as the accused can plead that the crime is 'political', that is, intended to secure a United Ireland and therefore non-extraditable under Irish law.

A comparison of the Republic of Ireland and the United Kingdom makes evident the difference between being a state 'and then some', and being 'not quite a state'. The Republic of Ireland has integrity as a state. It has a well-defined border, for Article 3 of the 1937 Irish Constitution establishes the 26 counties of Ireland as its territorial border, 'pending the re-integration of the national territory claimed in Article 2'. Within these borders, Ireland remained neutral during the Second World War, and has refused to join NATO since. Moreover, its leaders are extremely conscious that their first aim is to maintain the security of the 26-county Republic, and prevent disorder from breaking out there. The government claims a monopoly of force, and inherits authority from a regime that demonstrated this monopoly by winning a bloody civil war in 1922–3. IRA personnel and institutions operate within the Republic– but normally *not* as military organisations. The history of the Republic indicates that if the IRA were actively to challenge the Republic's authority within its 26 counties, it could be treated ruthlessly by the government (Bell, 1970). The legitimacy of the Republic has been demonstrated time and again by the failure of 'Republican' (that is, IRA-front) groups to win popular support at elections.

The Republic's governors have a policy of being a state 'and then some', for they also lay claim to a portion of the United Kingdom. The claim to a part of the Crown's domain does not detract from the Republic's position as a state; instead, it detracts from the status of the United Kingdom. Realising the claim of Ireland *irredenta* would, in the literal sense, mean the end of the United Kingdom.

As long as the claim for Irish unity was not actively pursued within the United Kingdom – whether by the Irish government *or* by Republican forces – it could be ignored. But the claim for Irish unity – which is also a claim for the break up of the United Kingdom – has been actively advocated by physical force Republicans within the United Kingdom since 1971. Irish unity is advocated too by the chief elected representatives of the Catholic minority, the SDLP. The advocacy was low-key when power-sharing appeared possible, but since then Irish unity has been increasingly prominent as an SDLP goal.

Ironically, Westminster has been anxious to establish a *cordon sanitaire* within the United Kingdom. In violation of the integrity of the United Kingdom as a state, Northern Ireland has been treated as a place apart. The segregation is complete politically, for the British Labour Party does not wish to sponsor candidates for Parliament in Northern Ireland constituencies, notwithstanding the desire of the Northern Ireland Labour Party, its former affiliate, for this to be done. Nor do the Conservatives contest seats in collaboration with one or another fragment of their old Unionist alliance, based, as Brian Faulkner (1978, p. 23) rightly noted, 'not so much on doctrinaire Conservatism as on mutual interest'. The object of Westminster's policy for public order was described by Home Secretary Reginald Maudling as 'an acceptable level of violence', indicating that a much higher level of violence would be acceptable for Ulster than for any part of England, Scotland or Wales. Shortly before being appointed as Home Secretary in 1979, William Whitelaw described his security policy as a 'determination to prevent violence in this part of the United Kingdom'.[9]

The *cordon sanitaire* is recognised in law by the Prevention of Terrorism Act, approved in 1974 in the wake of a Republican bombing in England that killed 19 people in two public houses in Birmingham. The Act gives the Home Secretary the power to exclude British subjects from moving from Northern Ireland to Great Britain, or to deport persons from Britain to Northern Ireland. The law results in an elaborate system of screening persons in transit between Britain and Northern Ireland. Ulster people are subject to a degree of scrutiny at the 'border' of Great Britain that would not be applied to Continental or American visitors to Britain. From first enactment to 31 December 1979, this has resulted in the exclusion of 217 persons from Great Britain into Northern Ireland, and the detention of 4500 for questioning as suspects (Flackes, 1980, p. 209).

On the Ulster side of the division within the United Kingdom, special powers unknown in other parts of the United Kingdom have been taken by the Army, police and other defence agencies. The suspension of *habeas corpus* has been approved by the Westminster Parliament as well as by the

Stormont Parliament. Special courts for trial without jury, and with novel rules for evaluating confessions, were authorised by Westminster following a report of Lord Diplock (1972; cf. Boyle *et al.*, 1979). British intelligence organisations such as MI5, MI6 and military intelligence have been very active in Northern Ireland, scrutinising journalists and elected office holders, as well as paramilitaries (see, for example, McKitterick, 1980; Campbell, 1980; Lindsay, 1980). Consistently since 1971 charges against the security forces of brutality and torture have required a series of investigations by committees appointed by Whitehall, and independently (see, for example, Dash, 1972; Amnesty, 1978; Taylor, 1980; cf. Widgery, 1972; Compton, 1971). The Special Air Service (SAS) has also been active in uniformed and non-uniformed activities in the historic nine counties of Ulster. It could be argued that the measures are exceptional because the circumstances of Northern Ireland are exceptional. A corollary of this is that actions taken in Northern Ireland would be taken in England if circumstances were similar. However, Parliament has chosen not to make the powers conferred upon the Crown applicable to all parts of the United Kingdom, but to confine them to the Province.

Neither the old Stormont regime nor Westminster's institutions of temporary direct rule could claim to be fully legitimate, that is, accepted by the whole of the population of Northern Ireland. The fundamental political difference is that the old Stormont regime defended its authority whenever it was challenged or appeared to be under danger of challenge. In particular, it was strict in drawing the distinction between its own legal coercive forces, and illegal armed forces. By contrast, Westminster has not shown the political will to maintain its authority. The idea of integrating Northern Ireland with Great Britain, in a single unqualified United Kingdom government, has been rejected out of hand by both Conservative and Labour governments. In consequence, the Province is governed by 'temporary direct rule', an annually-renewable charter of authority.

Westminster politicians do not regard direct rule as either desirable or capable of continuation indefinitely. Temporary direct rule has been described by one Secretary of State for Northern Ireland, Humphrey Atkins, as deficient for three reasons. It is disliked by the principal political parties in Northern Ireland and in Britain. Legislation for Northern Ireland is typically made by Orders in Council rather than by normal parliamentary procedures. Moreover, there are 'absolutely minimal' opportunities for Ulster people to assume responsibility for their affairs (House of Commons, *Debates*, vol. 988, cols 553f, 9 July 1980). Since direct rule was imposed in 1972, Westminster has sought to end it three times: by the ill-fated power-sharing Executive of 1974; by an abortive Constitutional Convention in 1975; and by

1979–80 inter-party talks in Northern Ireland. A framework of government that governors themselves do not wish to defend is not a firm basis for authority, especially when the state is already flawed.

The legitimacy of Westminster is even more dubious in the eyes of mass British opinion. Surveys since 1969 of British attitudes toward Irish unity show a consistent plurality approving the British government encouraging Northern Ireland to join the Republić of Ireland. Similarly, since June 1974, a majority of the British public have also believed that Westminster should begin to withdraw troops from the Province. In short, there is *disagreement* between majority opinion in Northern Ireland and majority opinion in Great Britain *about whether the United Kingdom should continue*. The bulk of Ulster opinion wishes to remain within the United Kingdom, but British public opinion favours 'pulling out' of the United Kingdom, turning Westminster into the government of a governable Great Britain (Rose *et al.*, 1978).

In office, no British government official has publicly expressed the view that Great Britain should 'secede' from the United Kingdom, or that Northern Ireland should be expelled. Ministers have repeatedly affirmed that Northern Ireland can remain a part of the United Kingdom as long as a majority wishes this. But memoirs written after leaving office clearly show that British ministers would welcome Northern Ireland withdrawing from the United Kingdom. The arguments for withdrawal may be based upon a stark pessimism, as in the case of Joe Haines, press secretary to Harold Wilson:

> The British Labour government withdrew from the Indian sub-continent in 1947 and the resultant fighting cost a million Hindu, Sikh and Moslem lives. Would anyone today say that Britain was wrong to withdraw? . . . I am not convinced that civil war, bloodshed and massacre on a scale greater in the long run than now exists would follow a British withdrawal. (Haines, 1977, p. 116)

James Callaghan, in his memoir of Northern Ireland, wrote that 'Britain cannot be expected to sit patiently and bleed indefinitely if her best efforts face deliberate sabotage by the elected majority of the Province'. Ideally, Callaghan (1973, p. 187) added, 'I would like to see Ireland come together again'. In a speech as leader of the Opposition in 1971, Harold Wilson described Irish unity as the eventual settlement of what he called the Irish problem (House of Commons, *Debates*, vol. 826, col. 1571ff, 5 November 1971). But for as long as it lasts, Northern Ireland is in fact the United Kingdom problem.

V   IS BRITAIN PART OF THE UNITED KINGDOM?

In a world of independent states, the United Kingdom is an unusual problem. It is 'almost a state'; that is to say, it is a state except for Northern Ireland. But the standards of international law require that the government of the United Kingdom treat its territory as a single integral unit, and not as a qualified state. A government that cannot guarantee the boundaries of its territory, or effectively claim a monopoly of force within its territory, is a problematic state. The integrity of the United Kingdom as a state has been disrupted for more than a decade by the troubles in Northern Ireland.[10]

The customary way to respond to any generalisation drawn from the experience of Northern Ireland is to argue that it is 'not really' a part of the United Kingdom. Evidence of differences and misunderstandings between Ireland and Great Britain is plentiful, and can be pursued back through the centuries. Just as well-intentioned Englishmen (including public officials) think of Ireland as like the Isle of Wight, a piece of Crown Territory detached from the mainland (Peck, 1978, p. 18), so too there is a temptation for a well-bred London politician to read Northern Ireland out of the United Kingdom. One might describe this as trying to 'Mississippise Ulster', reflecting the way that American Presidents once tried, when challenged about civil rights, to pretend that Mississippi was *not* part of the Union. But when challenges to authority came in the 1950s and 1960s, Presidents Eisenhower and Johnson were prepared to put troops into the field to maintain the integrity of Union.

The 'exceptionalist' interpretation of the United Kingdom proposes a series of propositions, each starting, 'Except for Northern Ireland . . .'. In exceptionalist terms, the United Kingdom can be said to be a state, because: (a) except for Northern Ireland, it defends a well-defined border; (b) except for Northern Ireland, the government maintains an effective monopoly of force; and (c) except for Northern Ireland, the United Kingdom is a fully legitimate state. This, however, is politics with the hard bits left out.

While the 'exceptionalist' interpretation is understandable and familiar as political rhetoric, it is deficient as constitutional or international law, for the supreme authority is a Parliament and Crown of Great Britain *and* Northern Ireland. Either the United Kingdom exists, in which case it fails to exist as a proper state, or there is what might be called 'the Great Britain problem', that is, a *de facto* state which lacks *de jure* status, because it must also accept responsibility for Northern Ireland.

The customary way for British politicians to solve the Great Britain problem was to distance Northern Ireland.[11] Prior to 1921, this was done by administering the whole of Ireland through an Irish Office; after 1921, it was done by giving the Stormont Parliament responsibility for maintaining an effective monopoly of force, and defending its borders. Leaders of the 1964–70 Wilson government gave clear evidence of their desire to keep Northern Ireland problems at a distance. Sean MacStiofain (1975, p. 353), head of the Provisional IRA Army, could also 'distance' the troubles of Ulster from the Republic. He justified breaking his hunger-and-thirst fast in January 1973, by declaring: 'I do not want anybody hurt or blood spilled on my behalf in the Twenty-Six Counties'. The publicity given to civil rights protests, the introduction of British troops, and the suspension of Stormont in 1972 destroyed the buffer between Westminster and Northern Ireland. Westminster can no longer ignore the problems of a territory for which it is directly responsible.

In effect, Westminster handles the problem of Northern Ireland by denying the integrity of the United Kingdom, that is, by *not* making defence of its borders and internal security a first claim upon Westminster's resources. By default, Ulster Protestants have had to regard the defence of their part of the United Kingdom as their own responsibility. About one in eight of able-bodied male Ulster Protestants of military age has shown readiness to bear arms in defence of Northern Ireland's place as part of the United Kingdom – in Crown forces or in 'extra-legal' forces. The readiness of Ulster Protestants to challenge Westminster's authority, or to show distrust of Westminster's ambiguous intentions, is sometimes misinterpreted as an indication of popular support for an independent Ulster. In fact, the opposite is the case: it is evidence of a demand, enforced by extreme ultra-loyal actions, to defend the present boundaries of the United Kingdom.

Whatever the perspective, Northern Ireland *is* indubitably different. But to explain Westminster's failure to defend the United Kingdom on the grounds of distinctive Northern Ireland conditions is to imply that, if conditions were the same within Great Britain, Westminster would behave as it has done in Northern Ireland. The question thus arises; are there any conditions within Great Britain that sufficiently resemble Northern Ireland's challenge to the state? While any answer to such a question will be hypothetical, it is prudent as well as appropriate to speculate about such possibilities.

The territorial integrity of the United Kingdom is challenged by Scottish Nationalists and Welsh Nationalists, as well as by groups in Northern Ireland. Whereas in Ulster the Westminster Parliament is ready to allow Northern Ireland to secede unilaterally, the 1974–9 devolution debate showed Westminster's adamant view that under no circumstances would Scots or Welsh be allowed to vote about independence in a referendum. Westminster is not prepared to admit that Scotland or Wales has the unilateral right to withdraw from the United Kingdom, should a majority there wish to do so.

The monopoly of force within Great Britain is reflected in the absence of any tradition of organising physical force challenges to government (cf. Marsh, 1977). Policemen do not carry guns, nor have Britons learned how to organise underground armies in response to military conquest. The absence of a physical force tradition in politics is particularly noteworthy in the West of Scotland, where anti-social violence erupts at football matches and in street fights. Welsh language protesters occasionally turn to violence against property, but not against persons, and such violence appears to be the work of a minority of the minority that constitutes Welsh language activists. British parties can use the violence in Northern Ireland as an argument against Nationalist parties in Britain.

The most evidence of politically-induced challenges to laws is found in Wales, where language demonstrators have demonstrated a willingness to break symbolic laws, e.g. about printing of motor car licences or road signs, in order to state their claim for greater use of the Welsh language. This challenge can be met in more than one way: by arresting the violators, by ignoring the violation, or by meeting the protestors' demands by increasing bilingualism in matters under government auspices. In the most striking challenge yet by language protestors, a proposed hunger strike in October 1980 by Plaid Cymru leader Gwynfor Evans in protest against the Conservative government's refusal to allocate a channel to Welsh-language television, Westminster responded by meeting the protestor's demand.

The greatest challenge potentially to compliance with the law in Great Britain today comes from interests that lack an identifiable national territory. Industrial relations in the 1970s showed that some trade unionists, under certain circumstances, are prepared to reject laws deemed important by the government of the day. Furthermore, some trade unionists are also prepared to organise visible defiance of these laws on the grounds that they are 'illegitimate', even if legal. Since 1969 successive Labour and Conservative governments first declared that legislation on industrial relations was in the national interest – only to abandon pressing the point when this threatened a trade union challenge to the authority of government.

Race relations too raise questions of political 'nationhood' within Great Britain, and of compliance with basic laws. In so far as race relations politics leads to protest demonstrations in the streets, then, as Ulster events have shown, there is the potential for counter-demonstrations, with the police trying to maintain both effectiveness and neutrality *vis-à-vis* decidedly non-neutral immigrant groups and National Front protesters. When police are party to a conflict, their status may be challenged by demonstrators. In

Northern Ireland, the Catholic minority was said to be unable to trust the RUC because only 11 per cent of its members were Catholic, in a society which was one-third Catholic (Hunt, 1969, pp. 13, 29) – an under-representation by one-third. In England and Wales, where approximately 3.5 per cent of the population is coloured, only 0.2 per cent of the police force consists of 'ethnic minorities', under-representation by 17 times (Central Statistical Office, 1979, Tables 13.23–4).

A government confronted with a challenge to its authority must defeat the challenger or learn to govern without consensus – if it is to govern at all. The continental tradition of politics is that 'the state defends itself', and both the Fifth French Republic and the Republic of Italy give public evidence of doing so in the face of armed attacks. The English tradition is to attempt conciliation, to ignore protests or, in the extreme case of Northern Ireland, to distance Westminster from a challenge. Yet there is no certainty that challenges to authority will always be confined to one part of the United Kingdom. An English voice may protest: 'But surely, it can't happen here!' To which an Ulsterman can reply in a voice loud and clear: 'But it has'.

NOTES

1. Clark consistently refers to the community as 'Great Britain'. Contrast Utley, 1975; Dyson, 1980, esp. pp. 36-47.
2. The index of Greenstein and Polsby's (1975) *Handbook of Political Science* gives only four passing references to the state; by comparison, systems theory has three times this number of references.
3. See R. Rose, 1970. It is typical of the confusion of the Royal Commission on the Constitution (1973) p. iii, that it could cite this term and also refer to 'countries, nations and regions'. The present paper modifies and extends the earlier analysis, by arguing that the United Kingdom, while still multi-national, is no longer properly considered a state.
4. See Rose, 1971a, pp. 28ff, for a detailed discussion of the concept of authority used here; and, for its particular relevance to Northern Ireland, see ibid., Ch. 5.
5. The term Westminster is here used to refer to what is conventionally called British government. This allows the term government to be used primarily to emphasise what is elsewhere called the state, and avoids the considerable ambiguity about the territorial reference of the term 'British'. In practice, most decisions are taken in Whitehall, rather than the Palace of Westminster, but they must, none the less, be supported and defended in Parliament.
6. Cf. the reaction to the same MP three years later when she physically assaulted the Home Secretary, Reginald Maudling, on the floor of the House of Commons in anger at the killings on Bloody Sunday (House of Commons, *Debates*, 31 February 1972, vol. 830, cols 264ff).
   For pro-Unionist views held by a small minority of dissident Conservative and Ulster Unionist MPs, see Norton, 1978, as cited in index.

7. Parties receiving a majority of Protestant and Unionist votes (35.4 per cent Loyalist, against 26.5 per cent Faulkner Unionist) were excluded from the Sunningdale Conference (see Rose, 1976b, p. 30).
8. The fact is often ignored in London; cf. press treatment of the same statement by the Taoiseach, Charles Haughey, as reported by Dennis Kennedy, *Irish Times*, 19 May 1980, 'Ending British Pledge Key to Haughey Policy', and Michael Jones, *Sunday Times*, 18 May 1980, 'Haughey's Peace Package'. In both cases, the principal point was that Haughey would accept many conditions – provided they were part of the establishment of an all-Ireland Republic. See also the text of the Haughey statement on Panorama (BBC-TV) printed in *Irish Times*, 10 June 1980.
9. The Whitelaw quotation was noted by the author at a 1979 Conservative party general election press conference at Smith Square, London. Maudling's comment is set in context by McKitterick (1979).
10. The lack of full legitimacy, because of rejection of authority by a minority of Ulster people committed to Irish unity, did not, up to the late 1960s, detract from the state of the United Kingdom, albeit that it did from its claim to unqualified legitimacy.
11. For a discussion of 'distancing' as a traditional tactic of 'high' status politicians in an earlier era of governing the United Kingdom by a dual polity, see Bulpitt, 1978, p. 180.

REFERENCES

Amnesty (1978) *Report of an Amnesty International Mission to Northern Ireland* (London: Amnesty International).

Barker, Rodney (1977) 'The Absence of the State in Explanations of British Politics', duplicated (London: London School of Economics).

Barritt, Denis P. and C. F. Carter (1962) *The Northern Ireland Problem* (London: Oxford University Press).

Bell, J. Bowyer (1970) *The Secret Army* (London: Anthony Blond).

Birrell, Derek and Alan Murie (1980) *Policy and Government in Northern Ireland* (Dublin: Gill & Macmillan).

Blake, J. W. (1956) *Northern Ireland in the Second World War* (London: HMSO).

Bowden, Tom (1977) *The Breakdown of Public Security: the Case of Ireland 1916–1921 and Palestine 1936–1939* (London: Sage Publications).

Boyle, Kevin, Tom Hadden and Paddy Hillyard (1979) 'Emergency Powers: Ten Years on', *Fortnight* (Belfast) no. 174 (Dec. 1979/Jan. 1980).

Browne, Vincent (1980) 'The Arms Crisis, 1970', *Magill*, May–July.

Buckland, Patrick (1979) *The Factory of Grievances: Devolved Government in Northern Ireland, 1921–39* (Dublin: Gill & Macmillan).

Bulpitt, James (1978) 'The Making of the United Kingdom', *Parliamentary Affairs*, XXXI, no. 2, pp. 174–89.

Burton, Frank (1978) *The Politics of Legitimacy* (London: Routledge & Kegan Paul).

Callaghan, James (1973) *A House Divided* (London: Collins).

Calvert, Harry (1968) *Constitutional Law in Northern Ireland* (London & Belfast: Stevens & N. Ireland Law Quarterly).

Cameron, Lord (1969) *Disturbances in Northern Ireland*, Cmd. 532 (Belfast: HMSO).

Campbell, Duncan (1980) 'Big Brother's Many Mansions', *New Statesman*, 8 February.

Central Statistical Office (1979) *Social Trends*, vol. 10 (London: HMSO).

Clark, G. Kitson (1959) 'The Modern State and Modern Society', *Proceedings of the Royal Institution of Great Britain*, XXXVII.

Clark, Wallace (1967) *Guns in Ulster* (Belfast: Northern Whig).

Commentary upon the White Paper, Cmd. 558 (1971) (Belfast: published by the *Irish News* for anonymous Catholic authors).

Compton, Sir Edmund (1971) *Report of the Enquiry into Allegations against the Security Forces of Physical Brutality in Northern Ireland arising out of Events on the 9th August 1971*, Cmnd. 4823 (London: HMSO).

Coogan, Tim Pat (1980) *The IRA* (London: Fontana).

Dash, Samuel (1972) *Justice Denied: a Challenge to Lord Widgery's Report on Bloody Sunday* (London: International League for the Rights of Man and National Council for Civil Liberties).

Deutsch, Richard and Vivienne Magowan (1973) *Northern Ireland: a Chronology of Events, 1968-71* (Belfast: Blackstaff Press).

Dillon, Martin and Denis Lehane (1973) *Political Murder in Northern Ireland* (Harmondsworth: Penguin).

Diplock, Lord (1972) *Report of the Commission to Consider Legal Procedures to Deal with Terrorist Activities in Northern Ireland*, Cmnd. 5185 (London: HMSO).

Dyson, K. H. F. (1980) *The State Tradition in Western Europe* (Oxford: Martin Robertson).

Evelegh, Robin (1978) *Peace Keeping in a Democratic Society: the Lessons of Northern Ireland* (London: C. Hurst).

Farrell, Michael (1976) *Northern Ireland: the Orange State* (London: Pluto Press).

Farrell, Michael (1978) 'Arms outside the Law: Problems of the Ulster Special Constabulary 1920-1922', M.Sc. dissertation in politics (Glasgow: University of Strathclyde).

Faulkner, Brian (1978) *Memoirs of a Statesman* (London: Weidenfeld & Nicolson).

Fisk, Robert (1975) *The Point of No Return: the Strike which Broke the*

British in Ulster (London: André Deutsch).

Flackes, W. D. (1980) *Northern Ireland: a Political Directory, 1968–79* (Dublin: Gill & Macmillan).

The Future of Northern Ireland (1972) (London: HMSO).

Gardiner Committee (1975) *Report to Consider, in the Context of Civil Liberties and Human Rights, Measures to Deal with Terrorism in Northern Ireland,* Cmnd. 5897 (London: HMSO).

Garvin, Thomas A. (1980) Book review, *Irish University Review,* x, no. 2, pp. 306–10.

Government of Northern Ireland (1971) *A Record of Constructive Change,* Cmd. 558 (Belfast: HMSO).

Green, A. J. (1979) *Devolution and Public Finance: Stormont from 1926 to 1971* (Glasgow: University of Strathclyde Studies in Public Policy no. 48).

Greenstein, Fred and Nelson Polsby (1975) *Handbook of Political Science* (Reading, Mass.: Addison-Wesley)

Haines, Joe (1977) *The Politics of Power* (London: Jonathan Cape).

Hezlet, Arthur (1972) *The 'B' Specials* (London: Tom Stacey).

Hunt, Lord (1969) *Report of the Advisory Committee on Police in Northern Ireland,* Cmd. 535 (Belfast: HMSO).

Hurd, Douglas (1979) *An End to Promises* (London: Collins).

Jessop, Bob (1977) 'Recent Theories of the Capitalist State', *Cambridge Journal of Economics,* vol. 1, no. 4, pp. 353–73.

Kelly, Henry (1972) *How Stormont Fell* (Dublin: Gill & Macmillan).

Kelly, James (1971) *Orders for the Captain?* (Dublin: published for the author).

Lawrence, R. J. (1965) *The Government of Northern Ireland: Public Finance and Public Services, 1921–64* (Oxford: Clarendon Press).

Lindsay, Kennedy (1980) *Ambush at Tully-West: the British Intelligence Services in Action* (Dundalk: Dundrod Press).

Lowell, A. L. (1912) *The Government of England,* vol. II (London: Macmillan).

MacIntyre, Tom (1971) *Through the Bridewell Gate* (London: Faber & Faber).

McKitterick, David (1979) 'Reggie's Biggest Contributions to North were his Blunders', *Irish Times,* 14 February.

McKitterick, David (1980) 'British Spies in Ireland', 'Information for Sale', and 'Setting Spy against Spy', *Irish Times,* 22, 23, 24 April.

MacStiofain, Sean (1975) *Memoirs of a Revolutionary* (London: Gordon Cremonesi).

Mansergh, Nicholas (1936) *The Government of Northern Ireland* (London: Allen & Unwin).

Marsh, Alan (1977) *Protest and Political Consciousness* (London: Sage Publications).

Marshall, Geoffrey (1971) *Constitutional Theory* (Oxford: Clarendon Press).

Maudling, Reginald (1978) *Memoirs* (London: Sidgwick & Jackson).

Nelson, Sarah (1980) 'Ulster's Uncertain Defenders', Ph.D. thesis in politics (Glasgow: University of Strathclyde).

Nettl, J. P. (1968) 'The State as a Conceptual Variable', *World Politics*, vol. xx, pp. 559–81.

Norton, Philip (1978) *Conservative Dissidents* (London: Temple Smith).

Oliver, J. (1978a) *Working at Stormont* (Dublin: Institute of Public Administration).

Oliver, J. (1978b) *Ulster Today and Tomorrow* (London: PEP Broadsheet no. 574).

O'Neill, Terence (1972) *The Autobiography of Terence O'Neill* (London: Rupert Hart-Davis).

Our Changing Democracy (1975) Cmnd. 6348 (London: HMSO).

Peck, John (1978) *Dublin from Downing Street* (Dublin: Gill & Macmillan).

Poggi, Gianfranco (1978) *The Development of the Modern State* (London: Hutchinson).

Rose, Paul (1970) 'The Smashing of the Convention', *Irish Times*, 3, 4 February.

Rose, Richard (1970) *The United Kingdom as a Multi-National State* (Glasgow: University of Strathclyde Survey Research Centre Occasional Paper no. 6).

Rose, Richard (1971a) *Governing without Consensus: an Irish Perspective* (London: Faber & Faber).

Rose, Richard (1971b) 'Ulster: the Problem of Direct Rule', *New Society*, 10 June

Rose, Richard (1976a) 'On the Priorities of Citizenship in the Deep South and Northern Ireland', *Journal of Politics*, vol. xxxviii, no. 2, pp. 247–91.

Rose, Richard (1976b) *Northern Ireland: a Time of Choice* (London: Macmillan).

Rose, Richard (1980a) 'From Steady State to Fluid State: the United Kingdom Today', in W. B. Gwyn and R. Rose (eds), *Britain: Progress and Decline* (London: Macmillan) pp. 129–54.

Rose, Richard (1980b) *Politics in England* (London: Faber & Faber, 3rd edn).

Rose, Richard and Ian McAllister (1975) 'Repartition not the Solution to Northern Ireland's Problems', *Irish Times*, 16, September.

Rose, Richard, Ian McAllister and Peter Mair (1978) *Is There a Concurring Majority about Northern Ireland?* (Glasgow: University of Strathclyde Studies in Public Policy no. 22).

Royal Commission on the Constitution (1973) *Report*, Cmnd. 5460 (London: HMSO).

SDLP Manifesto (1979) *Strengthen Your Voice* (Belfast: SDLP).

Stewart, A. T. Q. (1967) *The Ulster Crisis* (London: Faber & Faber).

Sunday Times Insight (1972) *Ulster* (Harmondsworth: Penguin).

Taylor, Peter (1980) *Beating the Terrorists? Interrogation in Omagh, Gough and Castlereagh* (Harmondsworth: Penguin).

Utley, T. E. (1975) *Lessons of Ulster* (London: J. M. Dent).

Van Voris, W. H. (1975) *Violence in Ulster: an Oral Documentary* (Amherst: University of Massachusetts Press).

Wade, E. C. S. and A. W. Bradley (1970) *Constitutional Law*, 8th edn. of E. C. S. Wade and G. Godfrey Phillips' work of that title (London: Longman).

Walker, Christopher (1979) 'Bright Future for the Terrorists', *The Spectator*, 14 July.

Watkins, F. M. (1967) 'State: the Concept', *International Encyclopedia of the Social Sciences*, vol. 15 (New York: Macmillan and Free Press) pp. 150–7.

Widgery, Lord (1972) *Report of the Tribunal appointed to inquire into the events on Sunday 30th January 1972*, HL 101, HC 220 (London: HMSO).

Wilson, Harold (1974) *The Labour Government, 1964–1970* (Harmondsworth: Pelican).

Windlesham, Lord (1973) 'Ministers in Ulster: the Machinery of Direct Rule', *Public Administration*, vol. LI, no. 3 pp. 261–72.

Part II
Mobilising Popular Support

5 Conservatism, Unionism and the Problem of Territorial Management[1]

JIM BULPITT

> An old government is a mass made up of congeries of little circles, each of which has its own fixed centre and point of radiation. Every county and district, and parish and village, has its settled heads and leaders through whom, as their natural organ, their sentiments and wishes are made known, and by whose influence they may be greatly impressed with the wishes and sentiments of others.
>
> (Sir James Mackintosh, 1809)

> The days and weeks of screwed up smiles and laboured courtesy, the mock geniality, the hearty shake of the filthy hand, the chuckling reply that must be made to the coarse joke, the loathsome, choking compliment that must be paid to the grimy wife and sluttish daughter, the indispensable flattery of the vilest religious prejudices, the wholesale deglutition of hypocritical pledges . . .
>
> (Lord Salisbury, on canvassing, 1859)

INTRODUCTION

This chapter attempts to trace and assess the development of Conservative party ideas and practices regarding territorial politics in the United Kingdom from 1867 to the present. Two immediate preliminary observations are required. The words 'conservatism' and 'unionism' refer to a specific political organisation which has existed over time. In any particular historical period there are a variety of individuals and groups which espouse positions which can be labelled conservative or unionist, but in this chapter we are concerned solely with the historic Conservative & Unionist party. The fact that its territorial ideas and practices have received on so many occasions so much support from others, is just one of the many black jokes of United Kingdom political development. The content of territorial politics can be defined as that arena of political activity concerned with relations between the central political institutions in the capital city and those interests, communities, political organisations and governmental bodies, outside that central institutional complex but within the accepted boundaries of the state, which possess, or are commonly perceived to possess, a significant geographical or local regional character. Territorial politics, then, means more than the relationship between central departments and local authorities, or devolution to Scotland and Wales, or the Irish question. It is *all* these things, and more.

As described the chapter can be justified on three main counts. First, and surprisingly, no general survey of the Conservative party's territorial ideas and operations appears to exist. Given the impact of the party upon United Kingdom politics, this represents a major research gap. Secondly, what analysis we have only highlights the ambiguities and confusions of the party. A reading of the literature leaves us only with a series of questions. Why has a party which has constantly stressed constituency organisation autonomy allowed so much influence and prestige to its Parliamentary party leaders? (McKenzie, 1955). Why has the party of 'localism' assisted in the nationalisation of local politics via the entry of the party in local government? (Gyford, 1976; Young, 1975). Why, in the 1960s and 1970s, did the party reform British local government in a manner which annoyed many of its grass roots supporters and seemingly increased central control over local authorities? (Brand, 1974; Jones 1973; Dearlove, 1979). And why, it might be asked, is the Thatcher government doing the same thing? (Stewart, 1980; Goldsmith, 1980; McAllister and Hunter, 1980; Burgess and Travers, 1980). Why should a party supposedly so committed to pluralism not espouse enthusiastically devolution to Scotland and Wales? (Bogdanor, 1980). Finally, why should the traditional Unionist party mount major attacks on that cause in Ireland in 1920/21 and 1972, and find it so difficult to articulate its Unionism during the devolution debates of the 1970s? (Boyce, 1972; Utley 1975; Drucker and Brown, 1980). If localism, local self-government, and Unionism are the traditional principles of Conservative territorial philosophy (as is so often said), why is it they have been ignored on so many occasions by national and local Conservative leaders? Is this the result of expediency, trickery, or what? Clearly, the party and its supporters have some explaining to do.

Thirdly, to preview a conclusion, it is possible to argue that Conservative party elite attitudes to territorial politics can be seen, in the comparative perspective of right-wing parties in the Western world, as highly effective, idiosyncratic, and subtle. As such they deserve examination because they represent a major alternative to existing models of territorial politics.

I PROBLEMS OF ANALYSIS

Justifying the exercise is one thing, pursuing it systematically is another. To begin with, we are concerned with the relationship between political ideas and doctrines on the one hand and political behaviour on the other. This is a notoriously difficult connection to make. If we are dealing with different levels of political activity – local/regional and national – these different levels may hold different conservative and unionist doctrines and behave in distinct ways. Again, if party doctrines are difficult to identify or systematise at any level, then the analyst may have to resort to inferring political ideas from perceived behaviour, and employ inferred ideas to explain that behaviour. In respectable academic circles this is known as a circular argument and should be avoided; in practice, 'everybody does it'. Nevertheless, the popularity of this ploy should not obscure the weakness of the original connection. Thus, a plausible case is the best that can be advanced here.

A second major problem of analysis is that Conservatism, at least its Nordic and Anglo-Saxon varieties, is an elusive, incoherent, reactive ideology. It promotes no picture of an ideal future, nor, for that matter, does it possess an ideal status quo (Huntington, 1957; Harris, 1972). It is pre-eminently a 'philosophy of imperfection', directed towards limited political ends and supporting restrictions on the scope of political action (O'Sullivan, 1976, p. 12). Consequently, it can be argued that there is no point in pursuing essential Conservative truths or principles, no need to search for a continuing 'crucial nucleus of doctrine', since no such nucleus exists (Greenleaf, 1973, p. 179). The content of Conservatism is variable, depending on the reactions resulting from what others propose: 'What they defend at any given moment of time depends on what is being attacked rather than prior assumptions' (Harris, 1972, p. 13). In Britain, doctrinal ambiguity has been compounded by a pragmatic elite culture, or 'presumptuous empiricism' as Toulmin Smith once put it. Some specific accidents in the Conservative party's history have also helped: successive waves of 'refugees' from more radical parties; a seeming propensity for coalition government; and the long period of time the party has held office. Taken together these factors have put a continuous premium on party elite manoeuvres at the centre, often blighted local party organisation, and reaffirmed the positive benefits of doctrinal ambiguity. In these conditions, both supporters and opponents have stressed the 'tangential' nature of Conservative doctrines in relation to Conservative practice, and the unwillingness or inability of Conservative politicians to articulate a coherent ideology (Ramsden, 1978, pp. ix–x).

The third problem concerns the present state of academic research in the field of territorial politics. It would be convenient if we could relate Conservative ideas and behaviour to existing political science concepts and models. Thus for many it would be rewarding to assess the Conservative party in terms of the practical support it has given to such values as local democracy, local autonomy and local self-government. Since these values are invariably given a positive connotation, it follows that if the party, on examination, were found not to favour them, then presumably it would lose a few points on the political preferences scale. Alternatively, the Conservative party could be assessed in terms of which general structural model of territorial politics it favoured. Do the party's preferences correspond to a federal or unitary, centralised or decentralised, internal colonial or integrated structural model? It should be noted that these values and models are not distinct: federal, decentralised, and integrated structures are, in the literature, believed to be more favourable to local autonomy than their opposites.

But the structural models mentioned are weakly formulated in terms of the *political* process. They tend to assume that the structure of territorial politics is a mere reflection of the constitution, formal central government resources, or the economic power map. However, the processes of territorial politics often make nonsense of such assumptions (Bulpitt, 1979; Davis, 1978; Tarrow, 1978). Thus, it is very difficult to determine which countries approximate to which model. Again, to argue in favour of the general and automatic benefits to be obtained from local autonomy, local self-government and local democracy is a piece of liberal ideology masquerading as 'scientific' theory (Langrod, 1953; Bulpitt, 1972). The content of these values is disputed and confusion exists about the most appropriate means to achieve them. More specifically, we cannot assume that local democracy is synonymous with the autonomy of elected local councils. Nor for that matter is it obvious that democracy in general suffers if local organisations of political parties have little influence over their national leaders. In both cases, we risk confusing the interests of local organisations with those of local citizens.

Defining territorial politics in broader than usual terms results in the subject becoming frayed at the edges: identifying territorial actors and issues becomes a very real dilemma. How do we separate territorial matters from the working of the larger political system? What do we look at under the general heading of territorial politics? Over the last two decades in Britain, for example, peripheral movements have arisen protesting at central government policies concerning industrial and race relations, monetary controls, and prices and incomes. None of these policies or protest movements is normally regarded as part and parcel of territorial politics. Do we ignore them? If we do, we risk neglecting major aspects of our subject (at least as important in intensity terms as local government or devolution) and, in the case of prices and incomes policies, a major force favouring central control. Yet accepting such an extended scenario means that we are close to denying the distinctiveness of our territorial management. It begins to approximate to a state and society framework.

(i) Territorial politics

For most of the discussion four dimensions of the subject will be examined, namely: (a) intra-party government; (b) local government in England, elected and non-elected; (c) the Irish (or Northern Ireland) question; and (d) special arrangements for managing Scotland and Wales. On occasions, however, it may be necessary to extend the scope of territorial politics to take account of the points raised in the previous section. Where the process of territorial politics is concerned, particular attention will be paid to the choice (often 'forced') of the centre's collaborators. 'Collaborator' is used here in a non-pejorative sense. It refers to people at the local and regional levels of politics who are available to assist the centre in its territorial operations (Robinson and Gallagher, 1961, 1962; Robinson, 1972; Louis, 1976; Bulpitt, 1978). All central authorities require territorial collaborators. They can include local social notables, local councillors, local party officials, pressure group leaders, civil servants working in the field, and public persons serving on nominated *ad hoc* agencies with a territorial structure. For the centre, each category possesses advantages and disadvantages, and a party's collaborative preference scale tells us something about its territorial 'philosophy', as well as the problems and opportunities it encounters in this field.

(ii) Political ideas and practice

We seek to avoid the two extremes; undue concentration on what counts as Conservative philosophy in Britain and too detailed scrutiny of the party's legislative preferences and manoeuvres. The approach adopted here is to employ, in a symbolic rather than systematic fashion, two conceptual tools,

namely the 'official mind' (Robinson and Gallagher, 1961) and the
'operational code' (George, 1969). Although devised in different academic
contexts, and not without critics (especially the former), both concepts
emphasise precisely those ideas which are nearest to practice: inherited
perceptions and loyalties, traditional strategies, and tactical calculations of
politicians which set boundaries to their behaviour and establish predisposi-
tions to certain kinds of action. In other words, they are essentially
concerned with what other ages described as 'statecraft'. Clearly only a few
Conservatives, primarily the national party leadership, will be concerned
with these notions. Consequently what follows is, for the most part, a central
elite perspective on territorial politics: their 'camp followers', at the centre
and in the localities will appear only in so far as they affect their leaders'
operational code.[2] Clearly, pursuing the code will be difficult. It will be in
many ways, 'the pursuit of intimations', of guessing from a few moves of a
game the strategy being followed (Oakeshott, 1951, p. 125), and may result
in the construction of 'an hypothetical theory, the theory Conservatives – or
at least some of them – would have if they needed one' (Harris, 1972, p. 13).
Nevertheless, a central perspective does usefully limit the exercise and is,
perhaps, the only way to attempt a United Kingdom-wide survey of the
subject.

(iii) The Conservative party

Thus our prime concern is the operational code regarding the territorial
politics of the Conservative party's national elite. The code can be
understood only in the light of what can be called the party's basic and
continuing dilemma. How can a relatively privileged, predominantly
English, minority group, once popular government has arrived, protect its
interests (established institutions, private property and, more broadly and
vaguely, capitalism) in a multi-national society with a traditionally weak
state machine and an increasingly dangerous external world? This was the
dilemma in 1867, and it was to remain so for the next century. As stated the
dilemma is cast in general terms, but it has clear territorial connections.
And it points to the obvious: for the Conservative party the United Kingdom
is, and always has been, a particularly difficult piece of political real estate to
manage.

   Given this basic dilemma we need to know what role the party's territorial
code played in attempts to resolve it. Was it a major influence in the party's
grand strategy, a supportive prop to that strategy, or of no great relevance at
all? Clearly, the code and its place in grand strategy may change over time.
Seemingly similar items in the code may have meant different things, at

different times, in different places. To understand the code, we need to examine the Conservative party's response to varying system challenges. In the period examined, three such challenges surfaced, namely: (a) the challenge of Popular Government, 1867 to 1900; (b) the challenge of Democracy and the Labour movement, 1900 to 1960; (c) the challenge of Remodernisation, 1961 to the present. Each of these challenges forced a general strategic response from the Conservative party, and each response included a territorial component of varying importance. Within this challenge/response framework, the major alternative strategies open to the party were as follows:

(a) *Accept permanent minority party status*, either as a party of English (or perhaps Ulster) territorial defence, or as an anti-regime Ultra group.
(b) *Pursue a defensive pluralist strategy*. Aim to be one minority group amongst many, and defend Conservative interests via a proportional representation electoral system, an entrenched Constitution, and positive support for local/regional autonomy.
(c) *Attempt a Tory, or 'High State' strategy*. Develop a powerful central state machine, emphasise its positive welfare functions and combine this with one or more of the following: a vigorous mass party, a strong Unionist ideology, and *ad hoc* populist appeals.
(d) *Pursue a corporatist strategy*, managing the system via continuous cooperation with powerful non-territorial functional estates of the realm. The centre would be colonised by business or trade union interests, or both. Territorial politics would be confined to the attic.

Most right-wing parties in the Western world have followed one or more of these strategies. Which one(s) did the British Conservative party pursue?

II POPULAR GOVERNMENT AND THE TERRITORIAL CRISIS OF THE 1880s

The challenge

For many Conservatives in the early 1880s the political prospects looked grim. The party had spent much of the 19th century in the political wilderness, subject to periodic acute factional divisions, and seemingly unable to find a strategy to challenge the Whig/Liberal electoral hegemony (Blake, 1972; Marsh. 1978; Stewart, 1978). The party appeared stuck in an English agricultural fortress, seemingly condemned to almost permanent

minority status: the Whig/Liberal coalition was the natural party of
government. Disraeli's victory in 1874 had appeared to promise a brighter
future, but the experience of that government and the electoral defeat of 1880
suggested that it was yet another false dawn (Smith, 1967; Marsh, 1978). An
unsuccessful past promised a deplorable future. Disraeli had left the party
with no obvious successor as leader, and the party organisation, as the events
of 1880 indicated, was in a poor state. More important the spirit of the age
appeared to have passed by the Conservative party: agriculture was at the
beginning of a twenty-year depression, society was becoming more and
more urbanised, even suburbanised, and the external world looked increasingly dangerous. In addition, the traditional domestic politics of parliamentary oligarchy was threatened by the franchise extension in 1867, plus the
high probability of further extensions and other changes in electoral
management. The prospect of popular government, something less than
democracy but more open and aggressive than the traditional system,
seemed yet another nail in the party's coffin.

If this was the general picture, the situation for territorial politics was just
as bad, if not worse. In the 1880s the whole basis of traditional
centre–periphery relations came under attack; the Union itself was
threatened, by a variety of forces which combined, presaged a territorial
crisis of considerable proportions. In formal constitutional terms the United
Kingdom was the creation of three parliamentary statutes in 1536, 1707 and
1800, establishing respectively the Anglo–Welsh, Anglo–Scottish and
Anglo–Irish unions. These had added to the old union of Crowns, a union of
Parliaments, established Protestant churches, and, in theory at least, a
common market of goods, labour and capital. The operation of this Union
had been influenced by the political supremacy of the territorial aristocracy,
the cultural hegemony of Westminster politics, and the failure of the central
authorities to establish a powerful state machine. In practice this meant that
throughout the United Kingdom the centre relied on a complicated system of
indirect rule to manage its estate: territorial administration was in the hands
of local and regional social elites who collaborated with the central
authorities, had considerable influence at Westminster, and who preferred
(though they did not always get) separated, deferential, depoliticised local
communities (Bulpitt, 1978). In the 1880s, this peculiar pre-industrial, 18th
century structure of territorial politics was challenged by a number of forces:

(a) Social modernisation: the impact of improved education, communications and the continued spread of urbanisation meant the break-up of
parochial deference communities, and suggested their replacement by a
national society, London-dominated and administered by 'new men' not part
of the old territorial aristocracy.

(b) The creation of nationally-organised, voluntary, mass political parties, based on universal principles which either challenged the established autonomy of existing local political elites, or would allow provincial politicians to dominate parliamentary politics.

(c) The reform of county government on the elective principle, a change which would at one and the same time threaten the traditional rural hegemony of the landed interest, and open up the prospect of more positive, spendthrift and propertyless county administrations.

(d) The reappearance of the Irish question in triplicate: new organisation and tactics (New Departure, 1879; Irish parliamentary nationalist party, 1880; Plan of Campaign, 1886), new and astute leadership (Parnell, Dillon and Davitt) and a new and plausible reform programme (Land Reform and Home Rule). In combination, these developments threatened the traditional Protestant Ascendancy, property rights and the existing Union structure They also set an awkward example for other dependencies within the Union.

(e) Increasing demands from Scotland and Wales for the redress of specific grievances, concerning, for example, Welsh Church disestablishment, land reform in the Highlands, and education in Wales. In addition, there were more explicit political demands for improved parliamentary treatment, the creation of Secretaries of State, and for some, elected Home Rule assemblies.

(f) The advent of a new positive 'government' ethic at the centre, involving the possible creation of powerful technocratic central bureaucracy, increased interference in local affairs, and more radical policies regarding property rights.

Given the general and specifically territorial scenario described above, it is not surprising that many political observers in the early 1880s saw little future for the Conservative party. As Harcourt put it in 1884, 'I don't see any hope for the Tories anywhere or anyhow' (Cooke and Vincent, 1974, p. 3). Many Conservatives would have accepted that. On this view, the best that could be hoped for was a permanent minority party with some influence on weak Liberal governments and some control over a few, primarily rural, local communities in England (Marsh, 1978).

The strategic response

Despite the prophets of doom a short-term resolution of its basic dilemma was at hand. From mid-1885 to 1905, with only two short gaps, the United Kingdom was subject to Conservative parliamentary dominance. This reversal of fortunes was not solely the result of independent action by the party: political accidents such as the O'Shea divorce in 1890, and the favourable initial impact of the Boer war, helped. So too, did the divisions in, and policies of, rival parties, as well as the fact that many of the emerging social forces proved less radical than originally perceived. Nevertheless the 'Great Transformation' occurred primarily because the Conservative party found an efficient leader, an effective strategy, and an issue to confront and exploit the challenge of popular government.

The leader was Lord Salisbury, a man who 'never seems to have quite the place in the Conservative pantheon which one would have expected' (Blake, 1972, p. 131). It was under his leadership (1885–1902) that the Conservatives made the jump from an unsuccessful, divided, minority country party, representing primarily the landed interest, to a major and successful national party (at least in theory) drawing support from both the working and middle class, rural and urban areas and able to *claim* to represent all parts of the Kingdom (Marsh, 1978; Smith, 1972; Curtis, 1963; Cooke and Vincent, 1974). Salisbury had obvious political disadvantages – membership of the House of Lords, unsociability, profound pessimism, and an early career of opposition to most reforms. Nevertheless, he possessed talents lacking in his rivals: a caustic speaker, a capacity for hard work and careful attention to detail, an ability to select and work with talented colleagues, and above all, a superb sense of political tactics. After he had 'seen off' Randolph Churchill in 1886, he had no rival in the Conservative party and was a worthy opponent for Gladstone. The modern Conservative party is his creation, and none of its subsequent leaders can approach his effectiveness given such difficult conditions. Only poor Neville Chamberlain showed signs of equalling him, before his domestic achievements were destroyed by Hitler and conveniently forgotten by the Churchill 'gang' after 1940.

A good deal of Salisbury's effectiveness stemmed from the fact that by the mid 1880s he too had a plan of campaign, a long-term strategy. Earlier in the decade he had doubted the capacity of the Conservative party to play a major role in the body politic (Marsh, 1978, p. 37). However, under the impact of the second Gladstone administration and the electoral reforms of 1883, 1884 and 1885, he devised a strategy to confront the challenge of popular government. The principal components of this plan were: (a) the protection of property rights and the established institutions of Crown, Anglican Church, and the two Houses of Parliament; (b) the defence of the Empire and imperial trade; (c) disciplining the new electorate such that political power remained at Westminster; and (d) the maintenance of the two party system (in other words no truck with multi-partyism in Britain or 'centre' parties). Put another way, Salisbury's main concern was the defence of the existing social structure and its national institutions. Imperialism, the primacy of parliament, and the two party system were regarded as the political means to that aim.

To achieve these goals Salisbury required an issue to break Liberal hegemony. The issue which surfaced was Irish Home Rule, a cause adopted by Gladstone in December 1885 and on which he was defeated in the Commons and at a subsequent election in 1886. Gladstone had predicted that Home Rule would cause 'a mightly heave in the body politic' (Curtis, 1963, p. 108). Presumably, he did not perceive that the party which would gain from such a 'heave' would be the Conservative party. As one commentator has put it:

> It was to be over Ireland that Lord Salisbury discovered a point where his desires, the interests of his party, and the prejudices of his country came together powerfully. He used the Irish question to consolidate his primacy over the party, to stiffen its reflexes, to forge an alliance with the Unionist defectors from the Liberal party . . . and to establish himself in office for almost fourteen years until he chose to lay the burden down.
>
> (Marsh, 1978, p. 68)

Ireland also served a basic Conservative 'truth': the social structure is best preserved by talking about something else (Cowling, 1977, p. 393). Though, it should be added, Gladstone would have accepted that as well.

The territorial code

In the mid-1880s the Conservative party was rescued, and Salisbury given the opportunity to implement his general strategy by a territorial issue, the Irish Question. Two questions arise from this: What policies did successive Conservative governments pursue in this arena during this period? And were these policies purely *ad hoc*, pragmatic adjustments to differing situations, or were they based on some general underlying operational code?

After 1885 the party drew its electoral support and activist rank and file from a more diverse socio-economic and territorial 'constituency' than previously. In particular the growth of 'Villa Conservatism' and 'suburban knights' began to rival the influence of the landed interest within the party organisation (Cornford, 1963; Pelling, 1967). The bargains and concessions associated with the Unionist alliance provoked further complications. The alliance was not a simple two-way affair but an awkward troika of Whigs, Radicals and Conservatives. Finally, Salisbury tried to run his cabinets on a loose rein, allowing considerable operational autonomy to individual ministers. All these factors were likely to reduce the coherence of

Conservative territorial policies. A superficial glance at the nature of Conservative legislation appears to confirm this point. Conservatives opposed, on principle, *any* scheme to establish Home Rule assemblies or disestablish the Church of Wales and Church of Scotland (Webb, 1977, p. 40). Nor was the party in favour of any special parliamentary committees for Scottish and Welsh business (W. Kinnaird Rose, 1895). The principle measures enacted by Conservative governments during this period were as follows:

(a) *Ireland*. The 'perpetual' Crimes Act, 1887 (the principal plank of the coercion policy); a Land Act, 1887, establishing machinery for the arbitration of tenant rents; a series of Land Purchase Acts, 1885, 1888, 1891, 1896 and 1903, which offered financial assistance to Irish peasants wishing to buy land from landlords and capital to landlords wishing to sell out. The creation in 1891 of the Congested Districts Board, an early regional planning agency in the West of Ireland; a reforming local government Act, 1898; the establishment of an Irish Department of Agriculture and Technical Instruction, 1898; plus many *ad hoc* schemes to facilitate economic and social development in the West of Ireland.

(b) *Local government*. The Local Government Act, 1888, establishing elected county and county borough councils in England and Wales and instituting a new financial system of assigned revenues; the reform of local government in Scotland, 1889; the creation of metropolitan borough councils in London in 1899; the Education Act, 1902, which abolished *ad hoc* school boards in England and Wales and placed their functions in the hands of the county and county borough councils.

(c) *Scotland and Wales*. For Scotland, the Conservatives established a Scottish Secretary with a Scottish Office (in London) in 1885, and expanded the functions of that office in 1887; they allowed the Crofters Commission, set up by Gladstone in 1886 to continue and created a Congested Districts Board for the Highlands in 1897. For Wales, an Intermediate Education Act was passed in 1889, and a Tithes Act in 1891 (a response to Welsh tithe riots in the 1880s) which made landlords not, as previously, tenant farmers responsible for tithe payments.

Coercion and conciliation in Ireland, the 'municipalisation' of local government, administrative devolution to Scotland, 'moral force' Unionism in the Highlands (Hunter, 1974), educational and religious reforms in Wales, a legislative package spread over twenty years, do not appear to yield any grand design or general operational code. Do we then conclude that Conservative governments' response to the new forces and demands in the territorial politics arena was purely pragmatic, containing no general theme? There are several reasons for thinking that this is too easy a conclusion,

especially if we relate Salisbury's approach to the alternative strategies for
right-wing parties set out above. Salisbury viewed government as an
impartial arbitrator, over and above sectional conflict. Thus, although he
talked about the defence of property and established institutions, he did not
see government acting as a direct representative of any particular interest or
wheeling and dealing outside parliament to find solutions to specific
problems. For him, *both* working class and capitalist interests were to be
kept at arms length (Marsh, 1978, p. 12; Cooke and Vincent, 1974, p. 8).
Hence Salisbury's strategy did not approximate to any corporatist design.
Moreover, although he admired the United States constitution, like most
British Conservatives, he was not interested in constitutional innovation.
Thus, a general pluralist strategy was not a serious option. The constitution
was to be preserved, not tinkered with (Dicey, 1886). Nor was Salisbury, or
the party generally, favourable to any High State solution on Bismarckian
lines to the Conservative dilemma. In the United Kingdom such a strategy
would have involved the *creation* of a cohesive and powerful central state
machine, an attack on the traditional constitution, and a potentially
dangerous threat to individual property rights. Salisbury was never a
systematic centraliser, though he was quite prepared to accept central
controls which existed or were developing covertly in terms of the
day-to-day relations between central departments and local authorities
(Dunbabin, 1977, p. 298; Bellamy, 1980). In addition, he was pleased with
the general depoliticised impact of local government reform in England
(Dunbabin, 1965). This conformed to the ideal, if not always the reality of
the traditional territorial order. Finally, Salisbury and the bulk of the
Conservative party had rejected a minority party or ultra strategy: they
played the game to win majority party status and control of political power at
the centre, Westminster and Whitehall. But this power was to be employed
to reconstruct not innovate: the aim was to retain as much of the old system as
possible in the face of the various challenges which surfaced in the 1880s.
Reconstruction for Salisbury was bound to emphasise the need for constant
vigilance in foreign affairs, and the primacy of Westminster over peripheral
territorial politics as necessary means to domestic tranquility.

   The second point concerns internal Conservative management of a party
that was very strongly English. Like the Liberals the Conservatives never
successfully crossed the sea to Ireland. Unlike the Liberals they were weak
on the ground in Scotland and above all, Wales. Even in England they had to
accept Chamberlainite predominance in the West Midlands 'Duchy',
although successful in largely confining their awkward partner's ambitions
to that region (Hurst, 1962). This suggests that, particularly after the reform
of local government, the extent to which the Conservative party could

colonise local affairs was restricted. The easy acceptance of these restrictions on local party expansion by the leadership also suggests a lack of continuous elite interest in politics outside Westminster.

Electoral reform necessitated an efficient mass party organisation. Under Disraeli, the skeleton of such a machine had been created (a National Union and Central Office) but little had been done after 1874 to sustain it as an effective force. What Gorst called the 'old identity' still predominated in party management in the early 1880s. Salisbury, with the help of Middleton, his Principal Agent, rebuilt this organisation and made it into a highly effective electoral machine (Marsh, 1978; McKenzie, 1955). But efficient extra-parliamentary organisations posed dangers: they could be captured by dissident members of the Conservative elite (for example, Randolph Churchill in 1883/4) or they could be used by the rank and file to influence, even dominate, parliamentary politicians on matters of High Politics (for example, tariff reforms). Although Salisbury was not particularly enamoured with Conservative MPs ('Why should I spend my evenings being trampled on by the Conservative Party?'), he disliked and feared provincial 'wirepullers' and local caucus rule even more. He resolved this particular problem on the basis of the division of labour: local matters for local Conservatives, national matters for MPs and leaders. In fact this principle echoed the demands of most Conservative activists. A memorandum written by Lord Randolph Churchill's supporters in 1884 declared:

> We recognise as fundamental principles in any Conservative organisation: Non-interference on the part of political associations with the direction of matters incident to the duties and policy of our member in Parliament ... (and) that every political Association responsible for the interests of the party in the various parliamentary districts ought to enjoy full independence in the management of its local matters.   (Cornford, 1963)

The result was that, although the Conservative party was a national organisation, a certain duality was present in both its constitutional form and the operational relations between its Westminster and local levels. Salisbury believed the leader owed the party rank and file a very general loyalty. Peelite schisms were to be avoided. On the other hand, his only real interest in constituency parties was as vote-gathering organisations in parliamentary elections (Young, 1975). What Conservatives did in purely local matters was not his concern. It was beneficial if MPs took an interest in constituency affairs, but any attempts to influence MPs on national matters were to be deplored. The autonomy of the parliamentary leadership on matters of 'High Politics' (foreign and imperial affairs, defence, the Crown and established churches and, more generally, parliamentary party manoeuvres) was to be preserved at all costs.

Thirdly, it is possible to identify a common theme underlying important Conservative legislative measures. If we consider administrative devolution to Scotland, the reform of local government, and conciliatory or constructive Unionist policies in Ireland, it can be argued that, in part at least, they were all designed to ensure that dreary and time-consuming local affairs were hived off to local agencies and agents. Elected county and county borough councils were created and financed to ease the burden of local affairs on the centre, the Cabinet (Keith-Lucas and Richards, 1978, p. 141). The Scottish Office and the Scottish Secretary served the same purpose (Hanham, 1969). Instead of building a central state machine, the Conservatives sought to *divest it* of as many as possible of its potentially new responsibilities. Government, in the sense of direct administration, was to remain where it had always been, in the hands of local elites. Much of this, with an added twist, applies to Conservative policies in Ireland. Constructive Unionism was administered, largely autonomously, by Dublin Castle. This was in keeping with the traditional role of the Irish administration (Cooke and Vincent, 1974, pp. 17–18). Of course, there was an Irish Secretary in the Cabinet. But these were a peculiar breed, in many ways divorced from both London and Dublin government. 'Bloody Balfour', for example, held that office for over four years, yet he spent a total of only 6 months in Ireland, and only once visited the West coast (Curtis, 1963, p. 402). Constructive Unionism in Ireland was largely a task for Dublin officials rather than the London Cabinet.

The other point about Conservative Irish policy relates to ultimate aims. It was designed primarily to eliminate a traditional and increasingly ineffective set of territorial collaborators, the Anglo–Irish landlords, and replace them with new and potentially more effective collaborators, Irish peasant farmers. Land purchase acts were the necessary financial prop for the new collaborators, and local government reform their political education and opportunity (Norman, 1973, p. 224). This latent function of constructive Unionism – the reconstruction of an effective system of indirect rule – was recognised by its potential victims, the southern Irish Unionists (D'Alton, 1978).

The Conservative party did not run away from, face constructively, or attempt to direct the challenge of popular government. Instead it tried, on the whole successfully, to emasculate it. It did this by seeking and achieving power at the centre. In territorial politics, the resulting operational code increasingly emphasised the advantages of *central autonomy from peripheral forces*: the primacy of Westminster politicians and their freedom to pursue 'High Politics', unimpeded by provincial demands. The strange result of the territorial crisis of the 1880s was a centre freer from territorial pressures than ever before. Unionism was essentially a *negative* concept. In constitutional terms it signified adherence to the existing 'fully incorporating' Union with no regional legislatures; in operational terms it meant the centre viewed all territorial sections as similarly irritating and to be kept at a distance. The paradigm for such an operation was internal Conservative party management. The United Kingdom estate was run on the same lines as the party: the division of labour principle operated. There was a place for everything and everything was in its place. The Conservatives had reactivated the 17th century distinction between Court and Country. The paradox, however, was that the old Country party was now operating on Court principles. Central autonomy is important because, as we shall see, in the future, the party would return to it again and again. In short, the development of modern territorial ideas in the Conservative party both began and ended with Lord Salisbury.

III DEMOCRACY AND THE RISE OF LABOUR, 1906–22

If for Salisbury 'delay was life' (Blake, 1972, p. 88) then he had succeeded, for a generation, in curbing the excesses of popular government. Perhaps just as important, he had obstructed blind conservative reaction. But from 1900 to 1905 Salisbury's 'system' went into decline. The most important single cause of this decline was the Boer War. Although initial reactions to this conflict had favoured the Conservatives, and the general election of 1900 reflected this, Salisbury had found the events of 1899 and 1900 disturbing: they revealed an electorate all too passionate in its opinions for his liking. More generally, the war had exposed the United Kingdom's weakness in the wider world and highlighted the limitations of British society and politics. It eventually gave rise to a culture highly critical of existing institutions and practices and to a widely supported reform programme demanding increased national efficiency (Searle, 1971). Little of this fitted Salisbury's conception of politics, and the Conservatives were placed on the defensive. There were other reasons for the decline. In many ways, the 'system' had worked too well. By the early 1900s, parliamentary Conservatism appeared cut off from much of the world outside (Cornford, 1967), and, after Middleton's retirement, the party's organisation became increasingly ineffective. Salisbury himself resigned the premiership in 1902 and with his habitual pessimism sensed a new and darker future for the party: 'Things will be in a very fluid state after my disappearance' (Marsh, 1978,

p. 321). The new prime minister, Arthur Balfour (Salisbury's nephew) proved to be both accident-prone and unpopular, a fatal combination. In 1903 Chamberlain resigned to pursue tariff reform and the party was deeply split on the whole issue. Moreover, the policies pursued by the Government managed to arouse its opponents (something which Salisbury, an enemy of politicisation had always sought to avoid): the importation of Chinese coolies to work the Rand mines horrified liberal opinion; educationists and non-conformists, particularly in Wales, objected to the abolition of School Boards and the scheme to subsidise church schools from rate income in the Education Act of 1902; the refusal to pass legislation to alter the Taff Vale judgement aroused and politicised the trade unions; and Wyndham's Land Purchase Act and flirtation with a scheme for legislative councils stirred up Unionist opinion in Ireland.

The Conservative government resigned in 1905 and, after a brief caretaker ministry under Campbell-Bannerman, the Conservatives were resoundingly defeated in the general election of 1906. Unionism was submerged by an electoral shift of opinion of 'seismic proportions' (Shannon, 1976, p. 378). Although it recovered somewhat in the two elections of 1910, the party was not to enter office again until 1915, and then only in a coalition created by war.

The challenge

The electoral defeats of 1906 and 1910 tell only one part of the story. Of greater importance was the fact that in the period 1902 to 1922, the Conservative party appeared to be operating in a political system in which the dice were always loaded against it. The party was challenged by a number of forces which appeared to threaten both its position as a major party and the social system and constitution which it existed to support. Conservative hegemony was a thing of the past; the 'spirit of the age' once more was against it, and the party was back to the early 1880s. The principal forces challenging the party were as follows:

(a) The renewed strength of the Liberal party, resulting from the electoral strength of the 'new Liberalism' creed or, after 1910, from a four-party parliamentary situation in which the Liberals were kept in power by the votes of the Irish Nationalists and Labour party. A party system had developed which appeared to relegate the Conservatives to almost permanent opposition status.

(b) After 1910 the Irish question moved into a new, and from a Conservative viewpoint, more dangerous phase. A Liberal government, resting on Irish Nationalist parliamentary support, abolished the permanent veto of the House of Lords in 1911. As a result the way lay open for a third, and this time successful, Home Rule bill. Once passed, it would be difficult for a Liberal government to resist demands for similar legislation for Scotland and Wales. At the same time, the new and more militant republican nationalism of Sinn Fein developed in Ireland, a nationalism which demanded not Home Rule, but secession from the United Kingdom. After the 1916 Easter Rebellion, Sinn Fein became the dominant movement in the south of Ireland.

(c) In 1910 only about 40 per cent of all adult males were on the electoral register (Blewett, 1965). In 1918 nearly all adult males and some women were given the vote. In 1928 all women over 21 became potential voters. The restrictive parameters of popular government were swept aside and, with minor qualifications, the Conservatives were forced to operate for the first time in conditions of electoral democracy. As Baldwin put it: 'Democracy has arrived at a gallop in England and I feel all the time that it is a race for life; can we educate them before the crash comes?' (Middlemas and Barnes, 1969, p. 503).

(d) The Boer War, the Great War, the increasing assertiveness of the White Dominions (not to mention incipient nationalism in India), the entry of the United States on the world stage, the development of Japanese power and a new regime in Russia, all made the external world a more dangerous place for the United Kingdom, at a time when her resources were stretched to the limit. Moreover there was a greater gap between elite and mass perceptions of Britain's world power than ever before (Howard, 1974, p. 80).

(e) The birth and advancement of the Labour party, drawing support from the growing industrial strength of the trade unions, and, after 1918, possessing a programme which threatened property and established institutions and an organisational structure which denied the supremacy of parliamentary politics and leaders.

(f) The 'new liberalism' and the expanded electorate, the dangerous international situation, and the development of the Labour party, all threatened the growth of a new and more positive state machine challenging peripheral autonomy and individual liberties.

The strategic response

One of these challenges, Home Rule, was an obvious territorial issue. The others also had territorial implications. But to understand Conservative operations in that arena we need to discuss the sequence of the party's general strategic response, to the challenges detailed above.

The first has been labelled *'blind and unrewarding negativism'* (Stubbs, 1975, p. 15). It applies to Conservative party operations in the period 1906 to 1914 and particularly 1911 to 1914, after Balfour had resigned the leadership and was replaced by Bonar Law. Before the Parliament Act of 1911, the Conservatives had used the House of Lords to obstruct the Liberal government's programme. After the passage of that Act, Bonar Law concentrated party energies on the question of Irish Home Rule. Opposition to that measure became the party's sole strategy. It served to unite the party, to give the rank and file new confidence in their leadership, and was still a popular cause on which to appeal to the wider electorate. Nevertheless, it had a number of awkward implications for Conservatives. It meant that the party became, in effect, a party of territorial defence, though the territory concerned was not its own heartland, but that of another group, the Ulster Unionists (Macdonagh, 1977, p. 68). It meant, given the Home Rule majority in parliament, that the defence of the Union had to take place outside Westminster, a repudiation of parliamentary supremacy which Bonar Law explicitly condoned in his famous speech at Blenheim in 1912 (Blake, 1955, p. 130). Yet, such a strategy led nowhere: it relegated all other issues to the second division and, if the Liberals persisted with Home Rule, could culminate in civil war. Although the strategy was adopted to regain power, in practice it forced the Conservatives to behave as if they had accepted the status of a permanent reactionary minority.

The second response can be labelled *coalitionism* and was the dominant strategy from 1915 to 1922. It amounted to support for a centre party alliance to pursue the war, tackle post-war problems, and oppose the Labour party. The war 'calmed and refined' the Conservative party (Stubbs, 1975, p. 14) and allowed it to appreciate the talents and popular appeal of Lloyd George, an appeal useful in tackling the threat posed by the Labour party. Coalitionism is interesting, because for a brief period some Conservatives became interested in constitutional reforms – Home Rule All Round, proportional representation, referendums, a restructured House of Lords – which, if pursued, could have acted as the basis for a more general pluralist solution to the party's basic dilemma (Boyce, 1972; Close, 1977; Morgan, 1979).

Coalitionism was defeated, for a variety of reasons, not least opposition from local Conservative constituency associations, at a Carlton Club meeting in October 1922. As a result, the party committed itself to playing for national power, on its own, and on the basis of *a moderate programme* emphasising 'tranquillity and stability at home and abroad'. In effect, this was a return to Salisbury's strategy, but in far more dangerous circumstances. A new political regime was born in 1922, a regime which, bolstered by the events of 1926 and 1931, was to last for nearly forty years, and during which the Conservatives were to be in office for all but nine years. A new era of Conservative hegemony had begun, but in 1922 the prospects looked less bright. There was a new, expanded, and unknown working class electorate to be won. Liberal votes had now to be gained directly and not via the old (and since 1912 defunct) Liberal Unionist party. Moreover, if the Liberal party was to be eliminated to allow the return to two-party politics, this meant confronting the Labour party alone and accepting that a two-party system could lead to a Labour majority in parliament (Cowling, 1971). This strategy accepted George Wyndham's maxim propounded as far back as 1906: 'socialists and imperialists were living men: the others are old women and senile professors' (Biggs-Davison, 1951, p. 184). But its dangers were compounded by the failure of the Conservatives to adopt any of the constitutional safety valves mentioned above (Close, 1977).

In territorial terms, matters were seemingly no better. There was no certainty that partition represented any sort of settlement to the Irish question. Home Rule remained popular in certain political quarters in Scotland and Wales, especially given Asquith's promise of action on this issue in 1914 and the report of the Speakers Conference on Devolution in 1920 (Cmd. 692, 1920). Municipal socialism, or Poplarism as it was often called, bolstered by the increasing spread of Labour party organisation at the grass roots and the advent of pauper voters, suggested the development of a new profligacy in local government, a challenge to the centre's authority, and a convenient base for a Labour take-over at Westminster (Keith-Lucas, 1962; Jones, 1973; Briggs and Deacon, 1973, 1974). Moreover, the fall of the Coalition itself appeared to presage an era of weak Conservative party leadership, allied to increasing interference from local associations and backbench MPs. Finally, social reconstruction, made necessary by the war, promised a more powerful central state machine, which could interfere with both individual property rights and corporate local autonomy.

The territorial code

The operational code of Conservative leaders regarding territorial politics in the period after 1922 until the early 1960s was directly the result of circumstances, of the way certain forces developed, or failed to develop, after the early 1920s. Combined, these served to reduce the influence of territorial interests at the centre, to depoliticise local politics and to introduce the United Kingdom to a period of territorial stability relative to its past, its future, and the situation in other countries in this period.

Three forces conditioning the nature of this regime are of special importance. First, the events of 1920/21, involving the partition of Ireland and the establishment of a new state in the South with Dominion status, produced a period of nearly fifty years when Ireland assumed no great importance in United Kingdom politics. Since Irish nationalism had always acted as one of the principal stimuli of Scottish and Welsh nationalism, this development was of considerable benefit to the Conservatives. Equally important, the departure of a considerable body of Irish MPs made the Westminster game less complex. In short, the Irish settlement of the early 1920s had a profoundly conservative impact on territorial politics.

Secondly, for a variety of reasons which it is not the task of this chapter to explore, the Labour party, at both the centre and in the localities, eventually adopted a set of practices and attitudes which also served to promote territorial quiescence. From the mid-1920s, the party progressively 'forgot' Home Rule for Scotland and Wales, and only rarely concerned itself with Irish matters (Keating and Bleiman; 1979). In the field of British local government, it increasingly dropped the tactics of Poplarism and confined itself to a kind of gentle, deferential, 'public person' labourism, which Conservative leaders, if not their rank and file, could easily accept as the price of the strategy born in 1922. Moreover, after the first taste of national power in 1924 the Labour party increasingly perceived politics in terms of gaining power at the centre: the working class was to be dragged into a primarily bourgeois-conceived socialist utopia, not via Bradford, Durham or South Wales, but through the traditional corridors of Westminster and Whitehall. For the Conservative leaders, Labour was altogether a far better territorial opponent than the Liberal party. The parliamentary Labour party could be relied on not to play many territorial cards. On the other hand, at the local level, Labour provided sound, if often dreary and pompous collaborative 'chaps' to manage the less salubrious areas of Britain, areas in which Conservative collaborators were often few and far between.

The third point concerns the Conservative party itself. The party of Baldwin, Churchill and Macmillan was a very peculiar creature. Leaders often emerged who were not interested in territorial politics, but obsessed with defence and foreign affairs. Churchill and Eden are obvious examples, but so too was Macmillan, at least by the time he became Prime Minister (Brittan, 1964, p. 195). Chamberlain would have been interested in territorial politics, but came to power at the wrong time. He dealt with Hitler as if he were an irritating, yet basically sound, chairman of the LCC, and suffered accordingly. Baldwin talked constantly of 'England', but it is clear that this did not represent any real interest in the details of local government, even less in Scotland, Wales and Northern Ireland. Similar comments could be made about Conservative MPs in this period: they were concerned with their individual constituencies (especially rural ones) but more as welfare officers or depoliticised community spokesman than as politicians. Most kept (or were kept) at a distance from their constituency parties, and very few bothered to develop any regional political base beyond their own constituency patch. Limited interests dominated most Conservative constituency associations (Bulpitt, 1976), which often expunged politics from party activity. Fund raising (even before the Maxwell-Fyfe reforms regarding candidate subscriptions) and running a good administrative 'show' at general elections were regarded as their main tasks. Local government affairs were left to councillors in those areas in which the party bothered to contest local elections. Any direct party interest in local council affairs was opposed on the grounds that this resembled caucus control (Young, 1975, pp. 113–14). Policy discussions were shunted off to separate groups, such as the local branches of the post-war Conservative Political Centre. In these ways, 'politics' would not intrude into executive council and branch committee meetings and obstruct the organisation of serious matters such as 'Donkey Derbies' and 'Nearly New Sales', all essential if associations were to satisfy the Central Office's increasingly onerous post-war financial quotas. Moreover, local Conservatives disliked positive local government; welfare Conservatism was the province of the national leadership. Local Conservatives operated in a ratepayers' culture as trustees of the ratepayers' (that is, property-owners) taxes. In addition, constituency party autonomy from central interference was a slogan which the rank and file would always support, even if its implications were not fully understood. More important, constituency associations did not wish to interfere with the responsibilities of the national leadership. Organisations which carried their localism over this self-imposed boundary, such as the National Union of Ratepayers Associations in the 1930s, had their party support withdrawn (Young, 1975, pp. 164–5).

All three of these developments injected a considerable element of *political* duality into the territorial arena: national and local politics were relatively divorced from one another. Such conditions were highly favourable to the central autonomy code of the party's national leadership. For Salisbury this had been a code consciously conceived and pursued. In this period Conservative leaders passively accepted the advantages that such a code gave them on a plate. The code was easy to operate because general conditions favoured it. With enemies like Sinn Fein and the Labour party, the Conservatives did not require territorial friends.

The operation was not totally passive, however. Peripheral parochialism, central autonomy and the dual polity were sustained for Conservative leaders by two defensive weapons – territorial appeasement and depoliticisation. Appeasement took a variety of forms. For Northern Ireland, it meant Treasury funds and an unwillingness to inquire too closely into the nature of Unionist management. For Scotland, it involved a willingness to extol the virtues of its distinctive cultural symbols, the development of the Scottish Office in Edinburgh, and formal acceptance of the Balfour Committee's maxim – 'In the absence of convincing evidence to the contrary, the machinery of government should be designed to dispose of Scottish business in Scotland' (Cmd. 9212, 1954). Local government interests were appeased by avoiding radical reform legislation after Chamberlain's Act of 1929, an Act which was opposed by many members of the Cabinet and local constituency associations (Feiling, 1946). The-war time field administrative system was also run down after 1951 as a result of local authority hostility, though considerations of economy were important as well (Smith, 1964, 1965). Nor, except in extreme cases, did a Conservative government attempt to supervise strictly the operations of local councils. Chamberlain's forceful policies towards municipal socialism in the 1920s were an exception. Depoliticisation was reinforced by *ad hoc* nominated agencies (especially in Wales and Scotland), and a desire to confine central–local government relations, even intra-party relations, to bureaucrats at both levels. Bureaucratisation and nomination were the tools employed to fashion depoliticised local and regional communities.

The best examples of the pursuit of central autonomy are to be found outside the generally recognised dimensions of territorial policies. Keynesian macro-economic demand management became popular with Conservative leaders, *inter alia*, because it allowed the centre, in theory, to control the economy from the Treasury, without interference from outside interests. A willingness to look at the supply side of the economy would have involved meeting and bargaining with awkward people, like trade unionists, businessmen, and even consumers. In the 1950s the immigration issue also illustrated the operation of the central autonomy code. Coloured immigration very quickly provoked hostile reactions from local councils and local Conservatives (Foot, 1965). But such opposition interfered with the centre's pursuit of 'High Politics', namely the important part the Commonwealth played in supporting the United Kingdom's international power pretentions. Hence, peripheral protests on this matter were for long ignored. It is not the rapidity with which Conservative governments attended to anti-immigrant attitudes which should be emphasised, but their success in maintaining central autonomy on this issue for so long.

IV   REMODERNISATION AND THE TERRITORIAL ECONOMY OF THATCHERISM

The territorial regime just described was remarkable in terms of both its principal characteristics and its longevity. After two world wars, an economic depression, the advent of the Cold War, and the birth of Attlee's welfare state, the United Kingdom entered the second half of the 20th century with a structure of territorial politics based, in principle, on something resembling a Court/Country division, and exhibiting, in practice, a greater divorce between central and peripheral politics than at any time in the country's peace-time history since the 1630s.

Despite its longevity, the regime was extremely fragile. In addition, it carried with it a hidden penalty for the Conservative party. To begin with, it lacked intellectual support. Few people, and certainly not the Conservative leadership, attempted to articulate and justify its major premises. As a result it was easy prey for those who wished to attack it, especially those who wrongly opposed it on the grounds that it was centralised *from* the centre (Robson, 1966; Mackintosh, 1968). Its continued existence depended less on central strength and more on the quiescence of peripheral forces, particularly in the Labour party. Moreover, this territorial structure separated national and local politicians. Hence it was not an effective base from which to launch any political programme which required their positive collaboration. The Conservative government in the early 1960s was the first to suffer from this characteristic. Again, because those who took over the Conservative party in 1940 saw no reason to defend the domestic policies of the National Government in the 1930s, after 1945 the party was continually embarrassed by its role during that decade. In territorial politics this meant that most members of the Conservative elite were determined that the tribulations of the 'North Parts' during the interwar years – the Stockton syndrome – would 'never' be allowed to return again.[3] Thus the base was laid for future hasty and ill-considered Conservative experiments if Treasury demand management failed to prevent unemployment there.

The challenge

The year 1961, a time of the Selwyn Lloyd credit squeeze, the birth of the NEDC (and *Private Eye*), the application to join the EEC, the Plowden report on public expenditure and the SNP's 18 per cent vote in the Glasgow Bridgeton by-election, can be taken as the symbolic start of the new era. From that date, politics became dominated by the theme of *remodernisation*; the necessity to remake United Kingdom society, economy and politics on more efficient and democratic lines in order to accommodate the system to new external and domestic problems.

On the domestic front, the remodernisation programme which triumphed was based on the new Croslandite social democratic ideology, as refined by Harold Wilson's vision of the 'New Britain', a programme which stressed the need for more social equality and welfare via faster economic growth, increased public expenditure, more positive economic planning and the need for new men and administrative techniques at both the centre and in the provinces (Crosland, 1956; Wilson, 1964). Although the Conservative government adopted many of these themes in the early 1960s (although for Macmillan the major thrust to remodernisation was the external gambit of EEC membership), the period from 1961 to 1975 was unfortunate for the Conservatives. The nature of the party's predicament can be illustrated by major challenges to its identity and existence at the accession of Mrs Thatcher to the party leadership in 1975.

(a) The Conservatives had lost four out of the last five general elections. Equally important its vote had dropped from 13.7 million in 1959 to 10.4 million in October 1974 and its percentage share of the vote from 49.4 to 35.8 per cent. The fact that there had been a general decline in the electoral fortunes of both the major parties was small comfort to most Conservatives. The Labour party was in power and appeared to have achieved Harold Wilson's ambition to be the natural party of government.

(b) The system of government now exhibited the following features: an expanded Civil Service working a complex central machine with a vast range of responsibilities; high public expenditure and high direct taxation; continuous close contacts between central departments and pressure groups; and increasing influence of external forces (EEC, OPEC, IMF and multi-nationals) on domestic policy-making. The system was variously described as corporatist or post-parliamentary democracy (Winkler, 1976; Richardson and Jordan, 1979) and its results as social democracy, overload or ungovernability (Brittan, 1975; King, 1975; Rose, 1979). Whatever the label, it was considerably different from the relatively, simple, restricted, and effective system of the 1950s and before. For Conservatives it posed a dilemma: most received some rewards from the system, but many feared its potential impact on property rights and individual freedoms. Above all, they objected to the influence that trade unions had managed to gain in the system.

(c) In territorial terms, three major developments posed problems for the Conservatives. First, the centre had ceased to maintain its own autonomy to pursue 'High Politics'. A series of prices and incomes policies involving ever-increasing detailed supervision of the economic activities of corporations and individuals was the most obvious example. Regional

economic planning schemes, inner-city programmes, and centrally pre-
scribed comprehensive education were other illustrations. As a part of this,
central government intervened radically to alter the formal constitution of
territorial government. The old Stormont parliament was abolished; the
structure of elected local government in London, the English provinces,
Scotland and Wales had been radically altered; the administration of water
resources and the National Health Service restructured, and an expanded and
more coherent field administrative system established. Secondly, peripheral
communities were no longer quiescent. Not only had the traditional
collaborative system broken down in many places, the periphery had also
come to town. Westminster politics were now plagued by four varieties of
nationalist MPs whose importance was increased by the Labour government's small (and soon to vanish) majority. The politicisation of the
periphery also affected local authorities, trade union shop stewards, and
local racist and anti-racist groups. Most significant of all, it included
renewed demands for Home Rule or devolution assemblies in Scotland and
Wales, demands which, in 1975, the Labour government was seemingly
ready to appease. Finally, effective peripheral management by the centre
had declined considerably. 'No go' areas in Northern Ireland were the most
obvious examples. More worrying, because more general, was the loss of
Treasury control over local government expenditure (Wright, 1977). These
developments appeared to indicate a very disunited kingdom. Unionism,
central autonomy and dualism, the principal features in the pre-1961
Conservative territorial code, were all weak or abandoned.

(d) Paradoxically, a prime reason for the Conservative predicament came
from within its own ranks. The Heath government of 1970 to 1974 had
mounted an effective challenge to the old system. It was Mr Heath who had
issued the ambiguous 'Declaration of Perth' in 1968, calling for a devolved
Scottish assembly. It was the Heath government which had pursued the most
ambitious prices and incomes policies to date, threatened trade union
autonomy by the Industrial Relations Act, restructured local government in
Britain, abolished Stormont, and developed a corporatist style of central
activity. Moreover, in the course of losing the 1974 elections, Mr Heath had
enhanced Labour's claim to be the only party capable of working with the
trade unions; simultaneously, he confused Conservatives by his talk of
coalition and national governments.

The strategic response

The strategic response of the new Thatcher leadership in its first 15 months in
government has involved four broad themes.[4] First, a renewed commitment

to the party pursuing national power and opposing Labour on its own. At the time of the 1975 leadership contest, it was sometimes suggested that a change at the top was required to enable the party to pursue successfully a national party or coalition strategy. This was rejected. The leadership (if not all sections of the party) has also resisted any attempts to protect the Conservative interest via proportional representation and House of Lords reform. Secondly, the party's basic idealogical stance has been altered to re-emphasise (often with considerable rhetorical vehemence) the necessity to roll back the expanding frontiers of state activity, re-establish the disciplines of the market economy, and increase the freedoms and responsibilities of the individual and public and private corporations. The publicly-stated grounds for doing this are that such a system is both economically more efficient and a necessary support to pluralist politics. Thirdly, the solution of one particular problem, inflation, is given priority. Any awkward short-, or even medium-term problems, which may result from the pursuit of that aim, such as unemployment, low investment, business failures, falling living standards and political support are regarded as the necessary price to be paid for bringing down the level of inflation. Fourthly, in pursuit of these aims, the Thatcher government has adopted policies involving public expenditure cuts, cash limits on government departments and agencies, reductions in direct tax burdens, the abolition of economic controls and the attempt to abolish or 'hive off' administration agencies and government commercial functions associated in the Conservative mind with the socialist or corporatist state.

Clearly this package of policies is a very high stakes strategy. The United Kingdom economy, the structure of government, the Conservative party, and the electorate has been subjected to a 'controlled experiment', a set of doctrines and policies which Lord Salisbury, but possibly no subsequent Conservative leader, could support. The strategy appears to have been adopted because of challenges described above, and particularly the need to distance the party politically from Heathism; the personal preferences of the new leadership group (Sir Keith Joseph's discovery of Adam Smith, and Thatcher's dislike of political appeasement); and opinion poll results in the 1970s indicating a growing dislike among Labour supporters for many aspects of the party's programme and positive support for less taxation and public welfare (Crewe *et al.*, 1977; Stephenson, 1980). The 'theoretical' popularity of the strategy appears to be indicated by the results of the 1979 general election, which gave the Conservative party its biggest majority of votes over Labour since 1935 and, at the same time, resulting in a pronounced territorial imbalance between the two parties (Pulzer, 1979).

The territorial code

What have been the implications of this Thatcher strategy for the Conservative's territorial code? The principal policies followed by the Government in this arena have been as follows.

(a) A package of public expenditure cuts adversely affecting regional aid programmes (including the abolition of regional economic planning councils), nationalised industries, especially in Wales, Scotland and the north of England, and enforcing economies on a wide range of local government activities throughout the United Kingdom. Local government has taken the brunt of the Government's economy offensive.

(b) A 1979 Northern Ireland initiative attempting, once again, to find some agreement in the Province for a move away from direct rule to a form of regional-wide devolved government.

(c) The repeal of the Scotland Act and Wales Act following the referendum results of 1979. This reneged on a variety of conflicting and ambiguous promises regarding Scottish devolution which the party had given in the period 1968 to 1979 (Bogdanor, 1980; Drucker and Brown, 1980).

(d) The Local Government, Planning and Land (No. 2) Act (introduced in the House of Commons early in 1980) which involves among many things: (i) the abolition of a number of detailed controls over local authorities; (ii) the institution of a new Block Grant, carrying with it, many believe, more rigorous control of local authority finances; (iii) the establishment of centrally-appointed Urban Development Corporations, initially in the dockland areas of London and Liverpool, and taking over powers formerly held by local authorities; (iv) the imposition of new restrictions on local authority direct labour departments; and (v) the requirement that local authorities provide the centre with a large amount of statistical data concerning their operations.

(e) The Education Acts, 1979 and 1980. The former removed the compulsion to organise secondary education on comprehensive lines; the latter abolishes the statutory duty of LEAs to provide school milk and meals (similar provisions regarding bus transport were defeated in the House of Lords), required LEAs to publish information on the activities and performance of individual schools, and promised parents greater choice of schools for their children. In addition, the Department of Education and Science is preparing, for the first time, a 'non-statutory national framework' for school curricula.

(f) The Housing Act, 1980, which requires local authorities to sell council houses to sitting tenants wishing to buy them.

(g) The proposed abolition of Area Health Authorities within the National Health Service emphasises the community level of organisation, and, in many areas, divorces health authority and local authority boundaries. In addition, in 1979, the Secretary of State replaced the Lambeth Area Health Authority by appointed commissioners following the Authority's refusal to cut its budget by £5.5 million, an action later declared illegal by the courts.

Initial comment on these policies has concentrated on the impact upon specific communities of nationalised industry closures, and the threat to local government autonomy resulting from expenditure cuts and local government legislation. In particular, the Local Government Act is regarded as the paradigm case of the government's desire to control local government finances at the expense of local autonomy (Stewart, 1980; Burgess and Travers, 1980; McAllister and Hunter, 1980).

But the relationship between the Thatcherite general strategy and its territorial code may be more complex than this. An alternative interpretation runs as follows:

First, Thatcherism is pre-eminently an attempt to deal with the political problems of the United Kingdom. It is not an economic theory in search of politics, but the reverse. Thatcherism is a piece of statecraft: a political code with a convenient economic theory. Monetarism is that convenient theory. Hence, for the political economy of Thatcherism, monetarism is a means to essentially political ends. It is convenient because it promises the centre the prospect of managing the economy through those policies over which it can claim some control – money supply, public expenditure and interest rates. These policies can be defended as part of the executive's preserve of 'High Politics'. They are less open to outside influence from, say, the trade unions, than are most matters on the supply side of the economy. In this sense the political difference between monetarism and 1950s style Keynesian demand management is one of degree only. Of course, no system of economic management can be completely independent of outside forces. A choice has always to be made concerning which forces are acceptable. Monetarism ensures that the accepted influences are domestic finance capital and international monetary forces.

Secondly, for the Government there are three, not two, actors in the territorial arena – central government, local governments and individual citizens. The attack is not on local autonomy *per se*, but on the whole range of territorial agencies (including local authorities) which have grown so powerful since the early 1960s and which, in the Government's view, obstruct the autonomy of local citizens. In the words of the Secretary of State for the Environment, Michael Heseltine: 'In general terms, we did not feel it correct to enhance the rights of local authorities at the expense of the individual' (House of Commons, *Debates*, 5 February 1980, col. 246). Hence policies such as promoting 'tenants' rights' in the Housing Act, parental influence regarding local education in the Education Act, requirements for more published data concerning local government operations in the Local Government Act, the abolition of Area Health Authorities and assistance to individual trade unionists in the Employment Act, all can be regarded as part of a syndrome emphasising anti-government and anti-corporatism views, and favouring individual rights.

Thirdly, on this line of argument, the Thatcher government appears to have adopted a very radical territorial code, forsaking the traditional reliance on intermediate collaborative elites for a direct link with the citizenry. There is an element of populism in this code, but only a very instrumental one. In fact, the populist elements may have another aim, the pursuit of a different form of autonomy. What may be called the 'efficient secret' of Thatcherism is this: under the guise of opposition to intermediate corporate power and the development of local citizen autonomy, the Conservative leadership is attempting to return to its traditional Salisbury code, seeking the re-establishment of central autonomy. This provides an explanation of its peculiar mix of interventionist and individualist policies, a mixture most apparent and confusing in the Local Government Act.

It can be argued that a government committed to so much intervention in local affairs – the first to attempt control of individual local authority budgets, for example – is hardly pursuing a central autonomy code. But the central autonomy code has always been ambiguous in terms of the means of achieving that end. In the past autonomy could be achieved by allowing a considerable degree of freedom to local collaborative elites throughout the United Kingdom, and this was the reason why a technocrat like Heath was willing to consider off-loading a considerable amount of central responsibilities to regional assemblies. The general point is that if local elites govern to central and local satisfaction, this is an ideal prop for central autonomy. This ambiguity over means is currently illustrated by secondary education policy. The Secretary of State for Education, Mark Carlisle, has found it difficult to follow a consistent line in adjudicating on LEA secondary school schemes. Does he support the parents concerned, the local authority, or some national principle in comprehensive disputes? In practice, and in a very roundabout way, he appears to support the local electorate. The Carlisle principle appears to be 'the usually reigning local party has the right to determine educational doctrine' (Butt, 1980). This merely serves to highlight the problems of which government – Town Hall or Westminster – represents citizens; a dilemma the Labour government resolved in 1965 by proclaiming comprehensive education through its central authority. Similar problems surround the Northern Ireland initiative. Any Westminster intervention in the Province may be regarded as a blow to the central autonomy code. But if the plan is to reduce direct rule, then this policy can be seen as an attempt to reconstruct a lost autonomy, albeit by regional institutions different from Stormont.

The means to central autonomy will always be influenced by political expediency and circumstances and the present government, especially the Prime Minister, is no exception (Stephenson, 1980). After 15 years of predominantly Labour (and Heath) government, the Conservatives now head a system laid down by opponents (within and without the party). Hence, as *The Economist* argued in a leader of 8 December 1979: 'The trouble with being a non-interventionist government is that in order to go from intervention to non-intervention you have to intervene to challenge the way things are done'. This explains much of present Conservative territorial policy, especially in the field of elected local government.

One final point requires brief comment. A national party elite in pursuit of central autonomy is particulary susceptible to influence by the higher Civil Service. It is not that the Civil Service necessarily agrees with the central autonomy code, rather that such a code, by divorcing politicians from outside support, leaves them open to easy capture by bureaucrats and bureaucratic norms. Certainly Conservative local government reforms since the early 1960s (in particular the Block Grant proposals of 1980), appear to have been much influenced by Civil Service ideas (Goldsmith, 1980). This is a general threat to the present Government since, despite its concern with statecraft, it lacks organisational support for its strategy. Even the Conservative party is publicly divided on the matter in the Cabinet, Parliament and the constituencies. A leadership group which came to power via a Westminster coup has still to build an organisational base to support its policies.

V CONCLUSIONS

The Conservative party is the party of central autonomy. The party of Salisbury devised the code, the party of Baldwin and Churchill refined it, and the party of Margaret Thatcher is making determined attempts in difficult circumstances to reassert it. While all national political elites desire autonomy at some time, none has pursued that goal so consistently and so successfully in a formally democratic polity as the leadership of the British

Conservative party. The autonomy it gained may have been only 'relative' but is significant nevertheless.

In pursuit of the code, the Conservatives became the Court or Whitehall party, a significant reversal of their traditional role in United Kingdom politics. As a Court party, they increasingly regarded all territorial sections of the Union (including England) as similar, that is, having an equality of access (or distance) to the centre. That, for the most part, has been the operational meaning of Unionism to the Conservative leadership. Central autonomy was sought because the party continually thirsted for national power, because both leaders and followers feared or disliked many aspects of democratic politics (particularly elected local government and local caucus rule), because the leadership increasingly lost social contact with the periphery, and because the leaders desired, above all, to play 'High Politics' (defence, foreign affairs, Parliamentary manoeuvres and, later, economic management) without peripheral interference.

In theory, a variety of territorial structures and policies could embody such a code. In the United Kingdom the Conservative leadership's search for central autonomy was associated until recently with a management ethic and with depoliticised indirect rule of peripheral communities, allowing considerable autonomy to local elites. For Conservatives the United Kingdom was just another piece of estate management, with absentee landlords in London. The code meant, in practice, that both centre and periphery should relate to each other with *mutual* deference and appeasement. Although the code was devised by Conservative leaders, it was sustained by their own rank and file, a general cultural distaste for conflict (Hayward, 1976) and the Labour party. The code is pre-democratic in origin and perhaps anti-democratic in sentiment. Hence, it has never been articulated explicitly, and the Unionist cause has suffered from this.

In a rational world, this sort of code ought to decline. Central autonomy may have a past, and fervent attempts are being made to give it a present, but its future looks grim. When that happens, most Conservatives will have to stop regarding local government as a dreary but dangerous institution and the party leadership may have to give a more positive role to local Conservative associations. However, the remarkable thing is how long the code has survived, and how much support it has received outside the Conservative party. Central autonomy deserves to be recognised as a peculiar and successful contribution of British Conservatism to political theory and practice in the Western world.

NOTES

1. The writer is a member of a local Conservative Association. In so far as the word 'activist' has any meaning for that party at the local level he can be labelled as one. Most accounts of the Conservative party have been written by its opponents or by its intellectual collaborators from Oxford and Cambridge. What follows is an English provincial Tory perspective on the activities of the national party elite. I dedicate this chapter to that monstrous regiment of administrative competence – Conservative women – who, until recently, have effectively expunged serious political discussion from local party operations.
2. In the present context the 'operational code' is preferred to the 'official mind', on the grounds that, as a narrower concept, it can be more suitably employed to refer to the beliefs of one particular set of politicians. The 'official mind' has a wider meaning, referring to the beliefs of an Establishment at the centre, composed of both politicians and bureaucrats.
3. After 1945 Mr Harold Macmillan's support for welfare Conservatism was often justified by reference to his experiences as Stockton's MP during the 1930s.
4. This section is a comment on the first fifteen months of the Thatcher government's operations. Policy changes may occur before the strategy has run its full course. The important point is that the strategy was adopted in the first place.

REFERENCES

Bellamy, C. A. (1980) 'Central–Local Relations 1871–1919: the Case of the Local Government Board' (London: SSRC Interim Research Paper).

Biggs-Davison, J. (1951) *George Wyndham: A Study in Toryism* (London: Hodder).

Blake, Robert (1955) *The Unknown Prime Minister* (London: Eyre & Spottiswoode).

Blake, Robert (1972) *The Conservative Party from Peel to Churchill* (London: Fontana).

Blewett, Neal (1965) 'The Franchise in the United Kingdom 1885–1918', *Past and Present*, vol. XXXII (December) pp. 27–56.

Bogdanor, Vernon (1980) 'Devolution', in Zig Layton-Henry (ed.), *Conservative Party Politics* (London: Macmillan) pp. 75–94.

Boyce, D. G. (1972) *Englishmen and Irish Troubles, 1918–1922* (London: Jonathan Cape).

Brand, Jack (1974) *Local Government Reform in England* (London: Croom Helm).

Briggs, E. and A. Deacon (1973) 'The Creation of the Unemployment Assistance Board', *Policy and Politics* (September).

Briggs, E. and A. Deacon (1974) 'Local Democracy and Central Policy: the Issue of Pauper Votes in the 1920s', *Policy and Politics* (June).

Brittan, Samuel (1964)*The Treasury Under the Tories 1951–1964* (London: Pelican).

Brittan, Samuel (1975) 'The Economic Contradictions of Democracy', *British Journal of Political Science*, vol. 5, pp. 129–59.

Bulpitt, Jim (1972) 'Participation and Local Government: Territorial Democracy', in G. Parry (ed.), *Participation in Politics* (Manchester: Manchester University Press).

Bulpitt, Jim (1976) 'English Local Politics: the Collapse of the *Ancien Régime*?', Political Studies Association Conference.

Bulpitt, Jim (1978) 'The Making of the United Kingdom: Aspects of English Imperialism', *Parliamentary Affairs* (Spring) 174–89.

Bulpitt, Jim (1979) 'Territory and Power: Some Problems of Analysis' (Coventry: Political Studies Association Workshop on UK Politics, University of Warwick).

Burgess, T. and T. Travers (1980) *Ten Billion Pounds: Whitehall's Takeover of the Town Halls* (London: Grant McIntyre).

Butt, Ronald (1980) 'Schools: Who Has the Final Say?', *The Times*, 15 May.

Close, D. H. (1977) 'The Collapse of Resistance to Democracy: Conservatives, Adult Suffrage and Second Chamber Reform, 1911–1928', *Historical Journal* (December).

Cmd. 692 (1920)*Conference on Devolution: Letter from Mr Speaker to the Prime Minister* (London: HMSO).

Cmd. 9212 (1954) *Royal Commission on Scottish Affairs 1952–1954, Report* (London: HMSO).

Cooke, A. B. and John Vincent (1974) *The Governing Passion* (Brighton: Harvester Press).

Cornford, James (1963) 'The Transformation of Conservatism in the late 19th Century', *Victorian Studies* (September) pp. 35–66.

Cornford, James (1967) 'The Parliamentary Foundations of the Hotel Cecil', in Robert Robson (ed.), *Ideas and Institutions of Victorian Britain* (London: Bell).

Cowling, Maurice (1971) *The Impact of Labour* (Cambridge: Cambridge University Press).

Cowling, Maurice (1977)*The Impact of Hitler* (Chicago: Chicago University Press).

Crewe, Ivor, B. Sarlvik and James Alt (1977) 'Partisan De-Alignment in Britain, 1964–1974', *British Journal of Political Science* (April) pp. 129–90.

Crosland, C. A. R. (1956) *The Future of Socialism* (London: Jonathan Cape).

Curtis, L. P. Jr (1963) *Coercion and Conciliation in Ireland 1880–1892: a Study in Conservative Unionism* (Princeton, N. J.: Princeton University Press).

D'Alton, Ian (1978) 'A Contrast in Crises: Southern Irish Protestantism, 1820–1843 and 1885–1910', in A. C. Hepburn (ed.), *Minorities in History* (London: Edward Arnold).

Davis, S. Rufus (1978) *The Federal Principle* (London: University of California Press).

Dearlove, John (1979) *The Reorganisation of British Local Government* (Cambridge: Cambridge University Press).

Dicey, A. V. (1886) *England's Case Against Home Rule* (London: John Murray).

Drucker, H. M. and Gordon Brown (1980) *The Politics of Nationalism and Devolution* (London: Longman).

Dunbabin, J. P. D. (1965) 'Expectations of the New County Councils and their Realisation', *Historical Journal*, vol. 3, pp. 353–79.

Dunbabin, J. P. D. (1977) 'British Local Government Reform: the 19th Century and After', *English Historical Review* (October) pp. 777–805.

Feiling, Keith (1946) *Life of Neville Chamberlain* (London: Macmillan).

Foot, Paul (1965) *Immigration and Race in British Politics* (London: Penguin).

George, Alexander L. (1969) 'The "Operational Code": a Neglected Approach to the Study of Political Leaders and Decision-Making', *International Studies Quarterly* (June) pp. 190–222.

Goldsmith, M. (1980) 'Conservative Governments and Local Government Reform 1960–1980' (York: SSRC Urban Politics/History Seminar).

Greenleaf, W. H. (1973) 'The Character of Modern British Conservatism', in R. Benewick, R. N. Berki and B. Parekh (eds), *Knowledge and Belief in Politics* (London: Allen & Unwin).

Gyford, John (1976) *Local Politics in Britain* (London: Croom Helm).

Hanham, H. J. (1969) *Scottish Nationalism* (London: Faber & Faber).

Harris, N. (1972) *Competition and the Corporate Society* (London: Methuen).

Hayward, Jack (1976) 'Institutional Inertia and Political Impetus in France and Britain', *European Journal of Political Research*, vol. 4, pp. 341–59.

Howard, Michael (1974) *The Continental Commitment* (London: Pelican).

Hunter, James (1974) 'The Politics of Highland Land Reform, 1873–1895', *Scottish Historical Review*, no. 155, pp. 45–68.

Huntington, S. P. (1957) 'Conservatism as an Ideology', *American Political Science Review* (June) pp. 454–73.

Hurst, M. C. (1962) *Joseph Chamberlain and West Midland Politics 1886–1895* (Oxford: Dugdale Society).

Jones, G. W. (1973) 'The Local Government Act 1972 and the Redcliffe–Maud Commission', *Political Quarterly* (April).

Keating, Michael and David Bleiman (1979) *Labour and Scottish Nationalism* (London: Macmillan).

Keith-Lucas, B. (1962) ' Poplarism', *Public Law* (Spring) pp. 52–80.

Keith-Lucas, B. and P. Richards (1978) *A History of Local Government in the 20th Century* (London: Allen & Unwin).

King, A. (1975) 'Overload: problems of governing in the 1970s', *Political Studies* (June–September) pp. 284–96.

Langrod, G. (1953) 'Local Government and Local Democracy', *Public Administration*, vol. 31, pp. 25–34.

Louis, Wm. Roger (1976) *Imperialism: the Robinson and Gallagher Controversy* (New York: Franklin Watts).

McAllister, Richard and David Hunter (1980) *Local Government: Death or Devolution?* (London: The Outer Circle Policy Unit).

Macdonagh, Oliver (1977) *Ireland: the Union and its Aftermath* (London: Allen & Unwin).

McKenzie, Robert (1955) *British Political Parties* (London: Heinemann).

Mackintosh, J. P. (1968) *The Devolution of Power* (London: Chatto & Windus).

Marsh, Peter (1978) *The Discipline of Popular Government: Lord Salisbury's Domestic Statecraft, 1881–1902* (Sussex: Harvester Press).

Middlemas, Keith and John Barnes (1969) *Baldwin: a Biography* (London: Weidenfeld & Nicolson).

Morgan, Kenneth O. (1979) *Consensus and Disunity: the Lloyd George Coalition Government 1918–1922* (Oxford: Clarendon Press).

Norman, Edward (1973) *A History of Modern Ireland* (London: Pelican Books).

Oakeshott, Michael (1951) 'Political Education', in M. Oakeshott, *Rationalism in Politics* (London: Methuen, 1962).

O'Sullivan, Noël (1976) *Conservatism* (London: J. M. Dent).

Pelling, Henry (1967) *Social Geography of British Elections 1885–1910* (London: Macmillan).

Pulzer, Peter (1979) 'The British General Election of 1979: Back to the Fifties or on to the Eighties?', *Parliamentary Affairs* (Autumn) pp. 361–75.

Ramsden, John (1978) *A History of the Conservative Party: the Age of Balfour and Baldwin* (London: Longman).

Richardson, J. J. and A. G. Jordan (1979) *Governing Under Pressure: The*

Policy Process in a Post-Parliamentary Democracy (Oxford: Martin Robertson).

Robinson, Ronald (1972) 'Non-European Foundations of European Imperialism: Sketch for a Theory of Collaboration', in R. Owen and B. Sutcliffe (eds), *Studies in the Theory of Imperialism* (London: Longman).

Robinson, Ronald and John Gallagher (1961) *Africa and the Victorians: the Official Mind of Imperialism* (London: Macmillan).

Robinson, Ronald and John Gallagher (1962) 'The Partition of Africa', in *New Cambridge Modern History*, vol. xi (Cambridge: Cambridge University Press).

Robson, W. A. (1966) *Local Government in Crisis* (London: Allen & Unwin).

Rose, Richard (1979) 'Ungovernability: Is There Fire Behind the Smoke?', *Political Studies* (September) pp. 351–70.

Rose, W. Kinnaird (1895) 'Scottish Grand Committees', in W. Kinnaird Rose and R. Macaulay Smith (eds), *The Liberal Platform* (London: Liberal Publications Department).

Searle, G. R. (1971) *The Quest for National Efficiency* (Oxford: Blackwell).

Shannon, Richard (1976) *The Crisis of Imperialism 1865–1915* (St Albans: Paladin).

Smith, Brian (1964 & 1965) *Regionalism in England* (London: Acton Society Trust).

Smith, Paul (1967) *Disraelian Conservatism & Social Reform* (London: Routledge & Kegan Paul).

Smith, Paul (1972) *Lord Salisbury on Politics* (Cambridge: Cambridge University Press).

Stephenson, Hugh (1980) *Mrs. Thatcher's First Year* (London: Jill Norman).

Stewart, J. D. (1980) *The Local Government Bill: No. 2* (Lewes: Solace).

Stewart, Robert (1978) *The Foundations of the Conservative Party* (London: Longman).

Stubbs, John (1975) 'The Impact of the Great War on the Conservative Party', in G. Peele and C. Cook (eds), *The Politics of Reappraisal, 1918–1939* (London: Macmillan).

Tarrow, Sidney (1978) 'Introduction' in S. Tarrow P. J. Katzenstein and Luigi Graziano (eds), *Territorial Politics in Industrial Nations* (New York: Praeger).

Utley, T. E. (1975) *Lessons of Ulster* (London: Dent).

Webb, Keith (1977) *The Growth of Nationalism in Scotland* (Glasgow: Molendinar Press).

Wilson, Harold (1964) *The New Britain* (London: Penguin).

Winkler, J. T. (1976) 'Corporatism', *European Journal of Sociology*, no. 1, pp. 100–136.

Wright, Maurice (1977) 'Public Expenditure in Britain: the Crisis of Control', *Public Administration* (Summer) pp. 143–69.

Young, Ken (1975) *Local Politics and the Rise of Party* (Leicester: Leicester University Press).

6 The British Labour Party: Centralisation and Devolution

J. BARRY JONES and MICHAEL J. KEATING

The subject of this chapter is the Labour Party's role in integrating Scotland and Wales into the British political system and its changing attitudes to Scottish and Welsh devolution. The devolution issue was an unusual one for the party in several respects. It raised the territorial dimension in politics in a form that the party had not had to deal with for many years, and which it was ill-equipped to handle. It forced the party to reappraise some of its basic beliefs in order to come to terms with a changing political environment. It interacted with a wide range of other elements in Labour's philosophy and cut across some traditional divisions in the party. Finally, and paradoxically, it confronted the party with the necessity of developing a policy of devolution through a centralised party structure.

Policy-making for a Labour party claiming socialist credentials and working class support and operating in a competitive party context is a more complex process than for a party which is either dedicated to a single ideology or whose purpose is simply to build the broadest possible electoral coalition. Three elements determine its policies: interests of the organised working class; the need to appeal to the widest possible electoral constituency; and its own ideology. Attempts to explain Labour policy by reference to only one of these can never be more than partially successful.

A party basing itself purely on working class interests would make no concessions to other interests and would have to draw its leadership, activists and membership from a single class. Exclusive dependence on one class has never been sought or attained by the Labour Party, which from its conception has been an amalgam of social and economic interests. A party seeking to maximise its electoral support would acquire policies indiscriminately with no regard to social origin, likely beneficiaries, or their consistency or continuity within an overall programme. While the Labour Party and, even more, Labour governments have displayed a readiness to respond to electoral pressures, they none the less have been constrained by class interests and ideology. An unambiguously ideological party would place supreme emphasis on doctrinal purity, and be unwilling to make any compromise with short-term or external pressures; it would be confident that, in the long run, its objectives would be realised and determined that new issues should be judged solely within an inflexible ideological framework. It is fashionable to reject the notion that the Labour Party has any ideological framework and to maintain that its policies are explicable entirely in terms of its efforts to maximise its electoral support. But policies and programmes have to be justified within the framework of the party's philosophy and ideology. Although that framework has become increasingly elastic with the passage of time, it cannot be dispensed with completely, without risking intra-party strife.

I   LABOUR AND THE STATE

The nature of the state presents a fundamental question for the British Labour Party which has *both* statist and anti-statist traditions. In its early days, greater credence was given to anti-state theories, which derived from both ideological and pragmatic considerations. The former included guild socialism, as preached by G. D. H. Cole, and its industrial equivalent, syndicalism, and the individualistic libertarianism inherited from 19th-century Liberalism. The latter involved the localised structure of the Labour Party, the trade unions' concern with local bargaining within the private enterprise system, and the need to reach accommodations with local Liberal parties. The statist view acquired increasing acceptance during the 1920s and 1930s as the depression deepened and revealed the apparent failure of private enterprise and the need for positive intervention by the state in the running of the economy. In this same period, the Labour Party, emerging as a potential party of government, became increasingly concerned with the mechanics and uses of government, in contrast to its earlier questioning of the nature and form of the state itself.

The debate on the role of the state has been confused by questions about the degree of centralisation of the state, which caused a series of ideological dilemmas for the Labour Party. The Fabian dilemma between decentralisation as a means to furthering democracy and popular control, and centralisation, in the cause of planning and equity, has never been resolved. In 1920, the Webbs stated the fundamental problem of any democratic re-organisation of British local government [which] . . . is how to provide for the administration, as a single environmental complex, of diverse services, retaining and even intensifying the bond of neighbourhood and the consciousness of common life, under one and the same body of elected representatives immediately responsible to their constituents – and yet to secure for each of the different public services . . . such an area of administration as will permit, in all of them alike, a maximum of efficiency and economy.

(Sancton, 1976)

The Webbs ultimately resolved the problem by advocating functional decentralisation, but the argument for territorial decentralisation was pursued by several of the early Fabians, and finds a reflection in the strong local government tradition in the party. The decentralist strand, linked with the anti-statism implicit in guild socialism and syndicalism, confronts a centralist tradition which emphasises the national, and even international, solidarity of the working class.

Since the First World War, pragmatic class and electoral considerations have become more important; both the interests of Labour supporters and the need to expand an electoral base have pointed towards centralisation. For example, in order to redistribute resources and improve conditions in regions of deprivation – which are heavily represented in the party – a centralising policy has usually been seen to be necessary. The political advance of the Labour Party coincided historically with the economic decline of old industrial areas and reinforced dependence on central provision of economic benefits. Electorally, Labour has traditionally drawn strength from the peripheral areas of the United Kingdom and has usually sought to retain the loyalty of these areas by policies aimed at helping the *regions*, and not simply social groups within them. The prevailing Labour (and, under Edward Heath, Conservative) view has been that electoral appeals should be made on the basis of the promotion of the regions' economies, which is best done through a centralised policy. The combination of electoral strength in the peripheral regions and a belief in centralisation has thus made Labour the major centralising force in British politics. But this did not prevent it from responding to distinctive Scottish and Welsh demands where this could be done without damage to its overall strategy.

II FROM HOME RULE TO CENTRALISATION

In its early days at the turn of the century the Labour movement in Scotland and Wales looked with favour on Home Rule, to which there were few doctrinal obstacles. Statist ideas of planning had not yet gained general currency. John MacCormick's description of the ILP in Scotland after the First World War was not far wrong:

> Socialism in those days was not the doctrine of the state-planned economy which it has since become. The ILP had inherited much of the old Radical tradition of Scotland and for the most part as a street-corner missionary, I was expected not to expound the theories of Karl Marx but merely to give expression to the general sense of injustice and aspiration for a better way of life which were very natural feelings among the workers of Clydeside in the years between the wars.   (MacCormick, 1955)

In any case, had there been inconsistencies between support for Home Rule and the other elements in the programme, the party, at this time remote from power, would scarcely have concerned itself about them. In Wales, the industrial wing of the movement, which might have been expected to exert a centralising pressure, was divided. The publication in 1911 of the *Miners Next Step* revealed a basic distrust of bureaucratic centralisation on the part of the South Wales miners and support for a particular form of syndicalism which 'was profoundly shot through with an integrated sense of community, in some sense insulated from the English world outside' (Morgan, 1963). In Scotland, too, there was an absence of strong centralising pressures. For example, the main ingredients of the Clydeside militancy were defensive craft unionism and a syndicalist form of socialism, both derived from a local community base and antagonistic to statism. Furthermore in the period around the First World War, the industrial wing of the movement actually took the lead in pushing for Home Rule (Keating and Bleiman, 1979).

In both Scotland and Wales, Labour inherited support, policies and, indeed, the personnel of 19th-century radical Liberalism. In Wales, the fledgling movement had to contend not only with the all-powerful Liberals, who had won 33 of the 34 Welsh seats in 1906, but also with a non-conformist culture that was still in the ascendant, and a Welsh-speaking community that accounted for almost half the Principality's population. All three were strongly identified with Home Rule, and a party seeking electoral advancement could not afford to ignore such political realities. In Scotland, Keir Hardie's earlier Scottish Labour Party had faced the same problem. With only weak support from the organised industrial working class, it was largely a coalition of various 'advanced' groups, such as Highland land reformers, the Socialist League and Irish and Scottish Home Rulers. Although the party in Britain was gradually moving towards accepting the paramount need for central economic control, it remained sympathetic to distinctive Scottish and Welsh aspirations. In 1918, Arthur Henderson, then General Secretary, asserted that 'given self-government Wales might establish itself a modern Utopia and develop its own institutions, its own culture, its own ideal of democracy in politics, industry and social life . . .'. In the same year the party's annual conference debated constitutional devolution and resolved 'there should be constituted separate statutory legislative assemblies for Scotland, Wales and even England'. In Scotland after the First World War, traditional radicalism and the new industrial militancy were allied within the Labour Party to produce a brief upsurge of support for Home Rule.

During the 1920s Home Rule agitation in both Scotland and Wales came to an end. The old radical issues which had produced the distinctive character of Scottish and Welsh politics were dying. The economic slump of the 1920s undermined the independence and confidence of the Scottish labour movement and, hitting its staple industries particularly hard, raised serious questions about Scotland's viability as an economic unit. The similarly catastrophic impact of the depression on South Wales had the same effect, and a conventional wisdom emerged which held that the economic problems of Scotland and Wales were to be solved only by gaining access to United Kingdom resources, and steering development away from the prosperous areas of England. Politically, the breakthrough of 1922 and the Labour Government of 1924 concentrated attention on Westminster. Thereafter efforts were directed at securing a Labour Government for the United Kingdom. Labour's Scottish and Welsh seats made a vital contribution to its strength at Westminster and the party hierarchy, impressed by the logic of the electoral arithmetic, now had an interest in retaining the two nations within a unified Westminster system. Attempts by Home Rulers to influence the Labour Governments of 1924 and 1929–31 were simply stone-walled, as Labour turned increasingly to the idea of planning as a solution to economic problems, particularly those of depressed areas like Scotland and Wales. This became the basis of its electoral appeal.

In the 1930s, the increasingly centralist emphasis in Labour's policies reflected not only economic necessity but also a significant ideological shift. Nationalism had become tainted by its association with right-wing movements in Europe. In Scotland it was further damned by the attacks on Labour by the National Party of Scotland (later the SNP), which was composed largely of people who had broken with Labour in 1928 over its failure to take their cause seriously. In Wales, the nationalist party, Plaid Cymru, was founded in 1925 but it was an intellectual, romantic association and politically insignificant. Labour could safely ignore it. The creation of the South Wales Regional Council of Labour in 1937 was intended not to fulfil a devolutionist role, but to confront Communist infiltration of trade union branches and constituency parties in South Wales.

The Second World War saw a further massive increase in government activity, and a tendency to further centralisation. The 1945–51 Labour Government introduced centralising measures, a move fully supported by both Scottish and Welsh Labour leaderships. Although there were during the 1940s and 1950s all-party campaigns for devolution in both Scotland and Wales, these were peripheral to Labour's major concerns. The Scottish Convention of the late 1940s gained widespread support within the party, but its activities soon became regarded as attacks on the Labour Government. In Wales, parts of the Labour Party, irritated by Attlee's decision not to appoint a Welsh Secretary of State, supported a Parliament for Wales campaign launched in 1950 as an all-party pressure group; but the most eminent and respected devolutionist within the party, James Griffiths, remained studiously aloof, judging that it went beyond that which the party as a whole would tolerate.

Labour's secure electoral position in Scotland and Wales, and the lack of an effective electoral challenge from the nationalists, meant that Labour was able to resist these pressures, while Labour government policies for planning and nationalisation faced the devolutionists within the party with a dilemma which they had avoided – how to combine Labour's programme of central planning and redistribution with radical measures of decentralisation. In Scotland, this led to the formal abandonment of Labour's Home Rule commitment in 1958. By the late 1950s, Labour was identified with centralisation and the British state.

Labour's position in Scotland and Wales reflects the policy trinity described above: electoral strategy, economic interests and ideology. The party's increasing electoral dominance in both Scotland and Wales in the 1950s and 1960s freed it from the worry that a third party could capitalise on Scottish and Welsh grievances and undermine its position. At the same time, however, the party was, to varying degrees, prepared to exploit these issues itself and provide a 'substitute' national party. In Scotland, this took the form of pushing for administrative devolution and attacking Conservative Governments for their alleged neglect of Scottish needs. In Wales, there were a series of specifically Welsh issues which could enlist the support of Welsh socialists without provoking the charge of threatening the unity of the Labour movement and of endangering the structure of the welfare state. The most important of these issues was the demand for a Welsh Secretary of State of Cabinet rank but local government reform was another 'legitimate' concern for Welsh socialists who, like Jim Griffiths, saw it in the context of establishing regional authorities. Economic interest also dictated support for the centralised economy through the 1950s and 1960s, particularly as the Labour Party increasingly emphasised regional policy as a positive means of redistributing resources to the depressed areas, including Scotland and Wales. This in turn increased the party's ability to make electoral appeals on regional rather than simply on class grounds. Ideologically, the mainstream of Labour thinking continued to identify socialism with centralisation, but the old decentralist strand was never completely broken, particularly in Wales where some of the leaders and activists, especially non-conformists, had a genuine belief in Home Rule (Griffiths, 1978). Similarly, in Scotland a portion of the left maintained the old belief in Home Rule, though few regarded it as one of the major issues of politics. Consequently, it is possible to identify a continuum between the pre-1914 Home Rulers and the post-1966 devolutionists within the party. By 1966, Labour's essentially centralist strategies in Scotland and Wales had received triumphant vindication at the polls. At the general election of that year, the party won 32 of the 36 Welsh seats, and 46 of the 71 Scottish seats. In both nations it appeared that Labour had successfully 'sublimated' the national issue and turned it to its advantage.

III   THE NATIONALIST CHALLENGE AND LABOUR'S RESPONSE

The first shocks to Labour's self-confidence in Scotland and Wales came almost immediately after the 1966 general election. Plaid Cymru captured Carmarthen in a by-election and in 1967 the SNP capitalised on the Labour Government's unpopularity to overturn a massive majority at Hamilton. Although it is possible to argue, in retrospect, that special factors were present in both constituencies, they nevertheless were evidence of better organised and more assertive nationalist movements and of the organisational weakness of the Labour Party. Plaid Cymru had already made some advances in local government in the early 1960s, capitalising on popular disenchantment with Labour rule, and the SNP had made inroads into the Labour vote at several by-elections since 1961. Labour's instinctive reaction was to attack nationalism and stress the economic benefits of centralisation. According to the dominant school of thought, nationalist successes were no more than the product of a protest vote and would disappear with economic recovery. In both Scotland and Wales, however, some argued that the causes that stimulated the nationalists' electoral successes could (or even should) be accommodated successfully within the party.

The Welsh reaction

In Wales, the Labour Party's centralist reaction stressed the economic dangers of separatism (a term deliberately coined in preference to independence), and the advantages that would accrue to Wales from proper Westminster management of the economy and regional aid programmes. The establishment of the Welsh Economic Planning Council, the creation and enhanced role for the Welsh Secretary of State in the development of Mid-Wales, and the unexpected decision to locate the Royal Mint in Llantrisant were all part of what might be termed managerial decentralisation. However, the continuing decline of Wales' basic industries largely nullified government economic initiatives and Welsh unemployment continued at almost twice the national average. In 1967 and 1968 the near disastrous Labour by-election results in Rhondda and Caerphilly evoked a reaction which verged on hysteria; Plaid Cymru was labelled an 'incipient form of fascism'. However, Labour devolutionists were already preparing a different response.

The nationalist threat gave added keenness to the Welsh Council of Labour's growing enthusiasm for policy formulation, a development which coincided with Emrys Jones' appointment as the Welsh Regional Organiser and Secretary in 1965. In May 1966, some two months before the Carmarthen by-election, Welsh Labour's Annual Conference approved a policy for an elected Welsh Council above a reorganised local government structure of most-purpose authorities. However, any suggestion of an elected Welsh Council, even within the framework of local government reform, caused considerable apprehensions within the Welsh Labour Group of MPs, and virtually divided them along linguistic lines (Butt Philip, 1975). The position of the devolutionist Welsh Secretary of State, Cledwyn Hughes, was consequently weakened in Cabinet discussions, and the July 1967 local government proposals made only passing reference to the possibility of further strengthening the 'all-Wales machinery in the light of the Royal Commission on the Constitution report and other developments'. To the Welsh Executive of the Labour Party the message was clear: if the proposals for an elected Welsh Council were to be denied in the context of local government, they would have to be brought in via devolution and the Commission on the Constitution. But there was still a need to placate the suspicions, if not hostility, of Welsh Labour MPs, and this is revealed by the evidence presented to the Commission by the Labour Party in Wales. It rejected an Assembly with legislative power because 'it would reduce the effectiveness of Welsh MPs and the influence of Wales in the UK, and would jeopardise the unity of the country as a whole', but persisted in its demand for an elected Welsh Council.

By comparison with Scotland, the Labour Party in Wales was able to respond more rapidly and more sympathetically to the nationalist threat, because of its dominant electoral position. By 1966, the most agricultural and Welsh-speaking parts of north and west Wales were all held by Labour, which was able to present itself as the 'national' party in Wales, sympathetic not only to the steel workers and the miners of the South but also to the hill farmers and dairymen of the north and west. The preparation and presentation of evidence to the Commission on the Constitution had a profound impact upon the Welsh Council of Labour. Its views had been criticised and opposed by the Welsh Office Ministers and practically half the Welsh Labour Group. It had been pressured by Transport House to modify its evidence and bring its proposals into line with those presented by the Labour Party in Scotland: i.e. total opposition to an elected council. Although much was conceded, the principle of a directly elected council was maintained, and the Welsh Council of Labour emerged as a credible political force.

During the 1970–4 Conservative Government, Welsh Labour's original contention that an elected Welsh Council should be established within a local government context was reiterated and re-emphasised. The Welsh Executive expressed concern that 'the Crowther Commission [had] not made approaches to the government to halt consideration of local government re-organisation until its report is available'. A similar theme was present in Harold Wilson's speech to the Labour Party Local Government Conference at Newcastle on 10 February 1973; he implied that devolution could be accommodated within the established ideological framework of the Labour Party.

Instead of transferring functions from local to central government, or proceeding with one after another ad hoc, more or less appointive body covering wide areas of the country, we need, not only to halt this process, but to do two other things. First, to decentralise and democratise more and more work presently undertaken by central government either from Whitehall or through their own regional machinery, and, second, to create democratic regional authorities accountable to the people they serve, to deal with those services for which local authorities are too small.

Wilson was referring specifically to the *English* regions, but his message was eagerly accepted by Welsh Labour at pains to persuade its own supporters that the devolution policy was not only, nor even mainly, a response to nationalist threats. During the course of 1973 the 'devolution' policy began imperceptibly to move towards a policy of 'extending democracy', a far more acceptable ideological concept within the Labour movement. In July 1973 a Welsh Labour Party Study Group document revealed Welsh Labour's anxieties to integrate its policy into a broader British context.

> When the evidence of the Welsh Council of Labour to the Commission on the Constitution was being prepared four years ago, there was still a strong belief in the necessity for strong central government direction if regional problems, particularly economic ones, were to be successfully solved. Today, this can only be effectively done if the wishes of the people in each part of Britain are directly heeded through democratically elected bodies and their support for the necessary policies mobilised.
>
> (Labour Party in Wales, 1973)

The new approach was largely responsible for winning over the doubters and opponents of devolution in the Welsh Parliamentary Labour Group.

A Conservative Government, in particular a Conservative Secretary of State at the Welsh Office, gave added respectability to Welsh Labour's devolution policy. The extension of Welsh Office powers in health, education and water resources and the creation of new *ad hoc* bodies were criticised by Labour because they were 'a concession to the devolution of centralised power to the executive and not to the Welsh people'. Furthermore, the principle of public accountability contained within the office of the Welsh Secretary of State was severely strained by the appointment of Peter Thomas, who represented a suburban London constituency.

Nevertheless, Labour in Wales was not unanimously behind the devolution proposals in either of the 1974 general elections. The materialist wing of the party still subscribed strongly to the idea of a unified working class movement with centralised institutions for social and economic planning; they were still a factor to be reckoned with. The October 1974 Welsh Labour Manifesto exhibited the problems of trying to satisfy both sides of the devolution debate. While the elected Council would in 'no way be akin to a legislature', the manifesto stated 'central government would legislate broadly, leaving an area of wide decision making to the Welsh Council'. The ambiguities were the product of compromise forced on a party seeking to accommodate its divergent wings, sympathetic to Welsh aspirations on the one hand, while fulfilling its responsibilities to the British Labour movement on the other.

By October 1974 there had been an influx of new Labour MPs reflecting a different generation of socialists with a middle class, professional background who proceded to displace the pro-devolution majority in the Welsh Labour Group. Given these increasingly vocal critics of devolution within the ranks of Welsh Labour MPs, and the inability of Plaid seriously to threaten Labour's industrial stronghold in the valleys, Welsh Labour might have deferred dealing with the problem. However, the establishment of the Wales TUC in 1973 was crucial in sustaining the party's attachment to the devolution policy during the difficult period leading up to the publication of the Scotland and Wales Bill in 1975 (Osmond, 1977). From its inception, the Wales TUC favoured legislative devolution on the same basis as that envisaged for Scotland. Welsh trade unionists had been disillusioned by the performance of the Welsh Office on industrial matters, and particularly critical of the Conservative administration in Wales. Many had come to believe that an elected Welsh Assembly with legislative powers and a built-in Labour majority would be able to improve the Welsh economic climate. The 'advanced' position of the Wales TUC on devolution was shown at a special Welsh Labour Conference in July 1974, when the Welsh Labour officers had to dissuade the trade unions from forcing through an endorsement of legislative devolution, and to settle instead for an elected assembly with executive and some (undefined) economic powers.

After October 1974, there was increasing opposition from several Welsh Labour MPs to the idea of an elected Welsh Assembly. They doubted the wisdom of such a reform in the immediate aftermath of local government reorganisation; they questioned the logic of undermining the authority and status of the Welsh Secretary of State and the Welsh Office by creating an alternative power centre; and they were also deeply suspicious of the role Welsh Assemblymen might play. But they did not criticise the party's policy directly; instead, they called for a referendum. These criticisms reopened the fundamental divide within the Labour Party in Wales between those who saw no contradiction between socialism and their Welsh national identity, and others who were primarily motivated by a materialistic belief in the pre-eminent power and influence of British State.

The Scottish reaction

In Scotland, the apparent fading of the SNP challenge after Hamilton gave credence to the prevailing Labour view that nationalism was no more than a passing protest. The evidence of Labour's Scottish Council to the Commission on the Constitution firmly rejected a Scottish Assembly, pointing to the dangers of economic separation, a stance supported by the Scottish Labour Conference in 1970 and 1971. However, things were never quite the same after Hamilton. Now that the issue was back on the political agenda, the traditional supporters of devolution began to be heard again.

Moreover, Labour was faced with controversial measures of the 1970–4 Conservative Government touching distinctly Scottish questions. The Housing (Financial Provisions) (Scotland) Act, questioned the traditional separate basis of Scottish housing finance. While, in England, the Conservatives proposed that local authorities should move towards market rents, in Scotland, because this would have meant enormous rises, they retained the historic cost basis of rents as an interim measure but envisaged a move to market rents by 1974–5. The proposal to assimilate Scotland to the English system of housing finance allowed Labour to resume its role as defender of Scottish interests. However, Labour was no longer able to take too hard a line on this issue, as to accuse the Conservatives of overriding Scottish interests on the basis of their United Kingdom majority would give credibility to the nationalist case. In any case, Labour's position in Scotland was far from secure; in the Dundee East by-election of March 1973, Labour almost lost to the SNP.

Already in January 1973 the Scottish Executive had decided to review its position on Scottish government in view of the forthcoming report of the Commission on the Constitution. At the same time, opinion within the parliamentary group was swinging towards devolution, with even Shadow Secretary of State Willie Ross coming to the view that it might not be possible to resist it. A Scottish Executive sub-committee was appointed, to consult with interested parties and draft a report. By October, with the Kilbrandon Report imminent and a by-election pending at Glasgow Govan, the report was ready. It flatly rejected the idea of an Assembly. Pro-devolution members of the Executive tried to get it amended, then to delay publication, but they were overruled and the document appeared one day before the Kilbrandon Report and just a few days before the SNP victory at Govan. *Scotland and the UK* (Labour Party, Scottish Council, 1973) was a firm restatement of Labour's position as developed since the 1940s. It ruled out 'any new-fangled Assembly' on the grounds that Scottish influence at Westminster would be reduced, an Assembly would have financial restrictions, pose a threat to the new local authorities, threaten the economic unity of the United Kingdom, and fail to bring any real benefits to the Scottish people. Instead, it argued, the new local authorities should gradually be given more powers, and the work of the Select Committee on Scottish Affairs and the Scottish Grand Committee should be expanded. A second document proposed the creation of a body (later to become the

Scottish Development Agency) to attack economic grievances assumed to be at the root of the discontent.

The compromise did not last long, for the Kilbrandon Report crystallised the debate on devolution. While the devolutionist wing of the party seized on its endorsement of an Assembly, the anti-devolutionists pointed to the recommendation for the abolition of the Secretary of State for Scotland and the reduction in the number of Scottish MPs. By falling short of Kilbrandon, the proposals of *Scotland and the UK* now had to be regarded as centralist. As a failed compromise, they fell by the wayside.

Nationalist successes at the February 1974 general election, and the minority status of the Labour government, put more pressure on the Labour Party to rethink its attitude. It was now the Scottish Executive which was the major obstacle to a change of policy. Having avoided a vote on devolution at the annual conference in March, and rejected all the proposed devolution schemes in June, it was prevailed upon by the National Executive Committee of the British Labour Party to recall the conference, which, in August 1974, voted overwhelmingly for the establishment of a legislative assembly. Ross and the parliamentary leadership became enthusiastic converts and the Labour government, in advance of the October 1974 general election, was able to issue a White Paper promising devolution.

Two questions arise from Scottish Labour's dramatic reversal of direction in 1974. The first is, why did it change direction? The second is, did this represent a major retreat from its centralist position? The change of policy has been widely attributed to cynical electoral expediency on the part of the national leadership, who then ordered their Scottish followers into line. Certainly, the role of the Prime Minister and government leadership was important in forcing the change of policy. Alerted by the opinion pollsters, they were extremely concerned at what was seen as the dangerous obstinacy of the Scottish Executive in holding out against devolution, and exerted great pressure upon them. They also lined up loyalist union leaders to push the devolution policy through the special conference. However, the conversion of the rank and file was not just a matter of electoral expediency. Labour does not abandon cherished ideological positions overnight, even when they are electorally unpopular. This implies that either the old centralist stance was not a matter of deeply-held ideology *or* that it had not seriously been infringed. There is some truth in both of these points. The issue was not one which divided the party on the usual right–left lines. The party did have a decentralist tradition, and was able very quickly to build an ideological justification, summoning the ghost of Keir Hardie in aid.

This still leaves the question of why the party chose to exercise this option. Most of the party believed there was no choice if the Labour Party was to remain the dominant electoral party in Scottish politics. Having exploited Scottish discontents to its own electoral benefit, Labour felt particularly vulnerable in the face of a party better able to exploit them. Having defended its role in terms of getting material benefits for Scotland, it was outflanked by a party which, with North Sea oil, could more than match anything in Labour's pork-barrel. The promise of a Scottish Development Agency, the latest of Labour's traditional devices to contain nationalism, had failed to stem the tide, leaving Labour facing a second general election in 1974 in a dangerously weak position. Its electoral hegemony, which had enabled it to contain the national dimension in Scottish politics, had disappeared, or was in danger of disappearing. In theory, Labour could have raised the saliency of British issues on which it possessed an advantage, but in 1974 there was a distinct shortage of these; even the economic issue was being used against it with a vengeance by the SNP. Therefore, Labour reluctantly aligned itself with the national dimension in Scottish politics, in the belief that a policy of devolution, as opposed to centralisation or independence, was what the great majority of Scots wanted. In the circumstances of 1974 there was no half-way house between having an Assembly and not having an Assembly, nor was there time for extended contemplation. Willie Ross had believed that, if the issue of devolution were raised, it would be difficult to resist, for the traditional Labour policy of administrative devolution had reached its limits, and 1974 seemed to prove the case.

The decision for an Assembly and subsequent developments indicate that the essential elements of centralisation remained. The role of the Westminster leadership in pushing the policy was a *prima facie* indication that drastic decentralisation was not contemplated. Within Scotland, and particularly among the Scottish MPs, support for the policy was secured only on the conditions that Scotland would retain its Secretary of State and its full complement of 71 MPs. The unions were brought in on the assurance that devolution would not affect economic centralisation and United Kingdom-wide wage bargaining. The devolution concessions made were the minimum which the party thought necessary in order to preserve the essential features of the centralised state, and ensure the survival of the British Labour Party. While devolution was adopted largely from electoral necessity, this was possible only after it had been established as ideologically sound in the form adopted.

The Labour Government's reaction

During the period over which the devolution policy was emerging, the attitude of the party leadership at the United Kingdom level can best be understood in terms of electoral expediency. The immediate response to by-election reverses during the 1960s was in terms of pork-barrel politics – for example, the establishment of the Royal Mint at Llantrisant and the series of special measures for Scotland from the car factories of the 1960s to the Scottish Development Agency – rather than constitutional change.

However, what characterised the mood of the party leadership was a lack of interest in, and ignorance of, the changing pattern of Scottish and Welsh politics. An exception was Richard Crossman who perceived the need for constitutional change but he was opposed by the Welsh and Scottish Secretaries, who reflected the prevailing centralist view within the party in Scotland and Wales. Consequently, all that was achieved by the 1966–70 Labour Government was the establishment in 1969 of the Royal Commission on the Constitution, seen by most ministers as a way of shelving the issue until after the next general election. The continuing strength of the centralist tradition was amply demonstrated by the party's attempt to ensure uniformity and consistency in the evidence to the Royal Commission presented by its Scottish and Welsh councils. After the 1970 General Election, the party in opposition was able to review its policies, but this did not include political devolution for Scotland and Wales. The only hint of a change of attitude came in Harold Wilson's Newcastle speech in 1973, when he revealed a concern with the regional dimension of government. It was the dramatic advance of the nationalists in the February 1974 General Election which re-established the need for Labour to have a distinctive Scottish and Welsh strategy, and this in turn brought the centralist–decentralist debate to the forefront.

The appointment of Lord Crowther-Hunt, a pro-devolutionist member of the Commission on the Constitution, as Wilson's constitutional advisor, revealed a serious attempt to confront the issue, a step confirmed by Wilson's parliamentary statement in March 1974. By June 1974 a policy of political devolution for Scotland and, to a lesser extent, Wales, had been decided on by Downing Street. This was pushed through a largely uninterested Cabinet and NEC, and forced upon a reluctant Scottish Executive. Although the government had grasped the decentralist nettle, the party had not yet come to terms with the implications of the policy, a fact that was to impose severe strains on support for the government's devolutionary proposals.

After the October 1974 General Election, the major issue at stake was whether the assemblies, but specifically the Scottish Assembly, should have significant economic powers. As the granting of economic powers to an assembly would strike at one of the fundamental elements of Labour's centralist beliefs, it was an issue which divided the party's committed decentralisers from the rest. Support for the devolution of economic functions came from two sources: the group around Jim Sillars, a 'mini-cadre' which had been pressing for devolution, and the trade unions in Scotland and Wales which had begun to see the possible value of assemblies as a means of securing economic advantages. In part, this reflected a disillusionment with the machinery of the Scottish and Welsh Offices, in part a feeling that it was essential to have an assembly which could look after Scottish and Welsh interests. There was little support within the Government for the devolution of economic powers, apart from one Scottish minister who tried to mobilise support within the party for his view. Furthermore, the trade unions were not prepared to break up the economic unity of the UK.

The debate in the Government and the Party was complicated by the immense pressure under which Labour in Scotland suffered after 1974. Continued nationalist successes at local elections and the subsequent breakaway of Jim Sillars and John Robertson to form the Scottish Labour Party combined to create the impression that Labour in Scotland was fighting for its life. In retrospect, the fears of a complete Labour collapse in its Scottish industrial heartland can be seen as premature and exaggerated. But the Government was deeply worried. In these circumstances, a retreat from devolution was more than it dared contemplate.

IV RECONCILING CONFLICTS

The 1975 White Paper represented the first detailed attempt by the Government to reconcile the conflicting pressures upon it. It attempted to satisfy Scottish and Welsh demands for devolution while not conceding any of the authority of central government; to undercut the SNP and Plaid Cymru while not splitting the Labour Party; and to benefit the Scots and Welsh while not appearing to change English interests. Press reaction to the White Paper vividly illustrated the void which the Government was trying to bridge. The *Daily Mirror* commented, 'It's the least that could be offered and the most'; while its Scottish sister paper, the *Daily Record*, complained, 'We were PROMISED more now. WE WANT MORE because, Harold, your deal is just not good enough'. Generally, the reaction to the White Paper was so hostile that the Government had to issue a *Supplementary Statement* (virtually another White Paper) in August 1976. This reduced the supervisory role of the Secretaries of State over the proposed Assemblies, which were also given greater powers over the Scottish and Welsh Development Agencies. Still, the conflicting pressures bore upon the Government. Every concession to one group was likely to lose it the support of another. The main cross-pressures arose from ministers and senior civil servants who were self-evidently reluctant devolutionists; the parliamentary predicament; the position of the Labour Party in Scotland and Wales; and the electoral situation.

Most ministers had been reluctant converts to devolution, and Harold Wilson's constant references to the subject in his account of his 1974–6 Government as 'boring' seems to reflect the mood of the Cabinet. In so far as ministers and senior civil servants were prepared to back devolution, it was devolution of a very 'centralist' kind, the handing over of matters of 'low level politics' to assemblies which would be tightly constrained, legally and financially, retaining for the centre all the major instruments of governmental power. The Parliament of 1974–9 did not contain a majority for devolution. The Conservatives, committed by 1976 to opposing devolution, together with anti-devolution Labour MPs, outnumbered those committed in principle to devolution. Lacking a working majority, and increasingly dependent for its survival on the votes of Welsh and Scottish nationalists and Liberals, the Government was obliged to persist with the attempt to put a devolution scheme on the statute book. The divisions amongst the Government's supporters were complex. A number of MPs were, in principle, opposed to devolution. These, who formed the basis of the Labour Against Assemblies Group, included Scottish and Welsh MPs, English MPs and expatriates like George Cunningham, a Scot sitting for a London constituency. Other MPs, predominantly from the north of England, were concerned that Scottish and Welsh devolution would disadvantage their own regions. However, MPs were prepared to follow the party whip, with greater or lesser reluctance, depending on their own view of the issue and their perception of the Government's seriousness on devolution. The most striking characteristic of the 1974–9 Parliament was the slender evidence of committed back-bench support for the scheme based on a genuine belief in devolution.

The government White Papers leading up to the Scotland and Wales bill in 1976 progressively clarified the devolution proposals. However, in Wales this removed ambiguities that had cloaked the inherent differences within the Welsh party, and arguments presumed to have been resolved were thus re-opened. Long-term opponents of devolution such as Leo Abse, who had reluctantly accepted the policy in 1973, renewed their opposition, and were joined by a group of new Labour MPs such as Neil Kinnock, Don Anderson and Ioan Evans, who argued that too much had been conceded to the Welsh radical wing of the party; that such concessions were unnecessary because Plaid Cymru had failed to match in strength their nationalist counterparts in Scotland, and that Welsh public opinion seemed unenthusiastic for the proposals. Subsequently, the arguments were refined to include the charge that Wales had no community of interest and that a Welsh-speaking elite would dominate an assembly. In the face of such attacks Welsh Labour produced a dual response; it exploited the 'loyalty factor' in an attempt to persuade the dissidents to follow the party's policy and, secondly, sought to link that policy more securely to the traditional economic and centralist elements of Labour party thinking.

The extension of the Welsh Office and nominated 'quangos' during the 1970s was used as an additional argument for the assembly. The Welsh Secretary supported the campaign, acknowledging in February 1975:

> On an All-Wales level of authority we already have a host of nominated bodies exercising enormous powers. Other decisions, some of them in great detail are taken by myself and while I am answerable to Parliament no one would pretend that Parliament's scrutiny of the Welsh Office's activities is adequate.   (Labour Party in Wales, 1975)

The original local government implications for an elected Welsh Assembly were also updated. In June 1976 a Labour Party Study Group, examining local government in Wales, rejected the two-tier Conservative structure and proposed single-tier all-purpose authorities under an elected Welsh Assembly. The local government context was deemed so important that the Welsh Executive insisted that the Wales Bill should specifically require the Welsh Assembly to review the local government structure.

The final phase came when the 1978 Annual Conference of the Welsh Labour Party was asked to approve a policy statement entitled 'Political and Industrial Democracy in Britain', which placed the devolution proposals within a continuum of a developing democracy, ranging from the extension of the franchise and reform of the House of Lords, to workers control and industrial democracy. The policy was approved by an overwhelming majority, the criticisms of dissident Labour MPs were blunted, and it appeared the Labour Party in Wales had come some considerable way to accommodating a policy of political decentralisation within the broader ideological and traditional working class ethos of the party.

It is the height of irony that, having talked about devolution for over half a century, the Labour Party in Scotland was rushed into a decision in 1974; yet, this was indeed the case. The party spent the next five years coming to terms with its decision. The 1974 Conference, despite the later protestations of anti-devolutionists like Tam Dalyell, had been unambiguous in its endorsement of a legislative assembly. Where it was unclear was on the vital issue of what powers the assembly should have. This was the issue on which the battle was now joined, with the pro-devolution forces retaining the initiative, the opponents seeking not to reverse the policy but to limit the powers of the assembly, and the bulk of the party searching for a reasonable balance which could be defended electorally while not prejudicing the party's basic aims.

At the 1975 Conference, the party's divisions came out in the open. A composite resolution from the T & GWU, calling for economic and revenue raising powers, was opposed by the Executive and defeated on a card vote, with most of the constituency parties voting with the Executive. This was something of an embarrassment to devolutionists within the Government, who were pushing for the devolution of the Scottish Development Agency. By the following year, with the Government's second White Paper to consider and a string of local government by-election defeats behind them, both the Executive and the Conference were in a more devolutionary mood. The Executive, whose report was accepted by Conference, demanded that the SDA be devolved, that the Secretary of State's veto be removed, and that the Assembly be given revenue-raising powers. The mood of the party at this time was accurately summed up by Geoffrey Smith in *The Times*. After commenting that many people believed that the Labour Party in Scotland was on the point of collapse, he went on:

There remain the convinced anti-devolutionists. But among the rest there is a general movement to a compromise position where the majority can stand and fight. There is a widespread recognition that something more than the White Paper will be needed to satisfy Scottish opinion. In some cases, that recognition is enthusiastic. More often it is the reluctant acceptance of political necessity. But one also encounters a feeling that, while there must be more devolution than the Government have yet proposed, there must nonetheless be strict limits as to how far it would be safe to go without jeopardising the integrity of the United Kingdom.

(*The Times*, 4 March 1976)

The delayed production of the Scotland and Wales Bill in 1976 did not serve to reconcile the conflicting pressures, and the Bill was effectively killed on 22 February 1977 when the Government failed to secure the guillotine motion necessary to restrict debate and thus get it through the committee stage. The defeat was inflicted by the combined opposition of Conservatives, Liberals and 22 Labour MPs. In addition, 23 Labour MPs abstained. Of the Labour MPs voting against the guillotine, two were from Scotland and two from Wales. Of those abstaining, two were from Scotland and five from Wales. Nine of the rebels were from the north of England. Thus, to construct a majority for devolution, the Government had to concentrate on three groups of MPs – the Liberals, Welsh, and north of England Labour MPs.

While public reaction in Scotland and Wales to the Bill's defeat was muted, the SNP continued to rise in the opinion polls and dealt Labour a severe blow in the 1977 local elections. Further, the precarious parliamentary situation left the Government dependent for survival on the Liberal and nationalist parties. A pact was therefore negotiated with the Liberals and, as a result of this, new and separate devolution bills produced for Scotland and Wales. Under the terms of the pact, devolution was a Liberal priority. The support of most of the northern English MPs was secured by the promise of regional committees of the National Enterprise Board and measures such as the acceleration of the order for the Drax B power station. All Labour MPs were told that a second rejection of devolution would mean the collapse of the pact and a disastrous general election defeat for Labour. Possibly the most crucial concession, however, had been made in order to secure the second reading of the original Scotland and Wales Bill, when the Government acceded to the demand for referendums in Scotland and Wales. This allowed Scottish and Welsh opponents of devolution to support the Bills – and thus the Government – while reserving the force of their opposition for the referendum campaigns. Moreover, in the case of Wales, public opinion polls suggested that the referendum would result in the defeat of the proposals. Consequently, the 43 Labour dissidents from the Scotland and Wales Bill were reduced to 16 for the separate bills.

As a result of the referendum concession, most of the debate on the details of the Scotland and Wales bills involved putting down 'markers' for the referendum campaign, rather than serious attempts to alter the legislation. One amendment, however, was of crucial importance and illustrated clearly the lack of a convinced majority for devolution in Parliament. This required that, unless the Acts received the support of at least 40 per cent of the electorate in Scotland and Wales respectively, the Secretaries of State would be obliged to lay orders for their repeal. The Government was unable to reverse this decision at the report stage of the Scotland Bill and subsequently adopted it in the case of the Wales Bill as well.

The 1979 referendum campaign divided the Labour Party in both Scotland and Wales. After the Scottish Executive had voted, by a majority, to give official backing to the Yes campaign, a Labour No campaign was formed, in January 1978. Besides such predictable figures as Tam Dalyell and Peter Doig, MP, this included MPs such as Robert Hughes, Richard Buchanan and Robin Cook, who had previously expressed their unease over devolution. The first real test of the No group was an amendment to ban the use of party funds in the referendum campaign, put to the 1978 Scottish Conference. This was heavily defeated and the party remained firmly committed to the devolution line. The Carscadden and Hamilton by-elections and the 1978 regional elections showed a dramatic improvement in Labour's fortunes at the expense of the SNP. Whatever the reasons for this improvement, within the party the devolution policy was seen as a vital element. It may not in itself have won votes, so the argument went, but it had deprived the SNP of a vital issue, and allowed Labour to attack the SNP on the issue which now marked the Nationalists off from Labour: separatism. Devolution was thus replaced by the issue of separatism versus the United Kingdom. This also enabled Labour to play up other issues on which it possessed an advantage, notably fear of unemployment, and the fall in the rate of inflation.

Ironically, support for devolution, which had previously been sustained by Labour's weakness, was now sustained by its reviving strength. However, the fall in Nationalist support was accompanied by a cooling of public enthusiasm for devolution as the referendum campaign opened. The campaign itself caught the Labour movement unprepared. Most party members had come to accept devolution as a more or less desirable necessity, conceded in response to perceived public demand rather than fought for. Few realised that it would have to be fought for in a referendum in the face of a No campaign able to capitalise on the voters' fear of change and on the sudden fall in popularity of the Government in 1979. Labour's devolution campaign was thus lack-lustre and lacking in conviction, while the No campaign hammered away very effectively at fears of more government, more bureaucracy, higher taxation and devolution as a step on the slippery slope to separatism. There was no effective party campaign for a Yes vote, and it seems that only about half the constituency parties actively campaigned. Whereas the Conservatives managed to rally most of their voters behind the No banner, Labour supporters were confused and divided. Labour's majority support in Scotland was enough to give victory to the Yes side but by the smallest of margins, 51.6 to 48.4 per cent, with a Yes vote falling well short of the required 40 per cent of the total electorate.

There was even less support for a Yes vote at the referendum within the Welsh Labour Party. A majority of constituency Labour parties in Wales publicly opposed the Government's devolution proposals, as did seven of the eight Welsh counties, including Mid-Glamorgan which includes Labour's strongest industrial seats. Anti-devolution Labour MPs (the so-called 'gang of six'), headed by Leo Abse and Neil Kinnock, launched a powerful campaign against the Government, which divided and disoriented the grassroots of the Welsh Labour movement. Differences between English- and Welsh-speakers and the north and the south of Wales were exploited, and the involvement of Plaid Cymru on the Yes side of the campaign promoted the popular view that devolution was but the first step on the slippery slope which would lead to the break-up of the United Kingdom (Jones and Wilford, 1979). In these circumstances a confused Labour electorate either abstained or voted for the status quo, with the result that in Wales 79.7 per cent of the votes were against the Government's proposal.

The Scottish and Welsh referendums, intended to release the Labour Government from the horns of its dilemma, only impaled it further. In Wales, the clear-cut rejection left no option but to repeal the Wales Act. The Scottish result, however, gave no guidance as to the correct course of action. The Government was obliged to lay an order for repeal for the Act, and had to decide how to recommend Labour MPs to vote on it. The issue thus returned to Parliament, forcing the Government to rebuild its coalition, not only to get itself off the devolution hook but also to stay in office. If it laid the repeal order and tried to whip its own back-benchers into voting it down, it would risk defeat by a combination of Conservatives and dissident Labour back-benchers. On the other hand, if it failed to secure an early vote on the order, it would risk defeat, in a vote of confidence, from a combination of Conservatives and nationalists. In the event, it tried to delay the decision and conceded the initiative to the anti-devolutionists. For the Labour Party, the survival of the Government for a few more weeks, until the opinion polls improved and the memories of the Winter's industrial troubles receded, became the all-important aim, and the party in Scotland failed to join the SNP in a forceful 'Scotland said Yes' campaign. As a result, the impression was established in the media that devolution had been defeated in Scotland as well as in Wales. The Government's offer of all-party talks was rejected on all sides and the fragile coalition, which had kept it in being through years of minority government, collapsed in the face of a combined Conservative and SNP vote of confidence. The incoming Conservative Parliament then proceeded to repeal the Scotland Act by 301 votes to 206 and the Wales Act by 191 votes to 8.

V CONCLUSION

The Labour Party in Scotland and Wales, with varying degrees of reluctance, has moved a long way since 1973 but it remains a self-consciously centralising force. The devolution proposals were presented as consistent with maintaining the integrity of the United Kingdom. What has changed, however, is its assessment of what constitutes the essential elements of unity and the degree of centralisation necessary for the implementation of Labour's social and economic programmes. The party is obliged to direct its attention to the operation of structures created to implement policies which have not always fulfilled the original hopes. Centralised planning, once the cornerstone of Labour's policies, has been called into question following the failures of the 1960s, while the world economic crisis of the 1970s and 1980s has undermined the confidence, characteristic of the immediate post-war period, in the capacity of government to provide all-embracing economic solutions. Attitudes current in the 1960s and 1970s, favouring workers control and community action, the product of disillusionment with the traditional institutions of government, have contributed to a further erosion of Labour's commitment to a centralised state. The one constant factor during this period of reappraisal is the continuing belief in a unified economic policy that can effectively redistribute resources on both a social and a territorial basis.

In the Scottish and Welsh Labour parties, the erosion of confidence in the centralist state enabled various decentralist traditions to be re-incorporated, in some degree, into party thought. This was easier in Wales, where the decentralist tradition was identified with Welsh radicalism, than in Scotland, where the presence of a significant separatist party tainted the tradition and restricted Labour's room for manoeuvre. The nationalist parties might have determined the timing and pace of devolution, but their impact was upon a party at least partially willing to move in that direction and was therefore a necessary, although not sufficient, cause of that change in policy.

In the face of such a change, the party bureaucracy in London remained and remains centralist in attitude and practice, concerned with integrating the Scottish and Welsh Labour movements into the larger British unit, so maximising Labour's strength. However, when that integrative task proves difficult, under the pressure of electoral circumstances, the party is quite capable of adopting the appropriate innovations, even when as in 1974 in Scotland this means backing its judgement against that of the local leadership.

The outcome of the 1979 referendums and general election in Scotland and Wales has presented new problems to the Labour Party. In particular, it poses serious questions about the strength and genuineness of the party's commitment to devolution. Devolution policy, initially intended to be a stabilising influence, is now likely to be the cause of further instability. In Wales, where the referendum result was a clear-cut rejection, the party's position is relatively clear. Because of its greater commitment to devolution, the item can remain on the party agenda, no doubt in some vague form, but the possibility of it being implemented is remote. In Scotland, on the other hand, there is a need to construct a new scheme capable of winning the support of the party's own devolutionists, and reconciling the commitment to the unified economy with the need to safeguard Labour from any future nationalist revival. It is not easy for Labour to let the policy lapse in practice, as in the 1920s, without formally rejecting devolution.

Whatever the future of devolution, Labour's role as a party of territorial defence remains important. In fulfilling this role, it must take account of the three elements in its policy-making process. Electorally, it faces conflicting demands: there is the need to safeguard its Scottish and Welsh flanks from nationalist attacks while, to win a parliamentary majority, it needs to gain substantial support in the south-east and midlands of England. The increased salience of territorial issues following the devolution episode and the heightened sense of regional consciousness and competition could render this problem intractable. In terms of its role as a vehicle for working class interests, a policy of territorial defence would be an implied admission of the divisibility of the working class movement, as well as raising practical problems for economic management. At the level of ideology, these problems suggest that the prevailing tone is likely to remain centralist. However, despite the traumas of devolution, the party is still far from a coherent ideology of political decentralisation and, indeed, of the British state itself.

REFERENCES

Griffiths, J. (1978), *James Griffiths and his Times* (Cardiff: Labour Party).

Jones, J. B. and R. A. Wilford (1979) *The Welsh Veto: the Politics of the Devolution Campaign* (Glasgow: University of Strathclyde *Studies in Public Policy* no. 32).

Keating, M. J. and D. Bleiman (1979) *Labour and Scottish Nationalism* (London: Macmillan).

Labour Party, Scottish Council (1973) *Scotland and the UK* (Glasgow: Labour Party, Scottish Council).

Labour Party in Wales (1973) *The Attitudes of the Labour Party in Wales Towards the Machinery of Government* (Cardiff: Labour Party).

Labour Party in Wales (1975) *The Welsh Assembly: Some Questions and Answers* (Cardiff: Labour Party).

MacCormick, J. (1955) *Flag in the Wind* (London: Gollancz).

Morgan, K. O. (1963) *Wales in British Politics, 1868–1922* (Cardiff: University of Wales Press).

——(1966) in Glanmôr Williams (ed.) *Merthyr Politics* (Cardiff: University of Wales Press).

Osmond, J. (1977) *Creative Conflict: The Politics of Welsh Devolution* (London: Routledge & Kegan Paul).

Philip, A. Butt (1975) *The Welsh Question* (Cardiff: University of Wales Press).

Sancton, A. (1976) 'British Socialist Theories of the Division of Power by Area', *Political Studies*, xxiv, 2, 158– 174.

7 United Kingdom Nationalist Parties: One Nationalism or Three?*

IAN McALLISTER

Although traditional theories of nationalism differ in many ways, most agree on one fundamental point: the core idea of nationalism is the congruence of a political and social community. Nationalism embodies the belief that a territorially distinct group bound together by a common sense of identity – whether based on language, race, culture or some other social attribute – should have its own form of government (see Kedourie, 1960; Gellner, 1964). The resurgence of political conflict on the peripheries of many developed Western nation states has undermined this traditional theory of nationalism. The political mobilisation of territorially distinct groups has shown that nationalism can take a variety of forms, emerging at different times, in different places, and under differing political, social and economic conditions.

Nationalist groups vary in their fundamental aims, for while all seek some political change, this can range from complete independence to limited autonomy. Often, this aim is combined with non-territorial aims, such as linguistic or religious reforms. They differ in the methods used to mobilise support from the community or nation which they claim to represent; some rely on pressure-group tactics, others on an electoral party approach, or a variety of methods. Most can mobilise only a minority of their community.

The United Kingdom represents an apposite example of diversity, since it sustains significant nationalist parties in three of its four constituent nations:

* This chapter was written while the author was employed in the Centre for the Study of Public Policy, University of Strathclyde. Financial support was provided by SSRC grant HR/4689 to study the Political Structure of the United Kingdom. My thanks to Professor Richard Rose, Peter Mair and Edward Page for commenting on an earlier draft of the chapter.

Scotland, Wales and Northern Ireland. The major nationalist party in each of these nations possesses the fundamental defining attribute of nationalism; that is, it seeks self-government for what it perceives as a social community. In Scotland, the Scottish National Party (SNP) defines this common social bond as Scottish identity or residence; in Wales, Plaid Cymru sees the bond expressed in Welsh cultural and linguistic values; and in Northern Ireland, the Social Democratic and Labour Party (SDLP) demonstrates the minority Catholic community's social, political and religious isolation from the majority Protestant community, and its historic links, reinforced by religion, with the population of the Irish Republic.

Each of the three parties examined here – the SNP, Plaid Cymru and the SDLP – have used a variety of political means towards their goals. Initially, party political organisation was viewed as a contingent and not a fixed activity. From the mid-1960s, the Scottish and Welsh nationalist parties began to reassess their strategy, and organised primarily as political parties to contest elections (McAllister, 1981; Davies, 1979). In Northern Ireland, the Nationalist Party refused to adopt a political organisation, and reforming elements within the Catholic community formed a competing political party in 1970, the SDLP.

The Ulster Unionist Party, historically the political voice of the Protestant community, has a distinctive communal base and a territorial attachment. Moreover, a substantial proportion of its supporters could be termed 'proto-nationalist', in so far as they give allegiance to a perceived Northern Ireland state and not to the sovereign authority, the Westminster Parliament.[2] Rose's survey (1971, pp. 240–4) demonstrated the existence of this latent Ulster nationalism within the Protestant community, in that a majority of Protestants would endorse violence to defend the Protestant state. In the past, various Ulster Unionist leaders, such as William Craig, have tapped embryonic Protestant nationalism by advocating independence for the Province and the severance of the British link. However, collectively the party has sought – and continues to seek – the retention of Northern Ireland's link with Britain and the maintenance of the United Kingdom territorial status quo; for this reason it is excluded from the analysis.[3]

The object of this chapter is to compare the three nationalist parties in the broad spectrum of their activities and outlook. One possibility is that the parties show *commonality* in their aims and policies, and a comparable pattern of electoral support. The alternative is that the parties show *diversity* along these dimensions. To test these two models systematically and consistently, the first section examines the aims and conference motions of the three parties. The second section examines each party's electoral performance and the territorial dispersion of its support. The third section assesses whether or not the three nationalist parties have a common record of success or failure in their impact on government policy toward the United Kingdom, which all seek to alter to a significant extent.

I   COMMUNALISM IN CONTENT

The political goals of a party are ultimately and relatively fixed. If and when they are achieved, then a party could cease to have a role. By contrast, policies are programmatic statements of action intended to obtain remedial action. For political parties, goals are long-term and non-negotiable; they unite the party faithful and ensure the purity of party doctrine. By contrast, policies are short-term negotiable objectives which accept the necessity of compromise and bargaining associated with electoral competition. Political goals can thus be seen as reflexive, or 'inducements to evoke adequate contributions from all members of the organisation', while policies are transitive goals which represent 'an intended impact of the organisation upon its environment' (Mohr, 1973, p. 476; see also Thompson, 1967, pp. 127–8).

Conventional political parties normally state goals as aspirations, ethereal in content and vague in interpretation. They concentrate efforts upon developing policies, which can form an opposition platform from which to negotiate and bargain, and a basis for governmental action. For nationalist political parties, however, an exclusive emphasis on policies is difficult; by their very nature, their ultimate goal of independence is inherent in their appeal: the goal of self-government for their community is what makes them nationalist. In addition, ultimate nationalist aims may be the single attribute uniting a politically heterogeneous membership. Consequently, nationalist parties exhibit a constant tension between goals, which must be continually emphasised to maintain their *raison d'être*, and the electoral necessity of putting forward policies to mobilise the maximum vote.

Given this distinction between goals and policies, there are two alternative patterns along which nationalist parties could develop. The first is that the parties could be policy-oriented, having ultimate goals which exist only as vague aspirations; in practice, they would concentrate on policies which would form an immediate basis for negotiation and compromise. The other alternative is that the parties could have one overriding, non-negotiable goal, which would either provide the exclusive basis for party policy or, where other policies did exist, dominate them. This section discusses these alternative patterns in relation to the policy aims of the SNP, Plaid Cymru, and the Northern Ireland Nationalists and SDLP, by examining constitutional goals, and whether or not the parties have been prepared to compromise these goals by accepting transitional policies, or by emphasising policies not distinctively nationalist in content.

The formal constitutional goals of the SNP have remained relatively static since the drafting of its 1949 constitution, which affirmed a commitment to Scottish independence achieved through electoral methods, and laid down that SNP members should not also belong to other parties. The drafting of the constitution was a response to various schisms within the party, between those who wished to compromise on a transitional form of limited autonomy prior to independence, and those who adhered to an absolute and non-negotiable commitment to Scottish independence (see McAllister, forthcoming). The formal goals laid down in the 1949 party constitution were:

(A) Self-Government for Scotland – that is, the restoration of Scottish National Sovereignty by the establishment of a democratic Scottish Government, freely elected by the Scottish People, and whose authority will be limited only by such agreement as will be freely entered into with other nations or states for the purpose of furthering international co-operation and world peace.

(B) The furtherance of all Scottish interests. (SNP, 1949, p. 1)

The goals have been preserved, although in 1968 a minor change was made by stating that Scottish sovereignty would be achieved through 'the establishment of a democratic Scottish Parliament within the Commonwealth' (SNP, 1968, p. 1).

Prior to the emergence of the devolution issue in the late 1960s, little attention was devoted to the practical steps to independence or the extent to which any advance would be by compromise. Indeed, it was often considered that independence was immutable. Scottish self-government was simply a desirable ultimate goal, justified on a variety of grounds. Early statements justified it on negative anti-English terms. For example, the 1955 election manifesto saw the SNP's first task as 'to undermine and ultimately destroy all vestiges of English state authority in Scotland'.[4] Other arguments have been based on morality, or Scottish nationhood (see Wolfe, 1968, p. 8). More recent justifications, fuelled by the discovery of North Sea oil, have been focussed on economics and the argument that Scotland, freed from England, would be an affluent and prosperous society (see Urwin, 1979).

Since the SNP was avowedly electoral and constitutional, it was assumed that the party would have a secure majority of Scottish support before self-government would be achieved. This policy was made explicit in 1968:

> When a clear majority of the Scottish Parliamentary seats are held by SNP MPs, they will ask the United Kingdom Parliament to set up a Scottish legislature with full control over all the affairs of Scotland. Failing such agreement in London, the SNP MPs and any other Scottish MPs who care to join them, will form a Scottish government, loyal to the Crown.   (SNP, 1968, p. 7)

Under this approach, the first Scottish government would submit a draft constitution to the electorate for approval, after which a general election would be held. A Scottish draft constitution was ratified by the 1976 SNP annual conference (SNP, 1976). In its evidence to the Kilbrandon Commission, the SNP merely restated its claim for full self-government, and outlined the principles upon which a Scottish constitution might be based.

The prospect of devolution under the 1974– 9 Labour government forced the SNP to consider whether or not it would accept a compromise or transitional stage between the present and independence. A lobby within the SNP successfully argued for such a compromise. The opposing lobby, based mainly on branch organisation, saw Scottish independence as an absolute, non-negotiable aim. The new strategy of compromise was justified on two grounds. First, it was argued that a majority of the Scottish electorate favoured some form of devolution, but that they were not, as yet, in favour of independence. Secondly, it was believed that 'an acceptably far-reaching scheme of legislative and executive devolution' would be 'an essential step in the process which will lead to Scottish independence' (SNP, n.d., p. 1).

Plaid Cymru's constitutional goals are greatly influenced by the party's origins as a movement dedicated to defending the Welsh language. The original list of goals excluded self-government, the party's main theoretician, Saunders Lewis, calling it 'an opportunity for endless disagreement within the party' (quoted in Davies, 1979, p. 44). The evolution of Plaid's constitutional aims has thus made Welsh independence the means of preserving Welsh cultural and linguistic values. Lewis underlined this in an influential statement (Lewis, 1975, p. 5; 1st edn, 1926) by arguing that nationalists should have 'self-government. Not independence. Not even unconditional freedom. But just as much freedom as may be necessary to establish and safeguard civilisation in Wales.'

The aims of the contemporary constitution are:

(a) To secure self-government for Wales

(b) To safeguard the culture, language, traditions and the economic life of Wales

(c) To secure for Wales the right to become a member of the United Nations Organisation. (Plaid Cymru, 1976, p. 1)

The only significant change in recent years was the 1966 addition of a phrase about safeguarding the 'economic life of Wales'. This change has been interpreted as an attempt to move away from 'a defensive, special interest association of the Welsh-speaking minority, to one seeking to promote Welsh interests and to build up support among the Welsh population as a whole' (Rawkins, 1975, p. 457).

Since the political goal of self-government has remained rooted in the party's origins, it has rarely been challenged. In common with the SNP, the establishment of the Commission on the Constitution forced a reassessment. The initial response to the Kilbrandon Commission was to produce a plan for the constitutional details of self-government, *The Peaceful Road to Self-Government*, which was ratified at a special party conference in Cardiff in March 1970. *The Peaceful Road to Self-Government* envisaged the establishment of a Welsh Parliament 'having powers and authority as full and complete in relation to Wales as the United Kingdom Parliament has over the affairs of the United Kingdom' (Plaid Cymru, 1970, Motion 1). This broad framework has remained Plaid policy on the constitution since 1970 and, while welcoming the Kilbrandon proposals 'as a first step' (Plaid Cymru, 1974a, Section 3.21), it argued that the Welsh Assembly should enjoy the same powers as the Scottish Assembly and include economic and industrial development powers (Plaid Cymru, n.d., p. 9). The Government's subsequent removal of legislative powers from the projected Welsh Assembly was opposed by Plaid on the basis that 'if the legislative, policy-making, function is divorced from the executive function, the policy-making body does not have direct experience of the way its policies work or fail to work' (Plaid Cymru, 1974b, p. 1). Throughout the devolution debate between 1974 and 1979, it was argued that the proposals for Welsh devolution should have parity with those for Scotland.

The constitutional goals of the Northern Ireland Nationalists and the SDLP differ considerably from those of the SNP and Plaid Cymru. First, the broad constitutional goal of all Northern Ireland politicians seeking electoral support within the Catholic community has been the Province's integration with another state, the Irish Republic, rather than the autonomy desired by Scottish and Welsh nationalists. The community for which they sought political change consisted of Ulster Catholics and the people of the Irish Republic, considered one community by religion and a common historical heritage. Secondly, the Northern Ireland Nationalists never formally organised as a political party and thus did not have a party constitution to state goals or an election manifesto or policy statement. On the contrary, goals were seen as inherent in the nationalist label. By contrast, the SDLP, while formally writing Irish unity into its constitution, also has socio-economic concerns, as its choice of name emphasises.

The constitutional goals of the Nationalists, therefore, were rarely adumbrated. They did not operate as an organised political party in the modern sense; elected representatives acted, as one Nationalist MP admitted, 'in harmony but not in harness' (*Irish News*, 1 November 1966). The single aim of Irish unity was accepted by all Catholic electors, and since voting was along sectarian lines, electors rarely felt the need (or had the opportunity) to elicit the views of their community's election candidates. As Eddie McAteer, the party leader throughout the 1960s, declared in a rare statement of principles, 'our task is to safeguard our mandate for a united Ireland' (*Irish News*, 13 December 1965).

The Nationalists' demise in the early 1970s and their replacement by the SDLP as the electoral representative of the Catholic community brought in its wake a new set of political priorities. The SDLP constitution stated, as one goal, the promotion 'of Irish unity based on the consent of a majority of people in Northern Ireland' (SDLP, 1975, p. 1). Since Northern Ireland has always had a Protestant majority opposed to Irish unity, this conditional clause freed the SDLP to compromise its constitutional aims in favour of reforming the contemporary structure of the Northern Ireland state. Crucially, the SDLP differed from the Nationalists in that they were prepared, in the medium term at least, to envisage political changes taking place within the context of the British link. Moreover, Irish unity was but one goal among many. The SDLP constitution also listed as goals cooperation with other socialist parties and trades unions, 'the abolition of all form of religious, political or class discrimination', and 'the public ownership and democratic control of such essential industries and services as the common good requires' (SDLP, 1975, p. 1).

After less than a year of parliamentary opposition, the SDLP withdrew from Stormont in July 1971 in protest against the British Army's shooting two civilians in Londonderry; this abstentionist policy was underpinned by the introduction of internment without trial less than a month later. The suspension of the Stormont Parliament in March 1972, and the introduction of direct rule, enabled the SDLP to re-enter parliamentary politics. The party's proposals for the 1973 Assembly elections combined the twin goals of power-sharing at the executive level of government and an in-stitutionalised link with the Irish Republic, which would have independent powers to bring about Irish unity 'by planned and agreed steps' (SDLP, 1973, p. 2). The SDLP willingly participated in the British government's 1973 plan to establish a legislative assembly in Northern Ireland, with a power-sharing executive formed from the SDLP, Alliance and the Ulster Unionists, and a Council of Ireland coordinating joint activities between Northern Ireland and the Irish Republic. Since the collapse of the power-sharing executive in 1974, the two goals have remained the fundamental basis of SDLP thinking on the constitution. Occasionally, one goal has been given prominence over the other to accord with the prevailing political climate. For example, during the 1975–6 Constitutional Convention, power-sharing rather than the Council of Ireland was emphasised. Since then, the Council of Ireland and the 'Irish Dimension' have achieved predominance over power-sharing.

In terms of constitutional goals, all three United Kingdom nationalist parties present both long-term non-negotiable goals, yet have been prepared to compromise on short-term policies which they have perceived to be advantageous. Between the parties, the degree of compromise varies. For example, the British government's 1973 plans for Northern Ireland were very close to the SDLP's declaration, and hence the party lost little by accepting them. The degree of compromise on fundamental goals in Scotland and Wales involved by devolution was large. This was reflected in the debate within the SNP and Plaid Cymru over whether or not to campaign in favour of the Labour government's devolution proposals in the referendum (Balsom and McAllister, 1979, p. 398), and in the reaction against the devolution compromise in both parties since the loss of the 1979 referendums. In short, nationalist parties have a commonality of ultimate goals, but differ somewhat about tactical compromise on constitutional policies.

A second way to test for commonality or diversity is to examine what emphasis, if any, nationalist parties give to socio-economic policies that are not distinctively nationalist. Manifestos present a readily available and consistent summary of party policies, but suffer from the drawback that they are drawn up by party managers and leaders, and may not accurately reflect the outlook of the party membership. For this reason, conference motions from grass-roots activists are examined here. It is worth noting that in the SNP and Plaid Cymru, an executive sub-committee decides which conference motions will be put forward for debate. In the SDLP, all submitted conference motions are theoretically debatable, a minority are composited, and the rest normally fall in default of conference time.

Table 7.1 gives a breakdown of 1979 conference motions in four headings, subdivided into various categories. Two main points emerge from the table. First, all three parties give some emphasis to each category. The

TABLE 7.1 Analysis of conference motions, 1979

	SNP %	Plaid Cymru %	SDLP %
National policy			
Devolution	2	7	11
Language policy	2	14	–
Total	(4)	(21)	(11)
Organisation			
Party strategy	4	4	2
Internal party affairs	9	14	11
Total	(13)	(18)	(13)
Socio-economic policy			
Environment, energy, local			
government, housing and planning	18	14	21
EEC, agriculture, education	16	4	15
Health and social services	4	4	10
Industrial policy, employment	17	7	14
Total	(55)	(29)	(60)
Other			
Administration of justice,			
law reform, policing	2	7	8
Miscellaneous	26	25	9
Total	(28)	(32)	(17)
Overall total	100	100	100
(N)	(54)	(28)	(138)

Source: SNP (1979); Plaid Cymru (1979); SDLP (1979).

second point is that although a majority of motions fall under the socio-economic heading in the SNP and SDLP, only 29 per cent of Plaid Cymru motions are so classified. Plaid's reduced socio-economic emphasis may be ascribed to the importance of the Welsh language as a conference issue encompassing, for example, education and the social services.

Overall, the three United Kingdom nationalist parties appear to operate at two distinct levels: at one level, there is a long-term non-negotiable territorial goal, enshrined in the party constitution and repeated in statements and manifestos; at another level there are short-term negotiable policies, often viewed as transitional steps toward independence. The salience of devolution as a political issue from 1974 to 1979 forced the parties to react to immediate political events without forcing a major compromise on long-term goals.

There are two main reasons to account for United Kingdom nationalist parties emphasising programmatic policies, both stemming from the adoption of electoral competition as a political means to achieving their goals. First, electoral competition involves a nationalist party in appealing for votes against competitors. As Downs (1957) showed, competition for votes forces parties to offer material inducements to the widest possible number of electors. A nationalist party is thus forced to emulate the tactics, style and scope of policies used by the other parties within the party system. Each of the three United Kingdom nationalist parties has been forced to compete for votes on the same basis as the dominant party, and to win a majority of the vote each has had to seek support in the dominant party's electoral domain. In Scotland and Wales, the SNP and Plaid Cymru have sought to build up the vote in the industrial areas dominated by the Labour Party (see Rawkins, 1978). In Northern Ireland, the SDLP has made occasional attempts over the past decade to attract Protestant voters away from the dominant Ulster Unionist Party (see McAllister, 1977, pp. 122–3).

Electoral expediency is the second reason why the nationalist parties have utilised consensus and bargaining. Only committed nationalist voters will support the party's fundamental long-term goal; the adoption of short-term policies may attract less committed voters. This is clearly illustrated in the constitutional options of nationalist identifiers in the three nations (see Table 7.2). In each case, identifiers are divided between the party's short-term policy (devolution of some form) and the long-term goal of independence.

In Scotland and Wales, those with a preference for devolution, not independence, *form the largest group of nationalist supporters*. In Northern Ireland, only a bare majority (52 per cent) of SDLP supporters favour some form of change which would alter the constitutional status of the Province in the direction of Irish unity *per se*. This dissonance between the aims of party leaders and the aims of voters is not unique to nationalist parties; on the contrary it is a phenomenon found in most political parties (see McCloskey *et al.*, 1963; Pomper, 1972).

TABLE 7.2 The constitutional options of nationalist identifiers, 1978–9 [a]

	Scotland (Sept. 1979) %	Wales (Feb. 1979) %	Northern Ireland (Summer 1978) %
No change	1	12	2
Devolution	56	47	46
Independence/ self-government	42	41	52
Don't know	1	–	–
Total	100	100	100
(N)	(154)	(95)	(164)

[a] Options for each question are as follows.

Scotland
No change: 'keep the present system'.
Devolution: 'non-directly elected Scottish Assembly; directly elected Scottish Assembly; Scottish Parliament'.
Independence/self-government: 'make Scotland completely independent'.

Wales
No change: 'no assembly at all, keeping the government of Wales much as it is now'.
Devolution: 'an assembly as currently proposed by the government; a strong assembly, similar to that proposed for Scotland with its own law-making powers'.
Independence/self-government: 'complete self-government for Wales'.

Northern Ireland
No change: 'direct rule from London'.
Devolution: 'devolved government based on majority rule or power-sharing'.
Independence/self-government: 'Irish unity, federal Ireland; independent Northern Ireland; condominium'.

Sources: Scotland, Sept. 1979 ORC survey; Wales, Feb. 1979 Abacus survey; Northern Ireland, Moxon-Browne (1979, Table 3.1).

II DIVERSITY IN ELECTORAL SUCCESS

Whether to adopt an electoral strategy is a major question facing any nationalist party. It can, additionally or alternatively, seek to achieve its goals by acting as a pressure group upon government through already established parties, and/or by extra-constitutional means. The case for being an electoral group is particularly arguable in the circumstances of the three parties considered here, since all are minority nationalist parties, that is, parties that could never hope to win a majority of seats in the 635-seat British

House of Commons because they nominate only 12, 36 or 71 candidates (Esman, 1977).

In the event, the SNP has given pre-eminence to electoral politics, and Plaid Cymru has given primary emphasis to electoral politics, while also having overlapping membership with language protest groups occasionally using extra-constitutional means. For example, Gwynfor Evans, Plaid Cymru President, threatened to fast to death for an exclusive Welsh language television channel, and the Government acceded to this pressure in September 1980. The Northern Ireland case is different, as the Province sustains two traditions of seeking political change: by electoral competition in the British style, or extra-constitutionally in the Irish style 'by all means necessary'. Groups and individuals can invoke *both* traditions in order to advance political aims. The emergence of the Provisional IRA in the early 1970s as the Catholic expression of the extra-constitutional physical force tradition created the conditions for a constitutional party to negotiate on behalf of the Catholic community, and the SDLP has filled this role.

For all three nationalist parties, the adoption of electoral competition has imposed particular constraints and imperatives. If patterns of support for each of the parties were the same, then success would mean a collective challenge to Westminster authority. Alternatively, if patterns diverge, a combination of success and failure would aid conflict management by the centre.

The three nationalist parties display very different patterns of post-war electoral growth (see Table 7.3). In Scotland, the SNP has volatile support: between 1964 and 1970 the party had a relatively consistent vote and saved a high proportion of its deposits in seats contested. In the 1970s the vote was unstable; and between February 1974 and 1979 the vote increased, creating more winnable seats. By contrast, Plaid Cymru wins a steady but low share of the vote, with a large number of lost deposits and no security of seats. Northern Ireland Nationalists, SDLP, and other Irish Unity candidates win a substantial portion of the vote where seats are contested and, where the vote is not split between competing nationalist candidates, some seats are winnable.

For a successful electoral strategy, the nationalist parties must gain cross-local support from within the territory. The more concentrated and localised their support is, then the greater will be the difficulty in mobilising voters outside their core group, even if this guarantees a few seats. Scotland, Wales and Northern Ireland are not only politically distinctive from England, but also there are important political differences between areas *within* the nations. This is aptly demonstrated by the within-nation dispersion of the nationalist vote. It has shown a distinct territorial imbalance

TABLE 7.3 Nationalist electoral performance in Westminster elections, 1945–79

Election	Scotland: SNP			Wales: Plaid Cymru			Northern Ireland: United Ireland [a]		
	% share of vote	Candidates	% share in contested seats	% share of vote	Candidates	% share in contested seats	% share of vote	Candidates	% share in contested seats
1945	1.2	8	7.6	1.1	6	6.3	18.8	3	30.5
1950	0.4	3	7.4	1.2	7	6.1	25.2	6	45.6
1951	0.3	2	12.2	0.7	4	5.9	27.2	4	49.1
1955	0.5	2	14.5	3.1	11	10.9	26.0	13	26.0
1959	0.8	5	10.7	5.2	20	9.7	11.0	12	11.0
1964	2.4	15	10.9	4.8	23	7.9	18.2	13	18.2
1966	5.0	23	14.3	4.3	20	8.3	21.1	8	39.2
1970	11.4	65	12.2	11.5	36	11.5	23.3	8	32.7
1974 Feb.	21.9	70	22.1	10.7	36	10.7	30.1	20	30.1
1974 Oct.	30.4	71	30.4	10.8	36	10.8	29.8	15	35.3
1979	17.3	71	17.3	8.1	36	8.1	28.0	22	33.4

[a] Includes Nationalists, Republican, Sinn Fein, Irish Labour, Republic Labour, National Democratic Party, SDLP, IIP, etc.

Source: Rose and McAllister (1982, Table 4.3).

that has remained largely independent of the growth or decline in the vote (cf. Hechter, 1975, Ch. 7).

In Scotland the rural areas outside the central industrial belt have been consistently stronger in their support for the SNP. In periods of nationalist electoral advance, this regional pattern becomes less marked, partly, at least, as a result of the differing patterns of candidacies caused by the Liberals. Plaid Cymru's support has been concentrated largely in the rural, Welsh-speaking areas of north Wales and little inroad has been made into the Labour vote in industrial south Wales (Cox, 1970; Balsom, 1979). In Northern Ireland, the Nationalists virtually withdrew from electoral competition in Belfast and the surrounding areas after 1949. This is paralleled in contemporary electoral politics by the SDLP's relative inability to find support in the urban east: the bulk of its electoral support is drawn from Catholics outside Belfast, and particularly in the rural areas west of the River Bann, which bifurcates the Province (McAllister, 1980).

There is both within-nation diversity in the electoral appeal of nationalist parties, and diversity between nations. Table 7.4 gives the mean, standard

TABLE 7.4   The within-nation dispersion of the nationalist vote, February 1974 to 1979 [a]

	SNP			Plaid Cymru			SDLP		
	mean	s. dev.	V	mean	s. dev.	V	mean	s. dev.	V
Feb. 1974	22.4	11.7	0.52	11.7	10.4	0.89	22.6	13.5	0.60
Oct. 1974	30.6	9.4	0.31	11.6	11.1	0.96	21.8	18.1	0.83
1979	17.5	10.7	0.61	9.2	10.9	1.18	20.3	15.3	0.75

[a] The table is based on the 71 constituencies in Scotland, 36 in Wales, and 12 in Northern Ireland. Uncontested constituencies are excluded.
S. dev.: standard deviation;   V (coefficient of variation): the standard deviation devided by the mean.

Source: Craig (1975) and newspaper sources for 1979.

deviation and coefficient of variation (V) for the nationalist vote in the February 1974 to 1979 General Elections. For each party, the degree of dispersion, measured by the coefficient of variation, has increased between February 1974 and 1979. Moreover, for the SNP and Plaid Cymru, the drop in their aggregate vote has resulted in a greater dispersion, particularly for the Plaid, which records the highest coefficient of all – 1.18 in 1979. The SDLP currently ranks second in the territorial variation of its vote, and the SNP has relatively least variation.

A nationalist party does not seek to win votes on as broad a front as an all-Britain party. First of all it seeks to mobilise the support of a core group. In Wales and Northern Ireland the core groups – Welsh-speakers and Catholics, respectively – represent a minority of the population. Only in Scotland does the core group of Scottish identifiers form a majority (56 per cent). To gain an electoral majority, nationalist parties would need to attract an overwhelming majority of the core group, plus a significant fraction of non-core group members in Wales and Northern Ireland. In practice, only the SDLP manages to win majority support from its core group; 65 per cent of Catholics support the SDLP (see Table 7.5). The Alliance Party receives the allegiance of 12 per cent of Catholics. By contrast, the SNP and Plaid Cymru win only the support of 21 per cent and 17 per cent of the core groups, respectively. The *total* vote for the parties varies, however, since the total

TABLE 7.5   Nationalist support and group mobilisation

(a) Scotland: National identification (1979)

| | | Voting intention: | | |
	SNP	Other parties	Total	(N)
Scottish	21	79	100	(327)
British	8	92	100	(217)
English	–	100	100	(10)
Other	16	84	100	(25)

Source: SSRC 1979 Scottish Election Survey, conducted by Dr J. A. Brand and Dr W. L. Miller, University of Strathclyde.

(b) Wales: Language (1978–9)

| | | Voting intention: | | |
	Plaid Cymru	Other parties	Total	(N)
Welsh-speakers	17	83	100	(992)
Non-Welsh-speakers	4	96	100	(2,577)

Source: Extracted from Balsom (1979, Table 2), based on aggregated surveys conducted in 1978 and 1979.

(c) Northern Ireland: Religion (1978)

| | | Voting intention: | | |
	SDLP	Other parties	Total	(N)
Protestant	0.5	99	100	(792)
Catholic	65	35	100	(329)

Source: Extracted from Moxon-Browne (1979, p. 13).

vote is a function of the *size* of the core group, as well as the proportion mobilised. All the parties fail to win any significant level of support outside the core group. The SNP is supported by 8 per cent of non-Scottish identifier group members, Plaid Cymru by 4 per cent of non-Welsh-speakers, and the SDLP by less than 1 per cent of non-Catholics. There is thus a commonality in confining support to a core group, but diversity in the degree of success or failure in gaining support within that group.

Cross-class support is a further indicator of a successful electoral strategy. Gaining nationwide support for nationalist political demands requires mobilising both middle class and working class support, since core group attributes are not class exclusive. All three nationalist parties have a common ability to draw support from both middle class and working class voters (see Table 7.6). Moreover, this pattern has persisted through a number of

TABLE 7.6   Class support for nationalist parties, 1978–9

	Scotland		Wales		Northern Ireland	
	Total %	SNP %	Total %	PC %	Total %	SDLP %
Social class AB	6	8	9	12	15	11
C1	19	28	21	23	25	22
C2	34	36	37	38	28	30
DE	41	28	33	27	32	37
Total	100	100	100	100	100	100
(N)	(579)	(90)	(3,569)	(272)	(1,121)	(218)

Sources: As for Table 7.5.

elections (see Jaensch, 1976, p. 313; Philip, 1973, p. 150). Plaid Cymru most nearly draws support from all classes, the SDLP second, and the SNP third. In Wales and Scotland, moreover, the nationalist parties tend to draw support more evenly in proportion to the class composition of the population than do the British parties. In Northern Ireland, all the communal parties – the Official Unionists and Democratic Unionists even more than the SDLP – tend to draw their support evenly across all classes.

Over all four measures, the three nationalist parties tend to follow established parties. Interestingly, British parties also have a significant amount of cross-class support in Scotland, Wales and England (cf. Butler and Stokes, 1975; Rose, 1980). Their most conspicuous common attribute is negative: a failure to mobilise sufficient electoral support to the level required for a parliamentary breakthrough by the first-past-the-post electoral system. On *present* patterns of support, none of the parties has any likelihood of gaining political power through constitutional channels.

III   UNITED KINGDOM NATIONALISMS: SUCCESS OR FAILURE?

In examining systematically and comparatively the similarities and differences between the three nationalist parties in Scotland, Wales and Northern Ireland, two models were proposed: a *commonality* model which suggested convergence between the three parties on aims, policies and electoral support; and a *diversity* model which stated the obverse. The evidence presented has not conclusively validated either model.

The nationalist parties' constitutional goals and programmatic policies suggested commonality: each party clearly possessed an overriding non-negotiable goal which was seen in a long-term perspective, together with a set of short-term negotiable policies on constitutional and programmatic fields. Each party has had a *dual* time perspective, which has enabled it to pursue each aim on a different time-scale. Each party also faces recurring difficulties in resolving competing claims for short-term and long-term success. The SNP and Plaid Cymru were each deeply divided over the propriety of campaigning for a 'yes' vote in the March 1979 devolution referendums. One group argued that, as an electoral party, they would have to support devolution as a positive step, even though it fell below their expectations; another group warned that such a course could undermine their credibility as a nationalist party seeking fundamental constitutional change. In both parties, the debate was resolved in favour of campaigning for a 'yes' vote, albeit by a narrow majority within Plaid Cymru. A similar dilemma faced the SDLP in late 1979, when the British Government launched talks on Northern Ireland's constitutional future. Participation could have undermined their public commitment to Irish unity, since this topic was excluded from the formal agenda; abstention could undermine their role as an electoral party committed to negotiation and compromise. After much internal conflict (including the resignation of their leader, Gerry Fitt) the SDLP decided on participation.

While both Scottish and Welsh nationalists believe in the economic viability of a small independent state, they differ in their philosophical outlooks. Welsh nationalism tends to be left or radical, even commending a syndicalist state based on self-sufficient small communities. In the words of founder Saunders Lewis: 'a free nation is a community of communities, and the hour has come for small communities to join together in a co-operative and diversified system in order to maintain freedom' (quoted in Osmond, 1977, p. 12). By contrast, Scottish nationalism endorses technological progress in a fully modern economy. The SNP declares that an independent Scotland could be an advanced, prosperous technological state, like Scandinavian neighbours. The SDLP is similar to the SNP in seeing itself as socially and economically progressive, rather than culturally defensive, like Plaid Cymru or an older generation of Irish nationalists.

In terms of voter mobilisation, the three parties show diversity; they differ in their mobilisation of core group and non-core group support, although they share the same inability to gain an electoral majority. Without an electoral majority, a party cannot argue that it has a mandate to implement its constitutional goals. Yet a political party need not gain an electoral majority to make a significant impact on the political system. As in the United States, the success of a minor or third party can also be gauged by whether or not it has succeeded in placing its central issue (or issues) on the political agenda.

As pressure groups, the United Kingdom nationalist parties have had a common measure of success. All three succeeded in placing their primary concern on the agenda of Westminster politics in the 1966–70 Parliament. They did this by the very novelty of their presence, and by disproportionate attention given to their questions in the Chamber. Moreover, they posed an *unknown* threat of future electoral difficulties. It is important to recall that the first MPs of both the SNP and Plaid Cymru entered the Commons by winning seats from the governing Labour Party at by-elections. The governing party, not surprisingly, sought to make concessions. It made gestures to political demands for distinctive national status, for example, the establishment of the Royal Commission on the Constitution, and pressures on the Ulster Unionists to adopt reform in Northern Ireland. Moreover, in the period in question, there was a tendency for public expenditure to rise. If per capita public expenditure is taken as a measure of influence, between 1964 and 1979 this increased in constant terms in Scotland and Wales by 68 and 60 per cent respectively (McAllister, Parry and Rose, 1979, p. 61).

The 1974 General Elections fortuitously placed the nationalist parties in an abnormally strong parliamentary position. The Labour Government quickly lost its overall majority and finally fell by one vote. In such circumstances, the small number of nationalist MPs enjoyed a dispro-portionate importance. The adoption of the 1978 Devolution Acts for Scotland and Wales, against considerable opposition from within the governing party as well as the Opposition, produced tangible proof of their parliamentary influence. The SDLP also secured firm government backing to guaranteeing it a seat in any devolved government for Northern Ireland, effectively vetoing the recommendation of the majority of the 1975 Northern Ireland Constitutional Convention.

If electoral gains are made the criteria of success, then none of the nationalist parties could ever win a British general election. But that is not their long-term goal, and short-term policies are directed towards territorial interest, not British office. Ironically, as pressure groups rather than electoral parties, all three have shown a significant impact upon Westminster government. The commitment to party competition within a constitutional framework has made each of the three groups political *parties* as well as *nationalists*. Unlike Sinn Fein, United Kingdom nationalist parties emphasise constitutional politics above simple nationalist appeals. The very fact that nationalists contest (and occasionally win) seats has led British governments to give some ground, thus allowing nationalist electoral parties to claim some success as pressure groups, while recording failure to date in pursuit of their long-term goals.

NOTES

1. Irish Nationalists and Republicans have consistently agreed that the Ulster Catholic community and the population of the Irish Republic constitute the Irish nation, but they have disagreed about whether or not the Ulster Protestant community constitutes a part of the Irish nation.
2. Protestant defiance of the sovereign Parliament has been traced to many factors. The most persuasive explanation is to be found in Miller (1978). He argues that the Ulster Protestants were by-passed by the nation-building phase in the early 19th century, and for this reason continue to give *unconditional* allegiance to the British monarch, but *conditional* allegiance to the Westminster Parliament based on a social contract theory deriving from Locke.
3. Ulster Unionist MPs at Westminster supported Scottish and Welsh devolution and voted for the two devolution bills. However, their support was tactical, in that they wished to see devolution returned to Northern Ireland, and saw this as a more likely occurrence if Scotland and Wales were granted it. They argued that devolution should take place only within the framework of the maintenance of United Kingdom unity.
4. John MacCormick, an SNP founder member who later organised the Scottish Convention, frequently underlined Scotland's 'historical and racial origins' (MacCormick, 1955, p. 46). See also Spence (1928, p. 70).

REFERENCES

Balsom, Denis (1979) *The Nature and Distribution of Support for Plaid Cymru* (Glasgow: University of Strathclyde Studies in Public Policy no. 36).

Balsom, Denis and Ian McAllister (1979) 'The Scottish and Welsh Devolution Referenda: Constitutional Change and Popular Choice', *Parliamentary Affairs*, vol. 22, no. 4, pp. 394–409.

Butler, David and Donald Stokes (1975) *Political Change in Britain* (London: Macmillan).

Cox, Kevin R. (1970) 'Geography, Social Contexts and Voting Behaviour in Wales', in E. Allardt and S. Rokkan (eds), *Mass Politics* (New York: Free Press).

Craig, F. W. S. (1975) *Britain Votes I* (Chichester: Political Reference Publications).

Davies, David Hywel (1979) 'The Welsh Nationalist Party, 1925–45: a Search for Identity', MSc. (Econ.) thesis (Cardiff: University of Wales).

Downs, Anthony (1957) *An Economic Theory of Democracy* (New York: Harper & Row).

Esman, Milton J. (1977) 'Perspectives on Ethnic Conflict in the Industrialised Societies', in Milton J. Esman (ed.), *Ethnic Conflict in the Western World* (Ithaca, New York: Cornell).

Gellner, Ernest (1964) *Thought and Change* (London: Weidenfeld & Nicolson).

Hechter, Michael (1975) *Internal Colonialism* (London: Routledge & Kegan Paul).

Jaensch, Dean (1976) 'The Scottish Vote 1974: a Realigning Political System?', *Political Studies*, vol. 24, no. 3, pp. 306–19.

Kedourie, Elie (1960) *Nationalism* (London: Hutchinson).

Lewis, Saunders (1975) *Principles of Nationalism* (Cardiff: Plaid Cymru, reprint of 1926 edn).

McAllister, Ian (1977) *The Northern Ireland Social Democratic and Labour Party* (London: Macmillan).

McAllister, Ian (1980) *Territorial Differentiation and Party Development in Northern Ireland* (Glasgow: University of Strathclyde Studies in Public Policy no. 66).

McAllister, Ian (forthcoming) 'Party Organisation and Minority Nationalism: a Comparative Study in the United Kingdom', *European Journal of Political Research*.

McAllister, Ian, Richard Parry and Richard Rose (1979) *United Kingdom Rankings: the Territorial Dimension in Social Indicators* (Glasgow: University of Strathclyde Studies in Public Policy no. 44).

McCloskey, Herbert, P. J. Hoffmann and R. O'Hara (1963) 'Issue Conflict and Consensus among Party Leaders and Followers', *American Political Science Review*, vol. 54, no. 2, pp. 406–27.

MacCormick, John M. (1955) *The Flag in the Wind* (London: Gollancz).

Miller, David (1978) *Queen's Rebels* (Dublin: Gill & Macmillan).

Mohr, Lawrence B. (1973) 'The Concept of Organizational Goal', *American Political Science Review*, vol. 67, no. 2, pp. 470–81.

Moxon-Browne, E. (1979) *Northern Ireland Attitude Survey: An Initial Report* (Belfast: Mimeo, Queen's University).

Osmond, John (1977) *Creative Conflict* (London: Routledge & Kegan Paul).

Philip, Alan Butt (1975) *The Welsh Question* (Cardiff: University of Wales Press).

Plaid Cymru (n.d.) *The Kilbrandon Report: An Interim Comment* (Cardiff: mimeo).

Plaid Cymru (1970) *Special Conference* (Cardiff: Plaid Cymru).

Plaid Cymru (1974a) *Rich Welsh or Poor British?* (Cardiff: Plaid Cymru, February 1974 election manifesto).

Plaid Cymru (1974b) *Power for Wales* (Cardiff: Plaid Cymru, October 1974 election manifesto).

Plaid Cymru (1976) *Constitution of Plaid Cymru* (Cardiff: mimeo).

Plaid Cymru (1979) *Conference 1979* (Cardiff: Plaid Cymru).

Pomper, Gerald M. (1972) 'From Confusion to Clarity: Issues and American Voters, 1956–68', *American Political Science Review*, vol. 66, no. 2, pp. 216–26.

Rawkins, Phillip M. (1975) 'Minority Nationalism and the Advanced Industrial State: a Case Study of Contemporary Wales', Ph.D. thesis (University of Toronto).

Rawkins, Phillip M. (1978) 'The Incidental Hero: the Nationalist Vision and Self-Imposed Limits to Political Advance in Industrial South Wales', paper presented to the Sociology of Wales Group, Cardiff.

Rose, Richard (1971) *Governing Without Consensus* (London: Faber).

Rose, Richard (1980) *Class Does Not Equal Party: the Decline of a Model of British Voting* (Glasgow: University of Strathclyde Studies in Public Policy no. 74).

Rose, Richard and Ian McAllister (1982) *United Kingdom Facts* (London: Macmillan).

Scottish National Party (n.d.) 'Comments on the Green Paper "Devolution Within the United Kingdom: Some Alternatives for Discussion"' (Edinburgh: mimeo).

SNP (1949) *Constitution and Rules of the Scottish National Party* (Edinburgh: SNP).

SNP (1968) *Constitution and Rules of the Scottish National Party* (Edinburgh: SNP).

SNP (1976) *Scotland's Future* (Edinburgh: SNP).

SNP (1979) *Conference Agenda* (Edinburgh: SNP).

Social Democratic and Labour Party (1973) *A New North, A New Ireland* (Belfast: SDLP).

SDLP (1975) *Party Constitution* (Belfast: SDLP).

SDLP (1979) *SDLP Ninth Annual Conference* (Belfast: SDLP).

Spence, Lewis (1928) 'The National Party of Scotland', *Edinburgh Review*, vol. 268, pp. 70– 89.

Thompson, James D. (1967) *Organisations in Action* (New York: McGraw-Hill).

Urwin, Derek W. (1979) *Politics, Cultural Identity and Economic Expectations in Scotland* (Bergen: Institute of Sociology and Political Studies Report no. 3).

Wolfe, William (1968) *Scotland Lives* (Edinburgh: Reprographia).

8 Variations in Electoral Behaviour in the United Kingdom

WILLIAM L. MILLER

How British is electoral behaviour in Britain? What are the similarities and differences between electoral behaviour in the component parts of the United Kingdom? The answers depend upon the component parts we select, upon the time when we measure the differences, and, not least, on our criteria for deciding which votes are equivalent to each other.

I TERRITORIAL UNITS

In keeping with the other chapters of this book I intend to base this analysis on the so-called 'national regions' of Scotland, England, (Northern) Ireland and Wales; that is, to look at social and political variations across units defined by the institutions of government and parties, rather than attempt to discover specially homogeneous political regions within the United Kingdom. Obviously there are also variations within each of these 'national' areas (see Miller, 1979), but few who detect within-Scotland variation would deny that there are also within-Strathclyde variations.

The national areas, despite an internal lack of homogeneity, have a special interest for a number of reasons. They are coextensive, almost by definition, with one of the gross determinants of electoral behaviour – the availability of parties to vote for. In the past, Irish Nationalists occasionally fought and occasionally won in English constituencies; but in recent years, the behaviour of party bureaucracies has restricted Scottish National Party votes to Scotland, Plaid Cymru votes to Wales, and Irish Nationalist votes to Ireland. Moreover, people in all parts of Scotland have had the opportunity to vote SNP just as everyone in Wales had the option of a PC vote and everyone in Northern Ireland had the option of voting for an Irish Nationalist party of one colour or another. Conversely, National Front voting is an almost exclusively English phenomenon, if for no other reason than the party's failure to contest seats outside England. In 1979, for example, the National Front had candidates in 58 per cent of English seats (297 out of 516) but in only 5 per cent of non-English seats. (Of the 6 National Front candidates outside England, 5 were in South Wales.)

A second reason why the national areas are especially interesting is that they have been the subjects of plausible schemes for institutionally separate political systems. Clearly Scotland and England have been divided by so much history and so many institutions, both ancient and modern, that the Scottish border would be a 'natural' break on the political map, even if political behaviour turned out to be identical on both sides. Similarly, while some would argue that Northern Ireland is less than a natural unit, few would dispute the significance of the dividing line between Ireland and Britain.

However, I have some misgivings about treating Wales as a unit separate from England. Apart from its cumbersome title, there is a lot to be said for treating 'England and Wales' as the natural unit, and Welshness as a characteristic of some people living in some parts of 'England and Wales'. Some administrative boundaries cross cut the 'Welsh' border, dividing Wales and binding different parts to portions of England. There is a high level of population movement in both directions across the border, homogenising by immigration. There have never been powerful political institutions coextensive with Wales, and the 1979 devolution referendum there strongly rejected beginning a process of building Welsh institutions of government. The Welsh language divides the territory of 'England and Wales' but *not* at the Welsh/English border. Communities there may be a plenty in Wales, but little evidence so far of a 'community of communities' equal to the whole of Wales. So were it not for the existence of Plaid Cymru candidates throughout Wales and nowhere else, coupled with the 1974–9 Labour Government's proposals for Welsh Devolution, I should be tempted to treat Wales as part of England (see Miller, 1977, Ch. 6, for such a treatment).

II THE SIZE OF VOTING VARIATIONS

It is impossible to discuss voting variations without looking at time trends, and giving thought to the units of account. Some territorial variations have been in existence so long that they may be termed traditional, while others ebb and flow in response to the issues of the day or the mood of the times. As for units of account, we may be happy to treat a Labour vote in Stirling as the equivalent of a Labour vote in Sheffield, but what about Unionist votes in Belfast and Birmingham or, conversely, do we really want to distinguish SNP votes in Dundee East from Liberal votes in Chester-le-Street?

As a measure of the variation in support for the major parties of government, let us take the variation in the Conservative lead over Labour expressed as a percentage of the total vote. Then for third parties let us take the Liberal share, the Nationalist share and the combined Liberal plus Nationalist share. Finally, we can construct a multi-party measure which summarises the overall difference between the voting pattern in one area and another:

$$MD = \sqrt{(dCON^2 + dLAB^2 + dLIB^2 + dNAT^2 + dOTH^2)/2}$$

Where $dCON$ means the difference between the Conservative share of the vote in the two areas and $dLAB, dLIB, dNAT, dOTH$ are defined similarly. The rationale for this measure is set out in the Appendix to this chapter. It has a minimum of zero, when voting patterns are identical, and a maximum of 100 per cent, when one area votes entirely for one party but the other area gives all its votes to a second party. It may sometimes be useful to treat votes for all the alternatives to the two parties of government as equivalent. Then the multi-party measure of voting difference becomes a three-option measure:

$$MD3 = \sqrt{(dCON^2 + dLAB^2 + dREST^2)/2}$$

where $dREST$ means the difference between the total third-party votes in the two areas. The formula is entirely symmetric and unbiased towards variations in any particular party's support.

Using these measures we can calculate the difference between voting in the different national areas. I shall compare Scotland, Wales and Northern Ireland with the norm defined by England. This is not the only possible approach but it has significant advantages. First, it does not require us to state any equivalence or lack of equivalence between Scots, Welsh and Irish Nationalists, such as would be necessary for direct Scots/Welsh comparisons. Secondly, it avoids comparison with a British norm, which also could not be done without taking a rigid definition of nationalist equivalences. Moreover the disparity in population between the four national areas means that a British norm is nothing more than a rather corrupt version of the English norm, a very weighted average of four highly divergent voting patterns.

TABLE 8.1 Multi-party and three-option measures of national voting deviations

Year	*Wales*		*Scotland*		*Ireland (NI only from 1929)*	
	Difference from English voting pattern in terms of					
	%MD	*%MD3*	*%MD*	*%MD3*	*%MD*	*%MD3*
1885	8	8	12	12	59	59
Jan. 1910	15	15	11	11	64[a]	60[a]
1929	15	15	6	5	34	34
1945	14	14	4	1	33	33
1950	15	15	2	1	31	30
1951	16	16	1	1	30	31
1955	17	18	1	0	36	36
1959	16	16	3	3	33	33
1964	15	15	6	5	27	24
1966	14	14	5	4	31	31
1970	18	18	11	10	30	27
Feb. 1974	15	13	19	8	64[b]	54[b]
Oct. 1974	15	13	25	16	72[b]	65[b]
1979	15	14	17	14	74[b]	71[b]

[a] The 1910 raw voting percentages in Ireland figures have been adjusted to take account of the very large number of unopposed returns.

[b] As equivalents of Conservative votes in Ireland from 1974 onwards, I have counted only the pro-Sunningdale Unionists and the UPNI. The Alliance Party is treated as an 'other'. Most Unionists, plus the SDLP and all other republicans are grouped into the 'local nationalist' column.

Sources: Craig (1976); Butler and Kavanagh (1980).

Table 8.1 gives measures of national voting differences at intervals from 1885 to 1979. It shows multi-party measures for the electoral deviation of Scotland, Wales and Ireland from the English norm.

Wales is distinguished by the relatively constant size of its deviation from English voting patterns. From 1910 onwards the Welsh figures for multi-party deviance all lie between 14 and 18 per cent. There were minor differences from year to year, and the political direction of Welsh electoral deviance varied sometimes to the advantage of the Liberals, at others to PC and sometimes more than usually strongly towards Labour. But, having admitted these minor variations in size and direction, the consistency of Welsh political deviance might well be described as *traditional*.

So, too, Northern Ireland exhibited a remarkably constant level of deviance from the inter-war years to 1970, with a multi-party difference measure ranging between 27 and 36 per cent. But Ireland as a whole had been twice as deviant as that before 1918. After 1970 Northern Ireland abruptly became still more deviant than old Ireland had been, principally because most Unionist votes now had to be classed as local nationalist rather than as British Conservative. So Irish deviance was partly traditional, partly definitional, caused partly by the behaviour of the Irish voters in Ireland, partly by the behaviour of their MPs at Westminster, and partly by the extent of Irish territory included in the United Kingdom.

Scotland however drifted slowly towards the English norm, then progressively diverged again. Differences between Scots and English voting were neither traditional nor were the trends caused by abrupt changes of definition. From the beginning of the century through to 1951 Scots deviance from England gradually declined until it was barely detectable. It stayed close to zero in 1955 before increasing to record levels in the 1970s.

As late as 1970, our measure of Scots electoral deviance was almost unaffected by grouping Scots Liberal and Nationalist votes together, mainly because there was little evidence that votes for the one offset votes for the other. Indeed, they tended to contest different subsets of Scots constituencies. But in 1974, the overall pattern of British voting suggests that Liberal and Nationalist votes expressed something of the same political mood, and Liberal candidates opposed SNP candidates throughout Scotland. While the SNP vote went up by over 10 per cent in February 1974, the overall tendency for both Scotland and Wales to support third parties more strongly than England actually declined. So while the multi-party measure of Scottish national deviance (MD) shows a sharp increase from 11 to 19 per cent, the three-option measure $(MD3)$, which treats SNP and Liberal votes as equivalent, shows a decline from 10 per cent in 1970 to 8 per cent in February 1974.

This three-option measure identifies the autumn election, in October 1974, as the critical time when Scots deviance doubled, from 8 to 16 per cent. And since this measure puts no weight on the division of third-party votes between Liberals and Nationalists, it shows a relatively modest decline in 1979 to 14 per cent. Thus, while both measures indicate that in 1979 Scots electoral deviance was higher than at any time prior to 1974, the three-option version suggests, in addition, that Scots voting patterns deviated more from the English norm in 1979 than in February 1974.

This is a rather surprising conclusion. The February 1974 result in Scotland certainly excited much more press and parliamentary reaction than the 1979 result. And it is true that while Liberal and Nationalist votes had something in common, they were not completely interchangeable. None the less, reactions to the February 1974 result overstated its significance, just as reactions to the 1979 result focussed on the SNP decline rather than the doubling of the national gap in Labour versus Conservative voting.

This variation over time in the Scots difference from English voting patterns suggests that issues, ideas, political debate and instrumental calculations have had a variable impact. Significantly, Scots could not be accused of volatility. Their differences from the English varied over time, but along the lines of longer-term trends: progressive convergence up to the early 1950s and progressive divergence thereafter.

Since 1974 it has been almost impossible to make a detailed comparison of Northern Ireland and English voting, because the differences have so obviously not been matters of degree. But the Welsh and Scots have had enough in common with the English to permit detailed comparison right through the seventies, and detailed Northern Ireland/English comparisons are possible until 1970. Using symmetric triangular representation (see Miller, 1981b, for a full description of this technique), Figure 8.1 shows Scots, Welsh and Northern Ireland electoral deviations in the years 1955, 1964, 1974 and 1979. In this representation, points near to a corner represent elections where one party gets nearly all the votes; points near to a side, but away from a corner, indicate that two parties shared nearly all the votes between them; points near the centre of the triangle represent elections where the votes were evenly split three ways, between Labour, the Conservative and third parties.

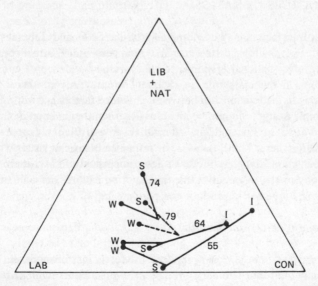

FIGURE 8.1 National deviations from English voting norms: 1955, 1964, October 1974 and 1979

In 1955 the Scots and English voted for just the same parties and in just the same proportions. The Northern Irish deviated very strongly in an anti-Labour direction and the Welsh strongly in an anti-Conservative direction. (Notice that anti-Conservative does not just mean pro-Labour in a multi-party contest; it also means pro-third party.)

In 1964 national differences were quite closely aligned along a Labour versus Conservative axis, with Wales at the Labour end, Northern Ireland at the Conservative end, and Scotland deviating a little towards Labour at the expense of both the Conservatives and third parties.

Third parties did well everywhere in the 1970s, so that the whole pattern moves up the diagram. The Welsh still deviated in an anti-Conservative direction as they had in 1955, though by a smaller amount. When Scots deviance was at its maximum in 1974, it was in a pro-third party, anti-Conservative direction, with Labour also suffering in Scotland. With the decline of third parties in 1979, Scots deviance changed, but the change was more one of direction than of size: it veered away from third parties and towards Labour. So, at least as far as national differences are concerned, we miss the point if we notice only the decline of the Nationalists in 1979.

III SOURCES OF NATIONAL DIFFERENCES

At least four factors may combine to produce national differences in party support. First, national differences in voting percentages might come from a uniform cross-national response to the varying incidence of causes, e.g. variations in the class mix in different areas. Second, there could be variations in the relationship between causative factors and voting. Again, two simple examples might be an across-the-board greater tendency to vote Conservative in England, or alternatively, a different degree of class polarisation there. Third, there is the influence of special issues which may cross-cut class divisions more or less imperfectly. Last, there may be variations in the aggregative mechanisms which put the partisanship of individuals together to produce the partisanship of constituencies.

(i) The uniform-response model

At its simplest, the uniform-response model suggests we should look for politically relevant socio-economic or attitudinal factors which affect votes in England, and the incidence of which varies between England and the other areas. Such variations are, of course, likely to provide better explanations of the long-run component of national differences than of changes in national deviance.

Let us start with socio-economic variations. Some of the statistics shown in Table 8.2 fit the variations in national voting, but others do not. The English are relatively prosperous, middle class and home-owning, with

TABLE 8.2   Social variation

	S	W	E	NI
% in agriculture (1971 census)	3.9	4.5	2.7	8.1
% males in class II (1971 census)	15.7	17.8	18.2	21.9
% males in SEGs 1, 2, 13 (1971 census)	10.9	10.5	13.0	9.0
% owner-occupiers (1971 census)	29.0	54.0	50.0	46.0
% council tenants (1971 census)	54.0	29.0	28.0	35.0
% TU family contact (BES 74)[a]	47.0	57.0	42.0	NA
% Catholic (BES 74)	12.0	7.0	9.0	NA
% Catholic marriages (1976)	15.0	6.0	9.0	39.0
GDP per capita as % of UK (1976)	97.0	90.0	102.0	78.0
% unemployed (1976)	7.0	7.4	5.4	10.3
cars per capita as % of UK (1976)	82.0	105.0	102.0	91.0

[a] 'BES 74' refers to the British Election Survey 1974, which had approximately 1200 Scots respondents, 135 Welsh and 2000 in England. Welsh figures are thus subject to high sampling variance, but the Scots figures are not.

Sources: Miller (1981a) for BES data on Scotland and England; McAllister, Parry and Rose (1979) for most official data; plus original analysis for BES Welsh figures and SEG measure of class.

fewer trade union contacts than the Scots or the Welsh, and so are quite reasonably more Conservative. But when we look in more detail at the table, some of the explanations based on uniform response to social conditions become less convincing.

The percentage in managerial occupations (socio-economic groups SEG 1, 2, 13) is a good index of an area's social class mix. It varies enough to explain the long-run tendency of Scotland towards Labour, but it provides no explanation of trends in Scottish deviance. It is also insufficient to explain Welsh support for Labour and powerless to account for Northern Ireland's lack of support for Labour. The alternative measure of the managerial classes, the per cent in social class II of the Registrar General's five social classes, makes Northern Ireland appear the most middle class of the four national areas, but this frequently quoted statistic is misleading when used outside England, because it incorporates self-employed farmers.[1]

England has the highest GDP per capita and the lowest unemployment rate, which matches its Conservative voting, but Northern Ireland inconveniently has the levels of GDP and unemployment usually associated with areas of left-wing hegemony in England. At the very least, this illustrates the subordinate role of economic conditions as an influence on Northern Ireland voting.

In contrast, some of the other social variations match the direction of political deviance but not its scale. Scotland, with 25 per cent more of its population in council houses than in Wales, and with 23 per cent less cars than the Welsh, should surely have been more, not less, Labour than Wales and also far more pro-Labour in comparison with England than it was, if these factors really do have a causal influence on voting (see Dunleavy, 1979, for a strong argument that they do).

Turning now to social attitudes which, though based on social structure, are considerably more fluid and open to choice (Table 8.3): the Scots and

TABLE 8.3   Variations in social attitudes

	S	W	E
% high religiosity (BES 74)	26	33	17
% religiosity (marriages 76) [a]	62	59	52
% read TU journal (BES 74)	36	40	57
% talk about politics (BES 74)	52	56	60
% working class identity (BES 74)	69	74	61
% working class identity of those with spontaneous identity (BES 74)	76	73	61

[a] On religiosity, measured by the percentage of religious marriages, Ireland scored a massive 91 per cent in 1976.

Sources: As in Table 8.2.

Welsh are significantly more religious than the English, they are less likely to read trade union journals, despite their high level of union membership, yet they have a higher level of working class identification than might be expected even from a higher level of working class occupations. Two of these three characteristics might be expected to help the Conservatives, the other Labour.

Views on general political issues were too similar throughout Britain to account for the differences in voting behaviour in the 1970s: the average English/Scottish difference on 13 issue questions was only 6 per cent; between Wales and England, 7 per cent, and between Wales and Scotland 8 per cent (see Table 8.4). The 1974 British Election Survey found Scots

TABLE 8.4 Variations in attitudes on issues

	S	W	E
% importance of prices	81	92	86
unemployment	68	81	73
EEC	56	72	70
housing	49	62	56
social services	55	69	60
redistribution	86	87	84
immigration	71	75	77
comprehensives	73	80	81
% cut social services	34	34	39
% stay in EEC	50	45	59
% very important to redistribute wealth	32	33	23
% repatriate immigrants	39	32	39
% very important to set up comprehensives	16	28	15

Sources: All data is from BES 74. Scots and English figures from Miller (1981a); Welsh figures from special analysis.

(though not Welsh) consistently assigning rather less importance to issues such as prices, unemployment, social services and immigration, which is consistent with their vote for a party which stressed other issues; but the national differences were small. Both Scots and Welsh were less keen to cut social services, or to stay in the EEC, and more favourable to a redistribution of wealth, all views which were consistent with pro-Labour deviation, however.

(ii) Special groups and issues outside England

There is a second type of social or attitudinal difference between national areas, namely the presence in Scotland, Wales and Northern Ireland of some groups and issues which scarcely exist in England. They are few in number but none the less powerful.

First, and most important of all, there was a degree of population segmentation: the English were English, the Scots were Scots, and the great bulk of the people of Northern Ireland were born there too. Over 9 out of 10 Scots residents were Scots-born. There was, therefore, a fairly high degree of identity between land and people. The same could be said of the Northern Irish, of the English, and even of the Northern region within England (McAllister, Parry and Rose, 1979). But there was much less identity between the Welsh land and people. Roughly a fifth of Welsh residents were incomers and a fifth of Welsh-born people living in the United Kingdom lived outside Wales. Moreover, these figures have been fairly stable for many years.

None the less, the fundamental social difference is that the populations of the different national areas are *largely separate groups of people*. Moreover, they are conscious of this difference, and a majority will normally choose to identify with the name of their national area rather than with the term 'British'. In Scotland, particularly, this separateness is reinforced by a largely separate daily and weekly press for both low- and high-brow readers, and separate governmental institutions present news differently (see Rose and McAllister, 1981).

Wales contains one social group – Welsh-speakers – who scarcely appear in England. But contains is the word, for these are not characteristic of Wales as a whole, and only the two most western and most sparsely populated Welsh counties have over a quarter of their population Welsh-speaking.

In all parts of the United Kingdom except England, however, constitutional relations with the central government are an issue. This is supplemented in Scotland by oil, in Wales by language and culture, and in Northern Ireland by sectarian relations. Where there are directly comparable figures, it is clear that long before the 1979 referendum, the Welsh were less interested in, or enthusiastic about, devolution than were the Scots or Ulstermen but the idea still appealed to more Welshmen than Englishmen (see Table 8.5). Fully 60 per cent of Scots declared that the devolution question was one important factor in *'deciding their vote'* in 1974. Scots

TABLE 8.5   Devolution and oil (1974)

	S	W	E
Weight of issue			
% importance of decentralisation [a]	86	78	72
% importance of North Sea oil	56	38	43
% importance of devolution	60	NA	NA
Position on issue			
% very important to decentralise	36	23	15
% share oil on British basis	31	82	82

[a] The figures for the weight given to decentralisation and to devolution can be compared across nations but *not* across questions, since the two questions were framed in very different ways. Note also that some of those who felt these issues were important were centralisers and anti-devolutionists.

Source: As in Table 8.4.

gave less weight to the question of North Sea oil as a factor in their voting decision, but at least they recognised oil as an 'issue' far more than did the English or Welsh, and the Scots took an overwhelmingly different position on it: 82 per cent of the English and Welsh wanted oil revenues shared on a uniform Britain-wide basis, but only 31 per cent of Scots agreed. (For a discussion of changing attitudes to oil revenues, see Miller, Brand and Jordan, 1980.)

How far do these special local issues and conditions fit voting variations? The separation of peoples, especially when reinforced by news media, provides just the sort of conditions required for divergent tendencies.

A Welsh language fits with a Welsh nationalist party and, within Wales, the pattern of Welsh-language-speaking fits nationalist party support and pro-devolution voting in the referendum. However, it is tendencies, not categories, that fit each other: only 24 per cent of Welsh-speakers and 34 per cent of those who wanted Welsh independence were willing to vote for the PC.

Rural areas in England, especially until the early 1960s, were centres of third-party support. It is fitting that the more rural national areas should also foster third parties. Though there are few parts of England with high levels of self-employed farmers, the places in Scotland, Wales and Northern Ireland where they are numerous have all tended towards a broad spectrum of anti-Conservative parties that has, almost randomly, included Labour, Liberal, Nationalists or Crofters.

And the fact that support for local constitutional reform of some sort was higher in Scotland and lower in Wales also matches the levels of non-British party support in these areas. Within the national areas also, support for constitutional reform varied closely with support for reforming parties. Those who wanted the greatest degree of devolution or separation from Westminster voted in much greater numbers for the nationalist parties (see Table 8.6).

(iii) Variations in response relationships: survey evidence

Class is a major determinant, if not *the* major determinant, of the balance between Labour and Conservative voting throughout mainland Britain. I shall restrict most of my discussion of varying class alignments to Britain because, as Table 8.7 shows, class was *not* an important influence on support for any major Irish party, except possibly the Alliance, which had a modest favourable bias in the middle class.

Taking the usual division of survey respondents according to whether their head of household had a manual or non-manual occupation, surveys in

TABLE 8.6   Devolution, oil, the language and voting

Degree of nationalist electoral support in various attitude groups

Constitutional preference	%SNP (1974)	Constitutional preference	%PC (1979)
status quo	0	no assembly	1
more understanding by UK government	12	assembly as proposed in referendum	15
more decisions in Scotland	26	stronger assembly	19
self-government	60	self-government	34
Attitude to oil revenues		*Relation to language*	
share on UK basis	14	cannot speak Welsh	4
more for Scotland	28	speak Welsh	10
most for Scotland	39	speak Welsh fluently	24
all for Scotland	47		

Sources: Scottish data from BES 74; Welsh calculated from BBC polls reported in Balsom, 1979. The BBC polls interviewed 3571 respondents.

Scotland, Wales and England indicate that Labour had about 30 per cent more support in the working class compared with its support in the middle class, whereas the Conservatives had a slightly smaller class bias the other way (see Table 8.7). There is evidence of a slight middle class bias towards the Liberals which accounts for the different strengths of Labour and Conservative class alignments. In the mid-1970s there was no evidence of any class bias in nationalist support. The National Front (NF) in England drew its support more heavily from the working class but, since it had so little support in total, the class bias in propensities to vote NF was negligible: its share of the working class vote was about half a per cent higher than its share of the middle class vote (see Harrop, England and Husbands, 1980, for the social basis of NF support).

The evidence from surveys suggests that the class alignment was remarkably unaffected by national differences or the growth of support for nationalist parties. While working class people were much more pro-Labour in Wales than in England, so, too, at a lower level were middle class people, leaving the class alignment (by which I mean the sensitivity and response of partisanship to class) unchanged. However, surveys do suggest a gradual decline in the degree of class polarisation over time.

Comparable measures of United Kingdom religious alignments are set out in Table 8.8. In contrast to the pattern of class alignments, Northern Ireland parties are the most socially structured by religious alignments. Indeed the

TABLE 8.7 Class alignments at the individual level

Difference between party per cent amongst non-manuals and amongst manuals

	Con	Lib	Lab	Nat
England (BES 1974)	27	4	−30	0
Scotland (BES 1974)	24	6	−30	0
Wales (BBC 1979)	28	0	−32	3

	Official Unionist	DUP	Alliance	SDLP
NI (1978)	−4	−3	14	−7

Note: The entries in Tables 8.7 and 8.8 are calculated in the following way. According to the 1974 SES survey, Scots living in non-manual households voted 38 per cent Con, 10 per cent Lib, 22 per cent Lab and 29 per cent SNP; and Scots in manual households voted 14 per cent Con, 4 per cent Lib, 52 per cent Lab, 29 per cent SNP. Thus the class effect of being middle class rather than working class helped the Conservatives by 38 − 14 = 24 per cent and Labour by 22 − 52 = −30 per cent, while having no effect on SNP support. Apart from rounding errors, coupled with the effects to excluded party groups, the entries in each row of the table sum to zero since one party's gain must be another's loss.

Sources: Scottish and Welsh data as in Table 8.6; Northern Ireland figures calculated from Moxon-Browne, 1979.

size of the religious bias in support for a Northern Irish party is purely dependent upon the gross size of the party, since over 98 per cent of SDLP voters are Catholic, and over 99 per cent of Unionist voters are Protestant. Only the Alliance Party, with 12 per cent of the vote in 1979, represents any significant escape from sectarian voting (Moxon-Browne, 1979). Ulster partisanship has always been largely determined by sectarian divisions, and the sectarian alignment in the late 1970s was even sharper than in the 1950s or 1960s (Rose, 1971).

Table 8.8 shows that religion also influences votes on the British mainland. For example, Scots Catholics were 47 per cent more likely to vote Labour than Church of Scotland members.[2] This 47 per cent Catholic bias looks close to the SDLP's 52 per cent Catholic bias in Northern Ireland. Yet for a complex variety of reasons, religion was a relatively unimportant influence on mainland voting patterns. First, no British party was limited to a single religious group. The Labour Party in Scotland had a comparable Catholic bias to the SDLP only because the Scots Labour Party took a far higher proportion of Catholic votes (78 per cent) than did the SDLP (52 per cent); so Scots Labour could do as well as any party among those in the Church of Scotland, yet still do 47 per cent better amongst Catholics.

The main religious division in both Scotland and England lies between the

TABLE 8.8 Religious alignments at the individual level

Difference between party per cent amongst specified religious groups and amongst those in established or dominant church

Party per cent breakdown of religious group

English religious groups (1974)

	Con	Lib	Lab
Anglicans (official)	45	21	34
non-conformist Protestant	33(−12)[a]	36(+15)	31(−3)
Catholic	31(−14)	11(−10)	58(+24)
irreligious	34(−11)	16(−5)	50(+16)

Scots religious groups (1974)

	Con	Lib	Lab	SNP
Church of Scotland (official)	30	7	31	32
Anglicans	44(+14)	12(+5)	19(−12)	25(−7)
Catholic	10(−20)	2(−5)	78(+47)	11(−21)
irreligious	16(−14)	6(−1)	43(+12)	35(+3)

Northern Ireland religious groups (1978)

	Official Unionist	DUP	Alliance	SDLP
Protestants	58[b]	17	16	0
Catholics	0(−58)	0(−17)	26(+10)	52(+52)

[a] Figures outside brackets show party percentages; figures inside brackets show differences between party support in official religious group and other groups.
[b] The percentages for party support in Northern Ireland do not add up to 100 per cent because a total of 12 per cent supported NILP, UPNI, Republican Clubs, Vanguard, etc.

Sources: Scottish and English figures from BES 74. Northern Irish figures calculated from Table 2.7 of Moxon-Browne, 1979.

appropriate national established church and the irreligious. Catholics and non-conformists may vote in distinctive ways but their numbers are relatively small. Middle class non-conformists in England gave 44 per cent of their votes to the Liberals, but they were a very small group. The most numerous group outside the established church, the irreligious, are numerous (the 1974 survey found over four times as many irreligious as Catholic in England), but their voting deviations are relatively small. Mainland Britain does not lack a multitude of interesting religious patterns in its voting, but it lacks the simple, gross, single religious pattern so evident in Ireland.

(iv) Variations in response relationships: constituency behaviour

We know that less than half the strength of the class alignment of parliamentary constituencies can be attributed to class alignments amongst individuals (see Miller, 1978). So the cross-national territorial uniformity we have observed amongst individuals in Britain need not apply when we contrast the behaviour of people in working class and middle class constituencies.

Scots and English constituency class alignments were very similar at all times from 1955 to 1979; there were distinctive features in Wales. Table 8.9 shows two measures of the power of constituency class alignments:

TABLE 8.9   Social alignments at the constituency level

Dependent variable	Social predictor	1955	1964	Oct. 74	1979
(a) Sensitivity: regression slopes in constituency regressions					
England Con lead over Lab	EMPL [a]	4.4	4.1	4.2	4.3
Scotland Con lead over Lab	EMPL	4.6	5.0	4.5	4.9
Wales Con lead over Lab	EMPL	5.7	6.8	5.6	6.3
N. Ireland Unionist lead over Irish Unity [d]	PROT [b]	1.7	1.3	2.0	2.0
(b) Predictability: R^2 values for regressions (% of variation explained)					
England Con lead over Lab	EMPL	64	66	77	78
Scotland Con lead over Lab	EMPL	67	76	75	78
Wales Con lead over Lab	EMPL	52	75	85	81
N. Ireland [c] Unionist lead over Irish Unity	PROT	57	61	88	86

[a] EMPL: per cent employers and managers in 1966 and 1971 censuses.
[b] PROT: per cent Protestant (of those with a religion) in 1971 census.
[c] The Ulster regressions for 1974 and 1979 omit two Westminster constituencies which had no Irish Unity candidate. This omission does *not* explain the rise in R^2 values in those years.
[d] Unionist, in this table, includes *all* varieties of Unionist, including UPNI. Irish Unity includes all varieties of republicans and the SDLP. The main groups excluded from both definitions are the NILP and the Alliance. In the earlier years, voting patterns in Northern Ireland were disturbed by massive and purposive abstentions.

sensitivity and fit. Both are derived from regressions predicting the Conservative percentage lead over Labour from the percentage employers and managers in the constituency. For reasons set out in Miller (1978), it is critical that we take this measure of constituency class. (The Northern Ireland entries show equivalent regressions predicting the Unionist percentage lead over Republicans from the percentage Protestant in the constituency.)

Sensitivity is defined as the variation in the Conservatives' percentage lead corresponding to a 1 per cent variation in the level of employers and managers. For Scotland, Table 8.9 shows this figure was close to 4.3, and for England 4.8, but for Wales 6.1. That is, there was a distinctly sharper relationship between constituency class and partisanship in Wales compared to the rest of Britain. Since cross-cutting alignments were no more powerful than elsewhere, the result was that Welsh partisanship was more predictable from class than Scots or English. In 1974, for example, variations in the level of employers and managers accounted for a staggering 85 per cent of Conservative/Labour voting variation in Wales.

Figure 8.2 illustrates the regressions for the three British areas at each of three elections from 1955 to 1979. Some of the important features of national class alignments can be seen very clearly in these diagrams.

First, the slope of the Welsh regression is sharper than for the other nations. Second, the reason why it is sharper is almost entirely due to an excess of Labour voting in the most working class Welsh constituencies. Middle class Welsh constituencies are not that different from English or Scots middle class constituencies, at least in terms of their Labour/ Conservative division. Once this point has been made by regression analysis, it is easy to check. Aberdare, Merthyr, Ebbw Vale, Abertillery and Rhondda all have about 5 per cent employers and managers and turned in an average Labour vote of 72 per cent in 1979. There are 8 Glasgow seats with 5 per cent or less managers, but their average Labour vote was only 67 per cent. And 5 Birmingham seats with 5 per cent or less managers averaged only a 56 per cent Labour vote.

We can see the Scots regression line slowly sinking as time passes. The dots on the lines show the mean constituency level of class and voting in each country. In 1955, the lower Conservative lead implied by Scotland's lower level of managers was exactly offset by a general tendency of all Scots constituencies to be more pro-Conservative than English constituencies with similar class characteristics. In 1955, a Scots *national* bias towards the Conservatives offset a Scots *class* bias towards Labour. In 1974, there was no Scots national bias either way and the Scots pro-Labour class bias explains the higher Labour lead in Scotland that year. Then in 1979 a Scots national bias against the Conservatives cumulated with a Scots class bias against them.

We can use the English slope coefficient from Table 8.9 in conjunction with the national class breakdowns from Table 8.2 to show how much greater or smaller the Conservative lead over Labour should be in Scotland,

Wales and Ireland on purely class grounds. The sensitivity coefficient is 4.3. Since Scots, Welsh and Irish had respectively 2.1, 2.5 and 4.0 less managers than England, the Conservative lead should have been 9 per cent less in Scotland, 11 per cent less in Wales, and 17 per cent less in Northern Ireland. Over the years since Labour became a great party, Labour's advantage in Scotland has approximated (on average) this target figure, but in Wales Labour has averaged well over twice the class-based advantage, and in Northern Ireland it has utterly failed ever to gain even a respectable vote, still less enjoy any advantage. These deviations from class-based predictions testify to the long-term special conditions in Wales and Northern Ireland – the pro-Labour valley culture of South Wales, and Ulster religious divisions.

But they also reinforce what was evident from our study of trends in Scots/English differences: whatever is special about Scotland, apart from a modest class difference, can be played either way between Labour and Conservative. The Scots class bias is inevitably anti-Conservative, but it is not large, and other Scots biases are clearly equally powerful and not inevitably anti-Conservative.

Similar class regressions can be computed for constituencies in Northern Ireland. They confirm the SDLP's link with the working class, and the Alliance Party's middle class bias, but the relationships are weak compared to Britain. In 1979 the R^2, for example, was only 25 per cent for the class-based regression predicting Alliance voting. Moreover, even if Irish class-based regressions had predicted Alliance voting better than that, they would obviously not be interpretable in the same way as British class-based regressions. The Alliance Party is not about social class, it is merely helped by the absence of a class milieu in which religious passions are intense.

More relevant to Northern Ireland conditions are the regressions relating Unionist versus Irish unity voting to the sectarian mix in the constituency. Table 8.9 shows that these religion-based regressions had a stronger predictive power (i.e. fit coefficient) in the 1970s than the managerial regressions in Britain. The sensitivity values appear lower for Northern Ireland, but this appearance is misleading. In the late 1970s, the slope value was 2.0. Thus, each extra 1 per cent Protestant added 2 per cent to the Unionist lead – by increasing the Unionist vote by 1 per cent and decreasing the Irish unity vote by the same amount.

(v) Variations in aggregative mechanisms

Aggregative mechanisms tell us more about a political system than data about individual social and attitudinal alignments. They explain a part – and often the major part – of alignments between constituencies and parties. That means they explain why parties get control of local councils and why

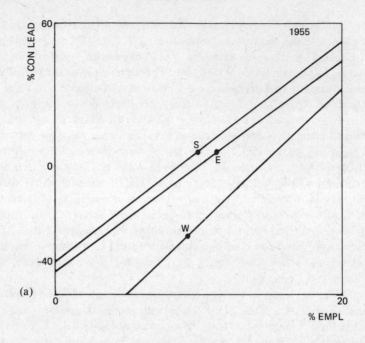

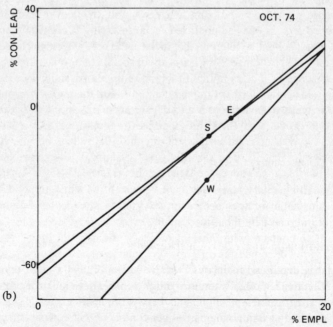

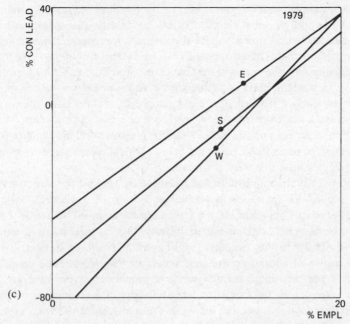

FIGURE 8.2   Class-based regressions for (a) 1955, (b) October 1974 and (c) 1979.

Notes
(1) The angle of the line shows how sensitive party support was to the level of employers and managers. Specifically, the slope shows by how many per cent the Con lead increases when the employers and managers increase by one per cent. For Scotland and England, the slope is about 4 or 5 to one.
(2) Parallel lines some distance apart indicate that constituencies in two countries are equally sensitive to variations in the class mix but that there is a purely national effect operating which makes one country's constituencies more Conservative than similar constituencies in the other country.
(3) The dots on each line represent the average class and partisan conditions in the appropriate country.

they win parliamentary seats. But, more than this, the nature of aggregative mechanisms tells us how people in a society *react to one another*. In particular, we can determine whether they react positively, negatively, or not at all, to contacts with other members of the same society who hold different views or come from different social backgrounds. In short, they tell us about the depth and intensity of differences at the grass roots; and how people react to each other when they differ may be more important than the differences themselves.

Throughout the British mainland, we can show, by comparing survey tables with constituency regressions, or by dividing survey respondents according to both personal characteristics and locality, that individuals are aggregated into a constituency class alignment by a consensual mechanism. Contact with members of the opposite class leads British people to vote more in accordance with the norms of that opposite class. So, middle class people who live in working class constituencies give far more (not a little more) support to Labour than middle class people in middle class areas. By contrast, we know from the almost total lack of cross-sectarian support for the Unionist parties and the SDLP, that in Northern Ireland contact with members of the opposite sect does not breed political consensus. In Northern Ireland aggregation is purely arithmetic.

Paradoxically, in both Britain and Northern Ireland, a 1 per cent turnover in the social mix (manual/non-manual in Britain, Protestant/Catholic in Ireland) produces approximately a 1 per cent turnover in the political mix (Labour/Conservative or Unionist/Irish Unity), but the mechanisms producing these similar results are entirely different. In Northern Ireland, it is a simple matter of adding up the individuals on one side or the other. In Britain, 1 per cent more manual workers produces a 1 per cent greater Labour vote, despite the fact that a large minority of those manual workers vote Conservative, because the local class mix influences the votes of *both* manual and non-manual workers in the locality.

These different mechanisms have implications for trends in constituency behaviour. Table 8.9 shows that constituency regressions confirm the survey evidence of a growing sensitivity to religious divisions in Northern Ireland. Both slope and fit coefficients increased in the 1970s. Yet, the table also shows that, despite survey evidence of declining class polarisation amongst individuals in Britain, British constituencies remain as class polarised as ever. As the individual component of British class polarisation has declined, the environmental component has increased. Class in Britain is steadily becoming an attribute of localities rather than individuals.

Some theorists have suggested that contact between occupational sectors will breed consensus, but contact between ethno-cultural groups will breed dissensus (see Esman, 1977). But not so in Britain. While sectarian contacts do not produce Catholic votes for the Unionists or Protestant votes for the SDLP, our 1979 Scottish Election Survey shows clear evidence that Scots who have had some contact with the English are more likely to vote Conservative and less likely to vote Labour or SNP. And this is true even after a control for the middle classes' greater contacts with England. The effect is small compared, for example, to the effect of living in a class environment, but then the measured stimulus is also weak. The direction of the effect is significant, none the less.

Similarly, we can look at aggregation processes in relation to the Welsh language or the Scots demand for devolution. According to the BBC's final pre-referendum poll in Wales, 39 per cent of Welsh-speakers intended to vote Yes, against only 20 per cent of non-Welsh-speakers. If this aggregated purely arithmetically, then for each 1 per cent more Welsh-speakers in a county, the Yes vote would rise by only one-fifth of a per cent. Clearly, the variation in Yes voting was far more sensitive to the language than that. But a mere comparison of the official returns cannot tell us whether the non-arithmetical aggregation process was consensual or not. Perhaps it was purely reinforcing.

Balsom's (1979) analysis of party preference in the BBC Wales polls points very strongly to a reinforcing and even reactive aggregation mechanism. Welsh-speakers were very much more inclined to state a PC preference. And Welsh-speakers living in Welsh-speaking areas were especially favourable to Plaid Cymru. But, in contrast to the class pattern, non-Welsh-speakers were no more inclined, indeed slightly less inclined to favour the PC if they lived in a Welsh-speaking area. So while Welsh-speakers were positively influenced by their social environment, whether it was Welsh- or English-speaking, the non-Welsh-speakers reacted against a Welsh-speaking environment (see Table 8.10).

TABLE 8.10   Reinforcement and reaction in Wales

| | % Plaid Cymru amongst | |
	Welsh-speakers	non-Welsh-speakers
N. W. and W. Wales (most Welsh-speaking area)	25	2
N. E. and Mid-Wales (intermediate)	16	1
South Wales (least Welsh-speaking area)	10	5

Source: Balsom (1979).

In Scotland, support for the SNP increased across the devolution spectrum. Those at the status quo end gave little support to the SNP, those at the independence end gave most, and, less obviously, there was a steady rise in SNP support across intermediate positions on this devolution spectrum (see Table 8.6). What happened in the areas where SNP candidates were elected to Parliament? Analysis of several surveys (Miller, 1981a) shows that these SNP areas were paradoxically *no* more favourable to devolution or independence than Labour or Conservative areas. The SNP built up a winning vote in specific places by getting an unusually high share of the vote amongst pro-devolutionists and pro-independence electors. These were everywhere the most likely to vote SNP, but they did so in varying proportions.

The SNP pattern has some similarities to the increasingly high Plaid Cymru support amongst Welsh-speakers in Welsh-speaking areas, but it is not quite the same. Those closest to the self-government end of the devolution spectrum gave specially high votes to the SNP in SNP areas, but the environment was not so much naturally strong on self-government as strong on SNP organisation. In short, the SNP captured seats in 1974 by the successful mobilisation of the pro-devolution and pro-independence vote; that is, by taking up its natural constituency.

In the successful SNP areas, the party's success was largely confined to the pro-independence end of the spectrum. It did not succeed in gaining many votes at the other end. If a good candidate and organisation enabled it to take up its natural constituency, they did not succeed in extending that constituency, though there was no evidence of any reaction by anti-devolutionists similar to that by the non-Welsh-speakers in Wales.

IV   CONCLUSION

The importance of class alignment is general throughout mainland Britain but not in Northern Ireland. On the mainland, cross-cutting voting influences are superimposed upon class alignment but are not so powerful as to obliterate class divisions.

Outside England, the most notable features of voting patterns are related to the special issues of devolution, language or religion, rather than to variations in factors which are important within England. Devolution attitudes, language and religion are not merely different variables; outside England they operate in a different way from the English class alignment. None shows the consensual pattern associated with class alignment, whereby people with different social characteristics tend towards each other's political norms when they come into contact with one another. Scots anti-devolutionists cannot be tempted to vote SNP, even in places where the SNP is, for some reason, specially attractive. English-speaking Welshmen are encouraged to vote against Plaid Cymru rather than for it, when they find themselves surrounded by Welsh-speakers. And Northern Ireland voters are so completely subject to their own religious attachment that there is not even the slightest tendency to go with or react against their environment. In short, the political responses of anti-devolution Scots, English-speaking Welshmen, and most Ulstermen, show a rigidity or intransigence that is absent from class divisions throughout Britain. They are beyond the reach of their political opponents' appeals, whereas social classes are not.

NOTES

1. In England the percentage in Social Class II is a reasonable substitute for a direct measure of the managerial classes, because this class includes 100 per cent of the farming managers plus about 80 per cent of industrial and commercial managers. But it is critical that Social Class II is *not* used for cross-national comparisons in the United Kingdom, partly because the larger agricultural sector outside England makes the bias inherent in the 100 : 80 per cent ratio unacceptable, but more especially because all self-employed farmers are allocated to Social Class II. Consequently, according to Social Class II, Northern Ireland is the most middle class nation in the UK, while the Highlands are the most middle class part of Scotland.
2. I have not burdened the reader by showing the effects of religion within class because most of the interesting effects evident in Table 8.8 survive class control. Two special points are worth noting, however.

   The high Labour vote amongst the Catholic middle class in Scotland frequently attracts comment, but the middle class Catholics are, in fact, no more deviant than the working class Catholics. Compared to Church of Scotland members in their own class, middle class Catholics were 43 per cent more Labour, while working class Catholics were 42 per cent more Labour. The 47 per cent Catholic effect shown in Table 8.8 reflects this uniform within-class deviance, plus the tendency of Catholics to be working class.

   The only example of a significant pattern revealed by class control is the large Liberal vote amongst the middle class non-conformists in England, which is not reflected amongst working class non-conformists.

REFERENCES

Balsom, D. (1979) *The Nature and Distribution of Support for Plaid Cymru* (Glasgow: Strathclyde University Studies in Public Policy no. 36).

Butler, D. and D. Kavanagh (1980) *The British General Election of 1979* (London: Macmillan).

Craig, F. W. S. (1976) *British Electoral Facts 1885–1975* (London: Macmillan).

Dunleavy, P. (1979) 'The Urban Basis of Political Alignment – Social Class, Domestic Property Ownership and State Intervention in Consumption Processes', *British Journal of Political Science*, vol. 9, pp. 409–43.

Esman, M. J. (ed.) (1977) *Ethnic Conflict in the Western World* (Ithaca, New York: Cornell University Press).

Harrop, M., J. England and C. T. Husbands (1980) 'The Bases of National Front Support', *Political Studies*, vol. 28, pp. 271–83.

McAllister, I., R. Parry and R. Rose (1979) *United Kingdom Rankings: The Territorial Dimension in Social Indicators* (Glasgow: Strathclyde University Studies in Public Policy no. 44).

Miller, W. L. (1977) *Electoral Dynamics in Britain since 1918* (London: Macmillan).

Miller, W. L. (1978) 'Social Class and Party Choice in England – a New Analysis', *British Journal of Political Science*, vol. 8, pp. 257–84.

Miller, W. L. (1979) 'Class, Region and Strata at the British General Election of 1979', *Parliamentary Affairs*, vol. 32, pp. 376–82.

Miller, W. L. (1981a) *The End of British Politics? Scottish and English Political Behaviour in the Seventies* (Oxford: Clarendon Press).

Miller, W. L. (1981b) 'Beyond Two Party Analysis – Some New Methods for Linear and Log-linear Analyses in Three-Party Systems', *Political Methodology* (in press).

Miller, W. L., J. Brand and M. Jordan (1980) *Oil and the Scottish Voter* (London: Social Science Research Council, North Sea Oil Panel Occasional Paper no. 2).

Moxon-Browne, E. (1979) *The Northern Ireland Attitudes Survey 1978* (Belfast: Queen's University, mimeo).

Rose, R. (1971) *Governing without Consensus* (London: Faber).

Rose, R. and I. McAllister (1982) *United Kingdom Facts* (London: Macmillan).

APPENDIX

We need a formula to calculate the difference between the multi-party outcome in one area and another. I shall start by dividing votes into Conservative, Labour, Liberal, (local) Nationalist, and Other – that is, into five groups; and take as my formula for *MD* the size of the difference between the electoral outcome in two areas:

$$MD = \sqrt{(dCON^2 + dLAB^2 + dLIB^2 + dNAT^2 + dOTH^2)/2}$$

where *dCON* means the difference between the Conservative share of the vote in the two areas, and *dLAB, dLIB, dNAT, dOTH* are defined similarly.

Intuitively, this formula has a lot to recommend it. Apart from the division by 2 and the square root, it is essentially the sum of the squares of the differences between party percentages in the two areas. It takes account of the differences in each and every party's support and it gives more weight (by squaring) to one large difference than to several small ones. Those brought up on least squares analysis procedures will feel an instinctive affinity for such a measure of multi-party difference.

However, the formula is not derived from intuition nor from common-sense reasoning. It is the formula for the distance between the points representing two electoral outcomes in a symmetric representation. In a two-party system, outcomes can be represented as points along a line ranging from 100 per cent Labour, say, to 100 per cent Conservative:

	Area *A*	Area *B*

100%   100%
Lab   Con

and the formula becomes

$$MD = \sqrt{(dCON^2 + dLAB^2)/2} = \sqrt{dCON^2} = dCON$$

(since $dCON = -dLAB$ in a two-party system). That is, MD simply equals the difference between the shares of the vote won by Conservatives in the two areas; and this must equal the difference in Labour shares of the vote.

In a three-party system, electoral outcomes can be defined by points within an equilateral triangle, and the formula

$$MD = \sqrt{(dCON^2 + dLAB^2 + dLIB^2)/2}$$

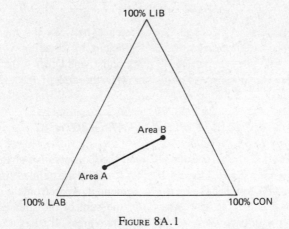

FIGURE 8A.1

equals the distance between the points representing the outcomes in two areas, provided the triangle is drawn to such a scale that each side has a length of 100 per cent.

In a four-party system, outcomes are represented by points within the solid body of a regular tetrahedron, and once again the formula for *MD* calculates the distance between the points representing the two outcomes.

I am using a five-party system which may be represented by a hyper-tetrahedron in four-dimensional space. That is very difficult to visualise, but I hope my readers can accept that the progression from two-party systems upwards indicates that the distance between points representing multi-party outcomes can be calculated using my formula for *MD*. See Miller (1981b) for a full description of this approach and its use in regression, log-linear analysis, and causal models.

Index